Created in the West Indies

Created in the West Indies

Caribbean Perspectives on V.S. Naipaul

Edited by Jennifer Rahim and Barbara Lalla

IAN RANDLE PUBLISHERS
Kingston • Miami

First published in Jamaica, 2011 by
Ian Randle Publishers
11 Cunningham Avenue
P.O. Box 686
Kingston 6
www.ianrandlepublishers.com

NATIONAL LIBRARY OF JAMAICA CATALOGUING-IN-PUBLICATION DATA
Created in the West Indies : Caribbean perspectives on V.S. Naipaul / edited by Jennifer Rahim and Barbara Lalla

p. ; cm.

Bibliography : p. – Includes index
ISBN 978-976-637-412-9 (pbk)

1. Naipaul, V. S. (Vidiadhar Surajprasad, 1932 -) – Criticism and interpretation
2. West Indies – In literature
I. Rahim, Jennifer II. Lalla, Barbara

Cover image of V.S. Naipaul by Israel Shenker courtesy of Redux Pictures.
Cover and book design by Ian Randle Publishers
Printed and bound in the United States

TABLE OF CONTENTS

ACKNOWLEDGEMENTS

This collection owes its greatest gratitude to the contributors, all of whom were patient and accommodating throughout the entire editing process. Appreciation for funding goes to the Campus Research and Publication Fund Committee of the University of the West Indies, St Augustine. Deep gratitude is also extended to graduate student, Andra K. Ramdeen, who worked along with the editors and the contributors. These papers include proceedings from the symposium, 'V.S. Naipaul: Created in the West Indies,' hosted by the Department of Liberal Arts, University of the West Indies, St Augustine, April 19, 2007. Others are from the university's Open Lecture Series devoted to the celebration of V.S. Naipaul's literary achievements and in recognition of his seventy-fifth birthday. Most of these essays appeared in *Anthurium: A Caribbean Studies Journal* 5, No. 2 (2007) and we express our deep appreciation to Sandra Pouchet Paquet of the University of Miami, Coral Gables. We thank all our colleagues in the Department of Liberal Arts for their support throughout the entire process. We also thank Rose-Ann Walker, who helped with the final proofreading of the manuscript.

Jennifer Rahim and Barbara Lalla
June 2010

INTRODUCTION

Jennifer Rahim

'To be a writer, I thought, was to have the conviction that one could go on. I didn't have that conviction.'[1] The statement is typically Naipaulian, fretful with that all too familiar confessional impulse and sly delight in the orchestration of paradox, for the doubt that inhabits his self-disclosure is, as we know, comprehensively nullified by a phenomenal response of over fifty years of seemingly inexhaustible creative versatility and will. For Vidyadhar Surajprasad Naipaul, the designation *writer* has meant many things: the childhood 'wish' without practice that became 'ambition' only when the 'idea of writing' emerged in him as an 'ennobling one;'[2] 'a form of incompleteness,' 'anguish, 'despair;'[3] and the reward of 'luck, and much labour.'[4] One can add more, but fundamentally, a writer is what Naipaul has succeeded in making himself. There is certainly no question about the place he occupies as one of the most talented and intriguing literary giants of our time. Along with his contemporary, Derek Walcott, he holds the distinction of also having won the prestigious Nobel Prize for Literature in 2001.

In July 2007, V.S. Naipaul crossed a significant threshold in the celebration of his seventy-fifth birthday. As part of an unprecedented initiative spearheaded by Pro-Vice Chancellor, Bhoendradatt Tewarie of The University of the West Indies, St Augustine campus, 2007 was selected to honour the life and work of this internationally acclaimed author and native son of Trinidad and Tobago. The year of celebrations featured a series of public events which served as a kind of homecoming for a man who has spent most of his writing career abroad and whose turbulent relationship with his West Indian origins is no secret. Significant among these events were the delivery of several lectures hosted by the University's Distinguished Open Lecture Series and an academic symposium organised by The Liberal Arts Department entitled, 'V.S. Naipaul: Created in the West Indies.' Together, these brought a number of distinguished Caribbean scholars and creative writers into a dynamic round of conversations with the academic fraternity, literature students and the general public on the work of a writer who has attracted the attention of a wide range of literary and cultural intellectuals, readers and enthusiasts of literature from across the globe. Presenters included Jean Antoine-Dunne, Edward Baugh, Bridget Brereton, Rhonda Cobham-Sander, Al Creighton, Merle Hodge, Barbara Lalla, Mark McWatt, Vijay Maharaj, Paula Morgan, Evelyn O'Callaghan, Brinsley Samaroo, Sandra Pouchet Paquet, Kenneth Ramchand, Jennifer Rahim, Gordon Rohlehr, Vishnu Singh, Lawrence Scott and Bhoendradatt Tewarie. The essays in this collection represent a selection of the academic papers and public lectures delivered at the St Augustine campus during the course of that year's activities.

Any attempt to compress into a single day the expansive field of themes and concerns that have preoccupied this most complex writer would have been an impossible task. The symposium was therefore designed to invite presentations on some of the core issues with which Naipaul's body of work has been associated and which continue to attract heated debate. Presentations were therefore invited on topics that included history and representation, home and belonging, and the 'self' and the writing process. Interestingly, most presenters at both the symposium and the public lecture series focused on the author's fictional works but all, in one way or the other, returned almost unavoidably to his early historical and travel writing in *The Loss of El Dorado* and *The Middle Passage* respectively. These two texts emerge in the discussions as foundational companions to his other works as they establish some of the major issues that have preoccupied Naipaul's writing life from the standpoint of his thematic explorations and his relentless interrogation of the question of form.

Not surprisingly, the common echo that reverberates through these essays is that now (in)famous line from *The Middle Passage*: 'History is built around achievement and creation; and nothing was created in the West Indies.'[5] This one statement continues to be the source of much accusative finger-pointing and is routinely evoked as evidence of Naipaul's rejection or abhorrence of his Caribbean origins. Although somewhat of a tiresome stomping ground for vigilante nationalists and regionalists on the lookout for literary treason, it remains an inescapable site of engagement. Naipaul is a most enigmatic writer who seems to relish the courtship of contention, even scandal, about a number of matters including his relationship to his homeland in particular, and the state of developing nations in general. The symposium's title, of course, was never innocent of the ironies that chuckle on its margins. It was intended not only to stimulate reflection but to release fresh insight and, with luck, brew new controversies around what is possibly the most quoted and, some would argue, misquoted statement that has haunted Naipaul's career.

Whatever the nature of his readerships' dissatisfactions, Naipaul's genius shines most brilliantly in his extraordinary capacity to astutely read social structures, to rigorously deconstruct the most complex of cultural and political systems, to perceptively render human motive and behaviour, and to simultaneously take risks in seeking out innovative routes to provide for the reader what he has been most faithful to – his particular way of seeing and feeling. Indeed, his lifelong writing project has been an exercise in clearing up his world and elucidating it, at best making fiction of a life whose only assurance is its offerings of 'partial truths.'[6] This is perhaps the best avenue for approaching the essays contained in the three sections of this collection: 'Circuits of Self-Refashioning,' 'Form Matters,' 'Rethinking Naipaul on the Threshold of History and New Horizons.' Regardless of how stringently his reading of the world may be opposed, the life and work of this writer cannot be easily contained or dismissed. The essays offer but ways of thinking about the man and the writer, both of whom slip the grasp much like the mystery of art-making itself to which Naipaul remains a staunch and unrepentant disciple.

The author's admirably large, exquisitely crafted, and controversially nuanced literary output has engaged societies, histories, traditions and landscapes that include those of his Caribbean homeland, Latin America, North America, England, Africa, India and the Far East. Quite early in his career, Naipaul had decided that he did not wish to be restricted by regional categories. In order to write without drying up, the world must be his primary subject and resource as he tells BBC interviewer, Harriett Gilbert: 'To be a writer you have to be out in the world, you have to risk yourself in the world....'[7] Yet, this *world* which Naipaul left Trinidad in 1950 to discover and to which his writing refers – its politics, its people and their complex histories that have preoccupied his creative imagination, directed his archival research and influenced his travel – is one that has been circumscribed by his colonial, Trinidadian origins. The centrality of that 'background' is confirmed in several places such as in *The Enigma of Arrival* where he writes:

> the island had given me the world as a writer; had given me the themes that in the second half of the twentieth century had become important; had made me metropolitan in a way quite different from my first understanding of the word....[8]

But having left home, the real project was to rediscover what he thought he knew about his island; it was to learn about life beyond the 'tall corrugated-iron gate' of the 'world at home,' that inward looking cloister of his 'peasant, half-Indian' upbringing ('Postscript' 2004, 187). Understandably, honouring the necessity to 'go back' would not be an uncomplicated process because return meant, among other things, more than a literal journey or the mining of a half-remembered personal history. Its fundamental requirement would be an educated and tangible expansion into the world through the de-familiarising familiarities of travel, painstaking archival research and much reading. For even those regions outside the island to which he longed to escape, he did not know, or rather knew in a particular way – it was a 'literary' knowledge, the 'fantasy' of place like the England given him by his colonial education (*Enigma* 1987, 23). Travel then would afford a reformed and enlarged awareness of place – the cities, cultures, peoples, histories and geographies that had at various historical moments intersected, even collided, on his 'small' island, the location that had given him 'the world as a writer' and 'had made him metropolitan' (140). In other words, *metropolitan* constitutes what it means to be Trinidadian, West Indian, and global – in short, radically *modern* with all its possibilities and handicaps. This is the awareness of self and sensibility at which he ultimately arrives and which had to become the shaper of his writing.

Notwithstanding the image of a man consumed as much by conflict as by the desire to succeed; notwithstanding the cultivated uncertainties about his allegiances and agendas – uncertainties often mischievously nurtured by the author himself and seemingly savoured by academics and the general public alike – what we can be sure of is that the island never left Naipaul. Also, rather than the accusation of abandoning his origins, or being a man without allegiances to his community, it is possibly truer to say that for most of his writing life he has lived in the gap of a nervous accommodation between his natal home and his chosen place of residence. This is starkly described in a 1954 letter to his mother where he wrote that the 'antipathy to a prolonged stay in this country [England] is as great as his fear of Trinidad.'[9] Drawing on a statement recorded in Patrick French's *The World Is What it Is*, Vishnu Singh captures Naipaul's most recent re-articulation of that sentiment when the writer says: 'to me departure is always more welcome than arrival.'[10] Some things apparently remain the same, although what definitely changed for Naipaul was the practice of return (literally and imaginatively) to a home where, as a young man, he had made this pledge to his sister, Kamla: '...I shall go away never to come back, as I trust' (*Letters* 1999, 8).

The need to negotiate new terms for making one's way in a world that had been dramatically and irreparably altered by the brutal and eruptive events set in motion by 1492 and its aftermath, has been the author's career-long engagement. His has been an intense conversation with the wreckage of that passage which has left in its wake insurmountable developmental challenges for plundered and fragmented societies, seemingly ill-prepared to survive the very capital-driven world that still exploits them. Repeatedly, his oeuvre has focused on the trauma of multiple displacements suffered by diasporic peoples in their countries of resettlement; the plight of the ordinary traveller/immigrant unmoored from the securities and familiarities of home; the absurd misadventures of postcolonial nations, their handicapped leadership and equally bemused and mimicry-prone populations in their struggle for liberation and independence.

Naipaul, of course, has been severely criticised for using the West as a measuring rod for 'civilization' and to support his consistently dim view of 'small societies,' usually ex-colonial and disadvantaged by various deprivations. His criticisms of the developing world have not altogether been unfair. However, to simply accuse him of venerating things Western is to miss a crucial point – that is, how the much referred to 'background' of the author has been responsible for shaping his particular attitude to or perception of reality, regardless of the geography or culture on which his literary eye is trained. Naipaul, for instance, asserts in *A Writer's People: Ways of Looking and Feeling*:

> I have said that I very early became aware of different ways of seeing because I came to the metropolis from very far. Another reason may be that I don't, properly speaking, have a past that is available to me, a past I can enter into and consider; and I grieve that lack.[11]

His stranger's cum traveller's condition, having come from 'afar,' therefore evokes the complicated histories of his other places of origin: those 'frightening,' 'haphazard,' island colonies and a colonial education that nurtured fantasies of another 'perfect world' to which he could escape and his partially remembered Indian ancestry and outsider's positioning in Afro-Creole Trinidad. These elements comprised the collective legacy of dislocation and grief that also bequeathed him the absence of a coherent 'past'. For Naipaul, such a beginning translates to an orientation towards seeing the world, not just the islands, in a state of decline. Ramchand had long ago drawn our attention to the author's habit of focussing on the 'lack,' and the fragmentation and loss that it implies. In the author's first England-based book, *Mr Stone and the Knights Companion,* which marks his shift from his purely West Indian based fiction, he notices that Naipaul's 'West-Indian nurtured vision of decay and ultimately illusory achievement is soberly transplanted to an English setting....'[12]

The eye for 'decay' defines the world view of Naipaul's entire corpus of work and reveals a preoccupation with the vulnerability of the human condition before the immutable governance of change, the only reliability. But change for him has always been equated with disintegration and 'shipwreck.' It is an attitude that for some signals his Brahmin detachment and for others evidence of an incurable ambivalence about the meaning of life itself manifested in the oscillation of his (semi)fictional characters between extremes of pleasure and revulsion, startling clarity and willed self-deception. The 'shifting about of reality,' in great and small measure, which consistently tips the balance between 'knowing and not knowing' would therefore become the familiar haunt of Naipaul's consciousness and the creative 'fever' of his imagination.[13] If the island had given Naipaul the world as a writer, his books would have to engage that world's historical and cultural complexities. Moreover, this engagement would be an arduous exercise of self-discovery. The scrupulous 'dredging' of his inherited 'areas of darkness,' which travel would help to remedy and would, as he claims in *A Writer's People*, provide the creative resource from which to also 'read and write himself' (2007, 52–54). However, the result of his conversation with human history, it is fair to say, has been an uneven balance of brilliant illumination and worrisome anathema.

Section One of this book, 'Circuits of Self-Refashioning,' contains essays by Edward Baugh, Evelyn O'Callaghan, Paula Morgan and Rhonda Cobham-Sander. They bring the act of writing to bear on the much considered chimera of identity and identification. At the heart of Naipaul's meticulous rapport with a self that is simultaneously known and unknown, embodied and performed, is the 'I,' that inescapable agent of seeing and experiencing. Not only is the exterior world an object of observation but the very self is interrogated, even when it is subjected to recognition by others or distanced by a third person perspective. This multiple positioning accounts for the tendency to refer to himself in the third person, 'the man' as Baugh would point out. Together these essays provide a compelling commentary on Naipaul's assertion in 'Reading and Writing' that 'Literature is the sum of its discoveries' (2004, 30), a statement that he apparently sets out to complete in his Nobel lecture, 'Two Worlds.' He offers the teasingly illusive self-disclosure, 'I am the sum of my books....I feel that at every stage of my literary career it could have been said that the last book contained all the others' (2004, 82–83).

Edward Baugh, '"The History that had made me:" The Making and Self-Making of V.S. Naipaul,' marshals a brilliant deconstruction of the author's literary personality by examining the intriguing interplay between the shifting borders of historical circumstance and the performance of self-invention, the fact of history and the invention of story, in which the author's fictional, autobiographical and non-fictional works have all participated. Naipaul's entire process of writing and the exercise of travel as an enabler of writing, Baugh argues, have been propelled by the need to understand self through the production of an identity or identities garnered from the history that had made him. That inescapable 'made in Trinidad stamp' and the India of his ancestry become endlessly evoked sites that incrementally explain personality – his 'nerves' and so on. Yet if, as Baugh argues, invention is for Naipaul the recourse of the incomplete self and so his books provide the collective stage for this 'self-in-performance,' then writing itself, with the book as artefact, is perhaps where his deepest allegiance lies. In the midst of an imperfect world, the fiction of wholeness which the well-written book represents is what triumphs, much like his admiration for Jack's garden. What we equally consume, then, as man and/or writer is 'in the best sense, a fiction,' Naipaul's supreme work of art.

The navigation of the endless labyrinth of personality is a constant source of intrigue for Naipaul, the writer. Often his reading of the 'other' mirrors his patient and passionate pursuit of self-knowledge and self-explanation. Rhonda Cobham-Sander's essay, 'Consuming the Self: V.S. Naipaul, C.L.R. James and *A Way in the World*,' probes this dimension of the author's writing by focussing on the strategies through which he discloses his evolution to the independence of personality and thought he has jealously guarded and defended. The reader is put in touch with a Naipaul who is aware of his approaching end which, for Cobham-Sander, is evident in the concern with influencing his 'critical legacy,' a major preoccupation in the novel, *A Way in the World.* There, the author's penchant for creating the 'illusion of fact' surfaces most obviously in the character, Lebrun, who is used as a foil to read his countryman, C.L.R. James, as well as his own fictional persona. Naipaul certainly proves himself to be the postcolonial Maverick in his unlikely evocation of James, a black intellectual and socialist, as an early 'role model' and parallel in ambition and achievement. The objective of the parallel is two-fold. First, Naipaul seeks to illuminate his self-saving path to individuation from ideological 'co-optation' to which Lebrun/James had in his own way been vulnerable. Second, Naipaul's consideration of James is propelled by his writer's desire to imagine the inner man behind the public persona James cultivated, and which provides a 'mirror' for his own self-reflection.

Self-irony is expertly managed as the author maps his struggle to resist compromising himself in a socio-political arena where race, ethnicity and class are recruited as powerful agents of persuasion. In a dangerous game of ideological control, the 'sticky' politics of inclusion/exclusion polices the 'slippery' borders between cultural difference and appropriation, international solidarity and individual freedom. Cobham-Sander meticulously analyses the symbolic ramifications of two meals of coo-coo and gefilte fish. Naipaul's almost pathological discomfort with the dish that represents the messy hybridity of Trinidad's Creole culture, is an important critique of what he holds to be its homogenising ideological limits against which he has struggled to safeguard his much celebrated avoidance of appropriation. But this attraction to the anti-heroic, and the inconsistencies of personality that attend it, perhaps offers access to the author's must humane recesses which stems, as Cobham-Sander suggests, from the conviction that the capacity to approach an understanding of the self from its most private, opaque regions is where, it seems, the bonds of our common vulnerable humanity are most genuinely wrought.

George Lamming's penetrating diagnostic of the literary environment in the West Indies during the first half of the twentieth century in *The Pleasures of Exile*, claims that writers 'simply wanted *to get out* of the place where they were born' because the 'atmosphere was too oppressive.'[14] Indeed, the book is a forerunner in the theorising of *exile* as being also concomitant with home. It is from this perspective of those 'who inhabit the "outsider" status at *home*' that Evelyn O'Callaghan's, 'Naipaul's Legacy: Made in the West Indies – for Export'[15] examines the criteria that deem some subjects 'made for export.' Beginning with Naipaul's representation of the region as a 'place where difference is rarely tolerated,' she argues this makes immigration to more accommodating spaces the preferred option for such identities. The essay expands Naipaul's well-known corpus of complaints about the displaced artist and gifted person in such an environment to include the need to escape 'gender fixity' and intolerance to 'same-sex desire' in the work of writers like Jamaica Kincaid and Shani Mootoo respectively. Further, O'Callaghan suggests that a new 'critical moment' has dawned that provides an opportunity to review responses to Naipaul's unfavourable criticism of the region which has been the main source of his ambivalent accommodation in the West Indian canon. The particular value of her cross-historical critical approach in reading the West Indian phase of Naipaul's writing with that of contemporary writers is that it facilitates the discernment of normally unconsidered continuities of experience and thought. One can appreciate, for instance, the manner in which a writer like Mootoo, who addresses the alienating effect of 'difference' from the perspective of sexual orientation, 'reconfigures Naipaul's legacy for the current generation.'

The numerous occasions of forced and willing uprooting from natal homelands that mark the 'modern' experience and are embodied in the figures of 'exile,' 'stranger,' 'traveller,' 'global citizen,' have also been extensions of Naipaul's fascination with self (re)invention and the quest for belonging. Such identities have also long been the loci of his mediations on the self-writer nexus. Naipaul, the man, is therefore never far removed from his interest in the condition of individuals who find themselves displaced and on the move for various reasons. Paula Morgan's essay, 'Consorting with Kali: Migration and Identity in Naipaul's "One Out of Many,"' provides a close reading of the plight of one such character, Santosh, the Bombay immigrant in Washington. Brought into focus is the inner chaos that attends the collision of worlds. The deep psycho-spiritual trauma of adjusting to the new cultural space whose social codes undermine the very foundations of Santosh's sense of self pivots on his sexual encounter with the black American, *hubshi*. His testimony to the debilitating 'no man's land of cultural liminality,' marked as it is by 'multiple sites of dislocation and non-belonging,' prompts Morgan to question the viability of Homi Bhabha's recommended shift of identity discourse to the politics of identity, as opposed to the old focus on essentialist 'ontological and epistemological imperatives.' The latter ways of identification, she contends, are never easily discarded. Old constructs persist. This is of course not entirely undesirable, only in Santosh's case, ethnically-derived notions of negative otherness short-circuit the possibilities for renewal in the inevitable 'contact-zone' of cultures.

The essays in Section Two, 'Form Matters,' by Gordon Rohlehr, Barbara Lalla, Jean Antoine-Dunne, Vijay Maharaj and Jennifer Rahim, consider Naipaul's wrestle with form, a concern that has preoccupied him from the very beginning of his career and is certainly evident in all the essays in this collection. 'Literature, like all living art,' writes Naipaul, 'is always on the move' ('Reading and Writing' 2004, 30). Literary form is therefore always a response to an age and the writer's responsibility is to engineer that change. In a world characterised by permanent displacements, the writer's task is to represent well, with fresh energy, 'the unaccommodating new reality' (31) of his time in forms that best yield to the complexities of that exercise. His alertness to the advent of the 'new' is sometimes manifest in a fierce dialogue with the traditions he inherited as a novelist and his views no doubt intersect with the canonical wars waged by an 'empire writing back' to the 'centre.' Yet Naipaul has never really been afflicted with the old postcolonial wound of 'an anxiety of influence.' With sobering clarity and uncommon humility he acknowledges a mammoth tradition of literary masters which means 'All of us who have come after have been derivative. We can never be the first again' (28). He is certain, however, that the old patterns cannot be merely repeated. Naipaul's most enviable gift is a creative restlessness that is at once adventurously open to stylistic experimentation and propelled by an exceptional capacity to meet the demands that his particular material and historical time make on him.

Gordon Rohlehr's essay, 'The Confessional Element in Naipaul's Fiction' allows one to consider a bridge of connection between the problem of form, with which Naipaul is endlessly engaged, and the thematic of trauma that characterises so much of the author's work, as well as the entire corpus of Caribbean literature. In the author's fictional output from the 1960s to the 1970s, which includes works such as *The Mimic Men, A Bend in the River, A Flag on the Island* and *In a Free State*, Rohlehr discerns an impulse towards confession. The 'direct' need for self-disclosure and exoneration evident in Naipaul's interviews, essays and travelogues finds 'indirect' expression in his fictional construction of protagonists who are invariably authorial masks, thereby reinforcing Baugh's claim that Naipaul, 'haunts himself in his characters.' Rohlehr's essay traces a progression or perhaps more suitably, a regression in the treatment of character from the comic, 'lighted-hearted' misadventures of the 'confessional trickster' types of the earlier fiction to the more grotesque, nauseated 'confessional anti-hero' or absurdist 'actor' types fashioned after the narrators of the European existentialists Dostoevsky, Sartre, Camus and others. These, according to Rohlehr, provided structural and theoretical prototypes for writing about his 'own uncreated and uncreative society.'

The rather chronic sense of void that Rohlehr sees as having intensified in the writing of the 1960s and '70s finds its precursor in Barbara Lalla's essay, 'Signifying Nothing: Writing About Nothing in *The Mystic Masseur*.' Much has been said about this Trinidad-based social satire, but Lalla unlocks new interpretative doors in her analysis of the novel. By applying the rigour of discourse analysis, she demonstrates its role as a conspiratorial agent in the reinforcement of a society defined by the total collapse of meaning in which the manufacture of nothingness thrives. The novel's ideological agenda, she argues, is oriented towards an 'implied authorial theory of chaos.' By cleverly trading on the dissolution of fiction and autobiography, Naipaul produces an entertaining but highly pertinent treatise about 'how nothingness can be discursively constructed.' Here, Lalla's insights echo the author's admission that he 'was used to living in a world where signs were without meaning, or without the meaning intended by their makers' (*Enigma* 1987, 120). Her analysis carefully unravels the ways in which the text both deploys various narrative techniques to signal this collapse of signification by recruiting the reader as primary evaluator of falsity whether of the main character, Ganesh, or the narrator who poses as pseudo-biographer. The illusiveness of identity, the deceptive *performativity* of self, the questionable 'truth' of history, the unreliability of written discourse, the untrustworthiness of personal witness are all 'setups of narratorial reliability' that reinforce the notion of void which, Lalla disturbingly concludes, 'cumulatively perpetuate the vacuum constructed by colonialism.'

'Narrative,' Lalla states 'is one means through which discourse constructs our perceptions of reality' and, in her analysis of *The Mystic Masseur*, Naipaul constructs 'insignificance.' It is a destination not unlike that at which Rohlehr arrives in relation to Naipaul's discovery of the existentialists. With much the same conclusion, Jean Antoine-Dunne's essay, 'Keeping an Eye on Naipaul,' examines the aesthetic cross-fertilizations between the techniques of cinematography and narration in the author's work, drawing on examples from texts like *Miguel Street, A Flag on the Island* and *Half A Life*. While the ability of characters to distinguish illusion from reality notably degenerates in the later works like *Half A Life,* the essay goes beyond the familiar discussion of postcolonial mimicry and the role cinema plays in providing identity-models for people who lack a secure sense of self, an interest Naipaul shares with other Caribbean writers. It examines the debt his approaches to characterisation and narration owe to cinema's montage 'techniques and structures' such as fragmentation, visual description, horror movie effects and the filmic caesura. This is certainly a promising trajectory that places Caribbean literary criticism in dynamic conversation with Film Studies. The link is reconfirmed by Naipaul's own acknowledgement of the role the 'glorious cinema' played in his 'imaginative life.' In this regard, he goes as far as to disclaim exaggeration, but at the same time dispenses judgement on what he saw as his society's philistinism when he states that, 'without the Hollywood of the 1930s and 1940s I would have been spiritually quite destitute' ('Reading and Writing' 2004, 31).

The majority of the critical readings of Naipaul's work concur in their assessment that the author's sensibility leans towards what Antoine-Dunne succinctly calls 'the shadow of the light of this world;' his inability to abide with 'anything half-and-half,' as Baugh argues; and his apparent disinterested acquiescence to life's mysterious illogic. Vijay Maharaj's 'A Mala in Obeisance: Hinduism in Selected Texts by V.S. Naipaul' provides an interesting counterpoint. She argues for the need to consider more carefully the author's creative engagement with the religious and philosophical aspects of his inherited Hindu background, one that intensifies as his writing career unfolds in spite of his confessed religious scepticism and ignorance of his ancestral belief system. Locating Naipaul in the categories of the sceptic and seeker-of-clarification, she supplies a different take on the issue of 'personality' where 'doubt, criticism, discussion and questioning' are defined in the context of the pursuit of faith and knowledge. Maharaj's analysis of Naipaul's speculations on a number of Hindu philosophical concepts certainly advances previous discussions on this dimension of the writer's work. In particular, she makes a case for seeing Naipaul's artistic practice as a reinvention of the long-standing tradition of the folk katha, originally used as a tool for the spiritual instruction of Indian indentured labourers and their descendents, but now expanded to engage a varied, modern audience.

A likely interface with Maharaj's essay is Jennifer Rahim's 'The Shadow of Hanuman: V.S. Naipaul and the "Unhomely" House of Fiction.' Drawing on the novel, *A House for Mr Biswas*, 'Prologue to an Autobiography' and the short story, 'How I Left Miguel Street,' the essay explores how the creative converge of travel, memory and narrative returns may serve to illuminate the author's inherited hybrid sensibility as the seat of his evolving poetics. At the centre of her argument is the figure of the Hindu deity, Hanuman, the ambivalent 'cosmic middleman,' whom Rahim argues is positioned as a totem of ongoing diasporic translation and transformation. Reading the use of the Hanuman trope in *A House for Mr Biswas* against Lakshmi Persaud's *Butterfly in the Wind* and Robert Antoni's *Divina Trace*, she sees Naipaul as ideologically occupying the middle ground between Persaud's protectionist poetics and Antoni's deconstructionist aesthetics. Naipaul deploys the deity as a symbol for the creative ambivalence that marks the slow process of 'adaptation and survival' in the Caribbean diaspora, the New World and beyond. This amalgamated sense of self, she argues, is the hard-won but still tentative acceptance of what it means to be 'modern' to which Naipaul appears to arrive in *The Enigma of Arrival*: 'We had made ourselves anew…. There was no ship of antique shape now to take us back. We had come out of the nightmare; and there was nowhere else to go' (1987, 317).

Section Three, 'Rethinking Naipaul on the Threshold of History and New Horizons,' provides an appropriate closure to this unique collection. It brings together essays by Sandra Pouchet Paquet, Lawrence Scott, Bhoendradatt Tewarie and Bridget Brereton that unlock new perspectives on the author by targeting the relevance of his richly cultivated 'historical sense' and what this facilitates: an informed consideration of history's ongoing making that is essential for charting a meaningful course forward on the individual and collective levels. Caribbean writers have characteristically invested in the vital role of imaginative literature in re-telling their histories which have been distorted and submerged in official historiographies oriented towards the lives of Western subjects, their cultural codes and knowledge systems. Although his methods may be different, his perspectives unpopular and his sceptic's route to recovery slow, Naipaul has not been entirely estranged from the requirement for '*a prophetic vision of the past*' which Édouard Glissant argues is necessary for the Caribbean writer whose relationship is to a submerged or 'obscured history.'[16] Paradoxically, just as Naipaul has often stood as judge at the bar of the New World's history, from which he too has been judged and found wanting, in these essays, his recourse to the past emerges as an essential starting point from which to begin the exercise of reassessing his contributions. This is not at all surprising as he has made himself a model of that fruitful practice of historical recovery as researcher and writer, going back almost ritualistically as far as possible to the 'beginning of things' for mere 'fragments of truth' from which to launch and re-launch his creative assessment of self and the world (*A Way* 1995, 9).

Sandra Pouchet Paquet's essay, 'V.S. Naipaul and the Interior Expeditions: "It is Impossible to Make a Step Without the Indians,"' serves well as an example of the humanising potential of historical (re) education. Naipaul has certainly exasperated his reading public with his discriminatory habits of representing race. Derek Walcott, for instance, bitterly complains about his derogatory references to peoples of African descent in his review of *The Enigma of Arrival.*[17] Whatever his many sins of attitude and representation, Paquet's discussion offers a ray of redemption. What she cautiously calls the author's 'unresolved incongruities in his representations' of the indigenous peoples of Trinidad and Guyana in his fictional and non-fictional works span a period of over 39 years. This body of work, she argues, demonstrates a progressive movement defined by two axes, if you will. The first is the 'absolute Otherness' that characterises early recordings of the Amerindian presence in *The Loss of El Dorado* and *The Middle Passage*. The second displays his compassionate evolution to an 'elegiac sense of loss' evident in his more recent re-visitations of his efforts to represent that community in *A Way in the World*, his Nobel lecture, 'Two Worlds,' and his essay, 'Reading and Writing.'

Importantly, Paquet's discussion continues the attempt to articulate a Caribbean literary poetics in the intersections she discerns between Naipaul and the Guyanese writer, Wilson Harris, who saw that the historical and cultural circumstances of the Caribbean required a new engagement with the novel. The radical reconstitution of form evident in the structural extravaganza of a 'multigenre' novel like *A Way in the World*, for instance, matches Harris's radical experimentations with form as well as exemplifies the maturation of the 'panfictionality' noted by Lalla, in her discussion of his early social satire, *The Mystic Masseur.* Ultimately, Paquet sees Naipaul's journey with the Amerindian presence as a kind of 'pilgrim's progress' that approaches Harris's notion of 'an art of compassion,' a humanising poetics that seeks to bring into conversation histories and peoples initially 'blocked' or 'eclipsed' by the imperial project and its biased historiographies of the region. This growth in consciousness, which is attributed to the filling in of gaps facilitated by archival research, is perhaps best compressed in the author's accidental arrival at the knowledge about the original Amerindian inhabitants of his natal village, Chaguanas. Documentary history and the childhood memory of reports about the seasonal crossings of aboriginal people from the mainland to Trinidad then crystallise, in his imagination as 'an unbearably affecting story' ('Postscript' 2004, 86).

Lawrence Scott's Open Lecture presentation, 'The Novelist And History – The Pleasures And Problems With Writing History,' contributes an interesting writer-on-writer perspective that combines the importance of the 'historical sense' with that of a Caribbean literary tradition. Scott acknowledges the value of being the beneficiary of a living tradition from which he can selectively draw; but for this writer who acknowledges 'no [literary] father..., but many fellow writers, comrades on this craft' of writing, Naipaul has been a necessary but not indispensable companion. For Scott, this loose affiliation springs from the irreconcilable tension between Naipaul's exquisite craftsmanship and his 'vision.' He recognises the influence of texts such as *The Loss of El Dorado* and *The Enigma of Arrival* on his efforts at writing historical fiction and experiments with marrying autobiography and fiction in *Witchbroom* and *Aelred's Sin*. Scott's admiration for craft, however, gives way to a critical rethinking of the author's purpose particularly his uncharitable representation of race and (homo) sexuality. Naipaul skirts responsibility for his biases, Scott contends, by upholding a claim to the disinterested objectivity of an 'I,' a fictionalised writer-self that deceptively blurs the boundary between the writer and the man, fact and fiction. In one sense, the critique raises the timeless debate about the location of artistic responsibility. Naipaul's response has been consistent. His first priority as a writer is to render 'the truth of [his] own responses' regardless of the reception.[18] For him, his originality and usefulness rest on that one fidelity. Yet this issue of the questionable agenda of the 'I' with which Scott struggles is native to the enigma of writing itself. It is, as Naipaul has always insisted, the locus where 'reality' and form cohere, where craft comes to harbour, and so is almost never engaged without its particular measure of pleasure.

The privilege of seeing with which Scott grapples is precisely the ground from which Bhoendradatt Tewarie's essay, 'V.S. Naipaul as Critical Thinker,' lays claim to the author's immense contribution to the contemporary world, not just as a creative writer, but also as a 'critical thinker' who is often found to be 'swimming against the current' of popular thought. Beyond Naipaul's brutally honest reading of the dilemmas faced by 'small societies,' Tewarie discerns in the author's oeuvre an almost prophetic anticipation of the radical reconstitution of the world order now dubbed globalisation. Naipaul is recognisably postmodern before the institutionalisation of the term, Tewarie argues. His primary investment is in the emerging new world order he calls, 'Our Universal Civilisation' and so fully he embraces its gifts of freedom of movement, access to knowledge, individual liberation and responsibility from which he has personally benefited. Of course, Naipaul cannot be exonerated for being persistently uncritical of the role so-called developed nations continue to play in perpetuating the conditions of disadvantage suffered by the very developing countries of which he is so critical. Tewarie suggests that, for Naipaul, 'barbarism' is the failure of individuals, groups and nations to meaningfully integrate the progressive elements of an evolving 'multicivilizational, multicultural world.' It is on the basis of this vision, although admittedly fraught with contradictions and unresolved biases, that Tewarie's essay champions the author's role as a critical-creative thinker. At the same time, however, ample room is left in his analysis for the continued interrogation and evaluation of Naipaul's thought.

If the writer's confrontation with history is inevitable, Bridget Brereton in her essay, 'Naipaul on History,' puts a different spin on that tenet by making a strong case for a closer partnership between the historian and creative writer. She revisits the very troublesome issue of Naipaulian 'historylessness' and invites a re-evaluation of the author's position in view of the commitment he has demonstrated as a creative writer to the importance of cultivating 'historical wonder' as a response to an inherited sense of discontinuity and absence. This, for Brereton, is one of his most valuable legacies and one for which he has been given little credit. In contrast to the more damning readings of Naipaul's echo of James Anthony Froude in his statement, 'nothing was created in the West Indies,' she argues that 'far from the dismissal of the historian's project as futile,' it is to the necessity of (re) constructing that history that he has been tirelessly committed as a writer, stemming from the conviction that a key index of underdevelopment and intellectual impoverishment of any people, nation or region of the world is the absence of sound historical narratives.

For Naipaul, Brereton contends, the real enemy of development, not only in the Caribbean, but (as he has demonstrated) in Latin America, Africa and India, is historical ignorance. This is the disease of mind and spirit that paralyses whole societies because of its power to interrupt the movement to self-knowledge which ultimately short-circuits the work of creative reconstruction. The author's personal commitment to the historical process is therefore of paramount value to a globe in which the collision of cultures can either yield deeper expressions of a common human community or generate retreats into ritualistic fundamentalisms, atavistic notions of purity and incomplete or biased national narratives. From this perspective, it follows that the true vitality of history, in which fiction participates, is not the production of static documentary study but the potential that engagement holds for fostering deep-level transformation and reformed relations among diverse but increasingly interconnected peoples. Naipaul poses the following question in *The Middle Passage*: 'How can the history of this West Indian futility be written?' (1969, 29). In an early study of the author's fictional engagement with this polemic, Rohlehr insightfully concludes that he 'is able to answer in terms of a creative sensibility a question to which he can find no satisfactory academic answer.'[19] Brereton's appreciation of the enriching dialectic between history and imaginative writing, modelled by Naipaul, corroborates, from the historian's vantage point, Rohlehr's evaluation.

Of course, Naipaul's work evokes a range of responses from his wide and varied readership. We may not always agree with him, but his unflinching commitment to telling his portion of reality; his consistent habit of re-examining his vision; his willingness to risk self-exposure, not sparing himself or his group his trademark ironic glance; his persistent quest for understanding; and his innovative adventures on the aesthetic terrain have laid a lasting foundation for a genuine and enduring dialogue with his work. Love him or leave him, Naipaul's voice is irresistible, even as it can disturb and exasperate, illuminate and vex us. This is a writer that leaves us few comfort zones or places of retreat from our common tenancy in the imperfect house of the human order, primarily because he claims no resting place for himself. He chooses instead a different quality of honesty, that is, to live creatively with the many uncertainties and large questions of our age. Perhaps his most enduring lesson is one that he seems to have slowly discovered, that is, the necessary submission to humility and flexibility as we make our way in a diverse, constantly changing and always mysterious world. There is no question as to which geography or historical circumstances had made him. Yet there is no contesting that, as a writer, he belongs to the world. The essays in this collection place him on the threshold of our ongoing conversations with the way forward in the shaping of a world civilisation that is genuinely welcoming to all peoples and nurturing of the greatest potentials of our common humanity.

Notes

1. V.S. Naipaul, 'Prologue to an Autobiography,' in *Literary Occasions: Essays* (London: Picador, 2004), 64.
2. Naipaul, 'Reading and Writing,' in *Literary Occasions*, 5.
3. Israel Shenker, 'V.S. Naipaul: Man Without a Society,' in *Critical Perspectives on V.S. Naipaul*, eds. Robert D. Hammer (Washington D.C.: Three Continents Press, 1979), 52.
4. Naipaul, "Postscript: Two Worlds," in *Literary Occasions*, 195.
5. Naipaul, *The Middle Passage* (1962; repr., Harmondsworth: Penguin Books, 1969), 29.
6. Kenneth Ramchand, 'Partial Truths: A Critical Assessment of V.S. Naipaul's later Fiction,' in *Critical Issues in West Indian Literature*, eds. Erika Sollish Smilowitz and Roberta Quarles Knowles (St Croix, Virgin Islands: Caribbean Books, 1984), 87.
7. Harriett Gilbert, 'V.S. Naipaul talks to BBC World Service about the threat to Britain from "council house culture," September 23, 2004. http://www.bbc.co.uk/print/pressoffice/pressreleases/stories/2004/09_september/23/naipaul.shtml.
8. Naipaul, *The Enigma of Arrival: A Novel* (London: Penguin Books, 1987), 140.
9. Gillon Aitken, ed. *Between Father and Son: Family Letters* (New York: Alfred A. Knoff, 1999), 8.
10. Vishnu Singh, 'The Colonial Goes to London,' a paper presented at the symposium, 'V.S. Naipaul: Created in the West Indies', St Augustine, Trinidad, 2007, 5.
11. Naipaul, *A Writer's People: Ways of Looking and Feeling* (London: Picador, 2007), 75.
12. Ramchand, *The West Indian Novel and Its* Background (2nd edn; London: Heinemann Books, 1983), 8.
13. Naipaul, *A Way in the World* (1994; rept. London: Minerva, 1995), 2.
14. George Lamming, *The Pleasures of Exile* (London: Michael Joseph, 1960), 41.
15. A earlier version of this essay appeared in *Lucayos*, 1 (2008): 106–17.
16. Édouard Glissant, *Caribbean Discourse: Selected Essays* (1989; rept. Charlotteville: University Press of Virginia, 1999), 63, 64.
17. Derek Walcott, 'The Garden Path: V.S. Naipaul,' in *What the Twilight Says: Essays* (London: Faber and Faber, 1998), 132.
18. Adrian Rowe-Evans, 'V.S. Naipaul,' *Transition* 40 (December 1971): 56.
19. Gordon Rohlehr, 'The Ironic Approach: The Novels of V.S. Naipaul,' in *Critical Perspectives on V.S. Naipaul*, 193.

Section One

Circuits of Self-Refashioning

1

'THE HISTORY THAT HAD MADE ME':

The Making and Self-Making of V.S. Naipaul

Edward Baugh

This paper examines two aspects of V.S. Naipaul's literary personality, that he signals by statements such as the following:

> Possibly, too, this mode of feeling went deeper and was an ancestral inheritance, something that went with the history that had made me.... (*The Enigma of Arrival*)

> And since no one can really see himself, I am sure that we would have been surprised and perhaps even wounded...by what the others saw. (*Half a Life*)

> I saw him as a very early colonial, someone with a feeling of incompleteness...someone who...had to reinvent himself. I saw in him some of my own early promptings (and the promptings of other people I knew). (*A Way in the World*)[1]

By literary personality I mean the personality that is embodied in the art of his books. One aspect is his acknowledgement, an analytical acknowledgement, of that personality as the product of historical circumstances, including, crucially, the time and place of his birth and early life. The other is the idea that the process of self-realisation, of the recognition of one's self as the product of one's origins and circumstances, is also, with Naipaul as with the rest of us, a process of self-invention. Further, these two aspects are integrally related in the matter of the recognition and construction of identity. In the identity-performance feature we may also read a 'made-in-Trinidad' stamp. There is in Naipaul, never mind the dispassionate, 'objective,' undemonstrative, transparent style for which he is famous, a subtle manifestation of that flair for the histrionic which he illuminates in his characters.

Naipaul's derogatory view of the West Indies is only too familiar a talking point, as is the outrage with which many West Indians have responded to that view. He would seem to have relished the role of goad to West Indian conscience and ego, and in this he is applauded by some critics, largely from the First World West, who see the outraged response simply as what is to be expected from insecure people afraid to look squarely at themselves. However, the popular construct of an absolute opposition of extremes is an over-simplification. There is some truth on both sides. Naipaul's apparent rejection of Trinidad and the West Indies is not as unqualified as it may at first appear.

His bleak report on the West Indies, whether, say, in *The Middle Passage* (1962) or *The Mimic Men* (1967) or in statements made to interviewers over the years, would seem totally dismissive, working to distance him from the region and to deny any debt to it. He has explicitly rejected the label 'West Indian writer' for himself. In a 1958 article, he argued, 'The only way out [of a too-limited audience and reputation] is to cease being a regional writer.'[2] Later he would be more cutting: '"West Indian" is a political word. It's all the things I reject. It's not me.'[3] We may ask, 'Why is "West Indian" a political word, as against, say, "British," "Russian" or "Japanese"?' That, however, is for another time.

So Naipaul, 50 years ago, in the first flush of success for his very Trinidadian 'social comedies' (to use his term)[4] was preparing to aim for wider horizons of subject matter, to cease being 'regional.' He had by 1958 published *The Mystic Masseur* (1957) and *The Suffrage of Elvira* (1958), and *Miguel Street* (1959) was imminent. Curiously enough, though, his next novel, his next book, which did not appear until 1961, and which was to be considered by many his greatest work and a classic of world literature, was the very Trinidadian *A*

House for Mr Biswas. It was only after he had published his West Indian travel book, *The Middle Passage* (1962), which started the 'tracing match' between him and the region, that he seemed to make a clean break and produced his 'English' novel, *Mr Stone and the Knights Companion* (1963).

So he took to the road, to become what the Jamaican painter and poet Gloria Escoffery mischievously called 'Mr. Big Time Naipaul,' who 'has left [his] home shores behind' to 'become the rootless internationalist he now claims to be.'[5] Naipaul had ended his 1958 article on the handicap of the regional writer by saying, 'Unless I am able to refresh myself by travel – to Trinidad, to India – I fear that living here [England] will eventually lead to my own sterility ….'[6] He has indeed travelled, not only to Trinidad and to India, but to the world of Islam, to Africa, Argentina, the US South, and to other places in the Caribbean, and his works, both non-fiction and fiction, continue to be the products of those travels. Of particular interest to my argument, though, is that at the outset, in as normal a statement as we could expect from any writer, he had identified Trinidad and India as 'source,' as the places to which he needed to travel for creative refreshment. He returned to Trinidad (and behind Trinidad, India) repeatedly and in different ways, whether literally, or for fictive locale and subject-matter, or by way of research into the history of the place. Taken together, these returns dramatise his effort to understand himself as the product of his beginnings. His work, taken as a whole in process, is a quest for that self which, to adapt Wordsworth's dictum, we simultaneously 'perceive' and 'half create.'[7]

There has been a certain touchiness about West Indian umbrage at Naipaul's derogatory remarks on the region, a touchiness which may be a sign of the sense of insecurity inherited by the ex-colonised. By contrast, Naipaul's sneering comments on contemporary English society or the Tony Blair government or Oxford University have raised no more than a ripple of amusement, perhaps a patronising ripple, in the British. There is no evidence that they feel threatened. One unfortunate result of all this is that some West Indians, in reaction to Naipaul's harsh, dismissive representations of the West Indies, his apparent dissociation of himself from the place, have for their part denied him any relevance to the region and dismissed him virtually unread. Yet there have been West Indians over the years who have continued to read Naipaul seriously and discriminatingly, recognising bias and limitation where they see it, while benefiting from his shrewd and challenging insights into our world, and delighting in his artistry. Running through this continuing attention is the conviction that Naipaul has not lost, cannot lose his West Indian connection.

The argument for Naipaul's indelible connection with his native place takes various turns. For example, Gloria Escoffery quotes from *The Mimic Men* two paragraphs in which the narrator-protagonist describes himself as a schoolboy in Trinidad being transported through rain by his father on his bicycle. Then she asks:

> How can a writer who can give the essence of an emotional experience between father and son in such a translucent, simple, deeply perceptive way be accused of being unsympathetic in his attitude to the people with whom he grew up? The same merits... appear in that masterpiece of humanity, *A House for Mr Biswas* (1981, 3).

Taking a cue from Escoffery, one may find all sorts of other examples to support the same question; to select just two: Naipaul's review of C.L.R. James's *Beyond A Boundary* and his short story 'Tell Me Who To Kill,' remarkable not only for its masterful use of Trinidadian Creole, but also for its intense compassion for the individual victim of society.

Commenting on one of Naipaul's more notorious pronouncements, 'Africa has no future',[8] Mervyn Morris notes:

> We know he doesn't literally mean what he has said, but we may bristle at what sounds like gratuitous rudeness....Some of these moments may perhaps be seen...as delightfully Trinidadian – Naipaul giving rein to verbal playfulness, outrageously following where the straight-man questioner has led. [9]

In other words, even at some moments when Naipaul may intend to be absolutely serious, we may read him as engaging in a kind of picong. There have been moments when, strange as it may seem, reading Lovelace and Naipaul, I have been struck by what seems to me a delightfully Trinidadian consanguinity between the two, notwithstanding important differences in their overall projects. At these times I sense an expressiveness characteristic of the land of 'mas,' and a flair for the moment when performance turns into pappyshow.

A leading idea in John Hearne's long-ago review of *The Middle Passage* is that Naipaul is never more West Indian than in his embarrassment at the

West Indies and in his readiness to put down the region. The idea is there, for instance, in Hearne's conceding that 'Naipaul is a great deal more than just another West Indian scholarship winner, bitterly ashamed of his origins.'[10] What perhaps stands out most from this statement is not the qualifier but the basic assertion, that Naipaul *is* 'another West Indian scholarship winner, bitterly ashamed of his origins.' Hearne posits that Naipaul 'is too intelligent not to recognize how many of these limitations he shares with his fellow West Indians...many of [the] limitations he finds in them' (1962, 66).

Still, Hearne began his review by conceding Naipaul's sharp eye for 'all that is pathetic, and so often contemptible, in our society' (65), suggesting in effect that West Indians need to pay attention to Naipaul, notwithstanding any shortcomings and biases in his way of seeing. Raoul Pantin is strong on this need to pay attention. He observes, cynically:

> Naipaul's painful misfortune may not only be his having looked Trinidad and Tobago and half the Third World straight in the eye and described what he's seen: the havoc colonialism leaves in its wake, all those 'half-made people and half-made societies,' so frail, so insecure, so full of mimicry, so mired in confused values.[11]

Early in *The Enigma of Arrival* there comes a paragraph germane to my argument. Reflecting on his feeling of the 'perfection' of the Wiltshire manor house in whose grounds he has come to live, and on the seemingly paradoxical idea that such signs of 'decay' as it presented were essential to his sense of the place's perfection, Naipaul wrote:

> To see the possibility, the certainty, of ruin, even at the moment of creation: it was my temperament. Those nerves had been given me as a child in Trinidad partly by our family circumstances: the half-ruined or broken-down houses we lived in, our many moves, our general uncertainty. Possibly too, this mode of feeling went deeper, and was an ancestral inheritance, something that came with the history that had made me: not only India, with its ideas of a world outside men's control, but also the colonial plantations or estates of Trinidad, to which my impoverished Indian ancestors had been transported in the last century – estates of which this Wiltshire estate, where I now lived, had been the apotheosis (1988, 52).

First, then, there is the basic acknowledgement that he was made by his history, and that Trinidad is a central fact of that history. Then there are some details which signify definitive factors in that making and in the product made: the references to 'nerves,' to 'the possibility, the certainty, of ruin,' to 'the half-ruined or broken down,' to his family's 'many moves,' and to 'colonial plantations.' These signifiers are consonant with major, characteristic features of Naipaul's writings, and they are key factors in the disposition and action, or inaction, of his characters. He haunts himself in his characters, even when he seems to distance them so markedly from himself.

These factors combine to produce the particular set of nerves that constitute the writer V.S. Naipaul. I use 'set' in two senses: as group or collection and as disposition, as in 'mindset' or 'set of face.' So the nerves are a result of the colonial condition. As Naipaul states in *The Enigma of Arrival*, 'I had taken to England all the rawness of my colonial's nerves, and those nerves had more or less remained…' (1988, 95). Again:

> The history I carried with me, together with the self-awareness that had come with my education and ambition, had sent me into the world with a sense of glory dead; and in England had given me the rawest stranger's nerves (52).

'Nerves' connotes a certain anxiety of self, an existential dread of the violation and reduction of self. This heightened sense of 'the possibility, the certainty of ruin' has a causative link to the reduced circumstances of his beginnings, to the impoverishment of his 'Indian ancestors [who] had been transported in the last century' to satisfy the greed and ego of the coloniser and the plantation system of indenture that had succeeded slavery. This original transportation and uprooting were followed only too inevitably by the 'many moves' of the family within the small space of the island, a movement, a restlessness and rootlessness fictionalised from early in the story of Mohun Biswas and repeated and repeated in his fictions on a global canvas, right up to the drifting of Willie Chandran, protagonist of his two latest novels, *Half a Life* (2001) and *Magic Seeds* (2004) from India to London to Mozambique to Berlin to India to London. This movement, fictive, fictionalised or autobiographical, is an antiheroic, postmodern, globalised variation on the picaresque.

This Naipaul, this personality, this particular set of nerves accounts for Naipaul's choice of the characters and societies which have been his focus. Frank Kermode has noted that, in *A Bend in the River*, 'a somewhat Naipaul-like character speaks of experiencing "a colonial rage…a rage with the people who had allowed themselves to be corralled into a foreign fantasy.'"[12] It is hardly surprising that Naipaul's artistic focus has been largely on the colonial, ex-colonial, neo-colonial, quasi-colonial Third World. To take the most recent example: Willie Chandran of *Half a Life*, is a confused, ineffectual throw-off of British colonialism in India. Named, by laughable accident, after the British novelist W. Somerset Maugham, he ends up in a Portuguese African colony (really Mozambique) when colonial rule is sputtering rudely to its end. The last third of the novel is a persuasively fictionalised report on the rude end of colonial rule in the country, and on the seemingly inevitable breakdown, decay and abandonment that ensue for what was already only a half-made, half-ruined society.

The set of nerves that is Naipaul makes a virtual fetish of wholeness and purity. It expresses itself in a horror of any violation of self, of hybridity, of damage or taint to pristine or wished-for completeness. It is deeply disturbed by anything 'half-and-half.' In labelling the life of Willie Chandran *Half a Life*, Naipaul was retrospectively labelling all the metamorphoses of the protagonist of all his books (and note 'protagonist,' singular) and they all relate to Naipaul. In *The Enigma of Arrival*, in quest of himself, reflecting on the fact that Jack, his English neighbour,

> ...lived among ruins, among superseded things....That idea of ruin and dereliction, of out-of-placeness, was something I felt about myself, attached to myself, a man from another hemisphere, another background, coming to rest in middle life in the cottage of a half neglected estate... (1988, 19).

In *The Enigma of Arrival* too, recalling his first journey away from Trinidad, he recalls how 'close [he was] to the village ways of his Asian-Indian community,' despite the fact that,

> Unhappy in his extended family, he was distrustful of larger, communal groupings. But that half-Indian world, that world removed in time and space from India, and mysterious to the man, its language not even half understood, its religion and religious rites not grasped, that half-Indian world was the social world the man knew (1988, 103).

Incidentally, the tactic of referring to himself in the third person, as 'the man,' dramatises the notion of autobiography as fiction, as self-construction.

Willie Chandran, a half-caste man with a half-and-half name and a half-Portuguese, half-African wife, finds, in the Portuguese African colony, that

> ...the world [he] had entered was only a half-and-half world, [where] many of the people...considered themselves, deep down, people of the second rank. They were not fully Portuguese and that was where their own ambition lay' (*Half a Life* 2001, 150).

So, for instance, Jacinto Correia 'had told his children, who were studying in Lisbon, that they were on no account to use public transport in Lisbon.... People must never think of them as colonial nobodies' (179). There were in the colony Portuguese, Africans and people of a 'half-and-half world'(150). It is the last named, his immediate circle, who are the focus of Willie's scrutiny. They are a fairly well-off clique of 'estate people,' but insecure in their half-and-half status, an insecurity deepened by the imminent collapse of such colonial order as exists.

To feel that one is a colonial nobody, a half-and-half person, to have one's individuality violated, one's wholeness tainted, or to suffer what Naipaul calls 'racial diminution' (*Enigma* 1988, 117), is about the gravest degradation that the Naipaulian persona can experience. Here again the roots of this feature may be found in Naipaul's childhood experience, as he himself relates it:

> I have always been fighting a hysteria that plagued me as a child....I mean the fear of being reduced to nothing, of feeling crushed. It's partly the old colonial anxiety of having one's individuality destroyed. And it also goes back to the family I grew up in – a typically Indian extended family (quoted in Michener 1981, 108).

This near-pathological horror at feeling that one has been thus tainted may occur in a variety of situations. In an interview with Margaria Fichtner, Naipaul once told of having been sent by someone a review he had written of one of Naipaul's books:

> It was meant to be very kind, but it was trivial, and I was so appalled at this kind of schoolboy attitude to this work that I felt, you know...sullied...I felt really violated...and for one day I was cast down with a kind of gloom of feeling sullied.[13]

This feeling has something in common with young Biswas's feeling ashamed of his place of domicile at Pagotes.

The nerves, the precariousness, the intimations of ruin, the dread of violation, taint, damage to the self – these are features of the self that Naipaul writes as he moves between autobiography, reportage and fiction. The travels and dislocations of the Naipaul persona at one and the same time represent the quest for self-knowledge as well as the self that is discovered or constructed.

The idea that people fashion identities for themselves has run through Naipaul's work from the beginning. This self-making has involved theatricality, performance. This feature has manifested itself at different levels. At first it was largely comic and satirical, an escape, for the characters, from the pressures of circumstance into play-acting and fantasy. However, it has also and increasingly been presented as an inevitable mode of the assertion of individuality. One performs one's idea of one's best self. Alternatively, one may collude in the violation of one's self by performing the degraded self which others more powerful impose on one. This collusion is painfully illustrated in the documentary opening and closing narratives of *In a Free State*: 'Prologue, from a Journal: The Tramp at Piraeus' and 'Epilogue, from a Journal: The Circus at Luxor.'[14]

In the former, Naipaul is enraged by the mocking cruelty meted out by his fellow passengers to the tramp; in the latter by the waiter with the camel-whip, for the pleasure of the tourists, to the boys grovelling for apples and bits of sandwiches tossed to them in sport. Naipaul, however, is also enraged at how, in both episodes, the victims seem, so self-degradingly, to accept the role of abject inferior and victim. The same principle is at work 30 years later in *Half a Life*, most strikingly in the brief episode of the 'big, light-eyed mulatto' tiler 'abused and shouted at by the Portuguese owner' of the restaurant on which the tiler is working (2001, 154). Willie Chandran's (and Naipaul's) sense of outrage is heightened by the tiler's compliance: 'He never replied to the shouts of the owner, whom he could so easily have knocked down. He just kept on working' (154–5). Then Willie asks, 'Who will rescue that man? Who will avenge him?' (155)

In *A Bend in the River*, role playing, as both idea and image, is essential. When the protagonist, Salim, visits London and falls in love with Kareisha, she shows what seems like a natural affection towards him, and he remarks: 'I luxuriated in this affection of Kareisha's, and acted out my man's role a little. It was wonderfully soothing. Acted – there was a lot of that about me at this time' (1979, 248). Here we see a major aspect of Salim's view of human behaviour – the idea that people, out of chronic need or weakness, are always prone to play-acting their lives.

When he says that 'there was a lot of that about me at this time,' he no doubt means that his behaviour at this time involved much role-playing. However, there is also a lot of acting about him all the time, in the sense that he is always noticing that people around him are putting on an act. Besides, it is not only on this occasion that he finds himself play-acting. One may even argue that the ultimate irony is that Salim's projection of himself as the painstakingly honest lifter of masks, exposer of the truth, is the novel's most elaborate instance of role-playing.

As is made explicit at the end of 'Prologue to an Autobiography,' the purpose of that narrative is to show how, by working back into his Trinidad history – into the family from which he emerged, and particularly into the stressful life of his father and his struggle to assert his individuality in the face of humiliating circumstances – he became V.S. Naipaul the writer, whom he was destined or willed himself to be. The process is in effect one of producing an identity by excavating and interpreting the history by which one sees oneself as having been made. The process of identity quest, of developing the idea of oneself, is re-enacted and extended in a subtle manner in *The Enigma of Arrival* and *A Way in the World.*

The Enigma of Arrival is centrally about Naipaul's view of his development, his journey as a writer, and how all that he has written has contributed to that quest for himself which he sees his writing as having been: 'Every exploration, every book, added to my knowledge, qualified my earlier idea of myself and the world' (1988, 154). The main movement of *The Enigma of Arrival* is towards the narrator's revision of his initial and indeed persuasive view of Jack's garden. The initial need and satisfaction were to see Jack's garden as a natural emanation of its locale, and Jack himself as an extension of that emanation, engaged in a natural, timeless activity instinct with the sacredness of antiquity. So initially it is with 'wonder' and 'envy' that Naipaul contemplates 'the satisfactions of his life – a man in his own setting, as I thought (to me an especially happy condition), a man in tune with the seasons and his landscape...' (*Enigma* 1988, 31). However, Naipaul comes to see that this view of Jack and his garden is like his picture of a Trinidad beach in a 'world before men, before the settlement,' that this view is also 'romance and ignorance.'

> So much that had looked traditional, natural, emanations of the landscape, things that country people did – the planting out of annuals, the tending of the geese, the clipping of the hedge, the pruning of the fruit trees – now turned out not to have been traditional or instinctive after all, but to have been part of Jack's way (*Enigma* 1988, 47).

'Jack's way.' Each of us must *construct* our life, not merely live it or endure it, must construct it according to our best idea of ourselves, *must*, in our way, make it, in the best sense, a fiction. Which is why I think that Naipaul is precisely and provocatively right to call *The Enigma of Arrival* a novel, when it is so transparently an autobiography. He is acknowledging that every autobiography, every biography, is ultimately a fiction, a construct, something shaped according to an idea, as indeed is every life, hence 'Jack's way.' The Chaplinesque, losing Biswas also has *his* way, even though in another sense he never has his way. Jack, even Jack, lives in the midst of ruin, of decay and flux, of newness and change; but he imposes his idea of himself on this futility, he shapes a garden, a world out of the seeming chaos, as the writer shapes a world.

A Way in the World incorporates the idea that the apparent truths that we see depend on our way of seeing, our way of looking. We each *make* (construct) our way in the world. In this collection of narratives, labelled 'a sequence' in the English edition, but, teasingly, 'a novel' in the American, the travel trope works to articulate the idea of personal self-invention, and how this idea connects with the issue of identity and the *agon* with history, the issue of understanding and coming to terms with the past, issues which have been virtual obsessions with so many West Indian writers of Naipaul's generation.

One of the links between the characters – real, historical or imaginary – in *A Way in the World* is that they are all travellers of one kind or another, or that their identities have been in some way determined by journeys of one kind or another. Take, for instance, the first one depicted in the book, a relatively minor personage, who might seem at first glance not to fit this pattern, but whose story introduces what are to prove central concerns of the book. He is Leonard Side, who 'dresses' dead bodies at Parry's Funeral Parlour, but also does flower arranging 'on the side' and teaches the members of the Women's Auxiliary Association to make bread and cakes. This is just the sort of bizarre juxtaposition that Naipaul delights in. There are others. For instance, although the schoolteacher who tells the story to Naipaul knew that Side 'was a Mohammedan,' he was at the same time

> …so much a man of his job – laying out Christian bodies, though nobody thought of it quite like that – that in that bedroom of his he even had a framed picture of Christ in Majesty, radiating light and gold, and lifting a finger of blessing (*A Way* 1995, 8).

The schoolteacher's shock involves the knowledge 'that the picture wasn't there for the religion alone: it was also for the beauty, the colours, the gold, the long wavy hair of Christ' (8).

Ultimately the sense of the incongruous, the bizarre, even the morbid, that attaches to Side is symptomatic of an incompleteness of self-knowledge, an incompleteness related to his loss of ancestral inheritance, his displacement, his loss of history:

> He knew he was a Mohammedan, in spite of the picture of Christ in the bedroom. But he would have had almost no idea of where he or his ancestors came from. He wouldn't have guessed that the name Side might have been a version of Sayed, and that his grandfather or great-grandfather might have come from a Shia Muslim group in India. From Lucknow, perhaps; there was even a street in St James called Lucknow Street. All Leonard Side would have known of himself and his ancestors would have been what he had awakened to in his mother's house in St James. In that he was like the rest of us (10).

That last sentence – 'In that he was like the rest of us' – is crucial to my argument about Naipaul's understanding of how Trinidad made him.

Further, Naipaul drops hints, here and there throughout the book, of his sense of identification with these characters, and of the idea of himself and his own quest for self, inheritance and 'home' as also being subjects of *A Way in the World* (the title of the Side chapter is 'An Inheritance'). The first sentence of the book is 'I left home more than forty years ago' (3). That word 'home,' uttered so easily, so 'normally,' has a remarkable ring, coming as it did at that point in Naipaul's writing journey, and the narrative that follows, through the stories of the various characters, is threaded by Naipaul's various returns to Trinidad. These returns mark stages in his own self-invention. Perhaps it is significant that the final chapter, which ends with the grimly ironic return of another Trinidadian, as a corpse in a coffin, to be 'dressed' in Parry's Funeral Parlour – perhaps it is significant to Naipaul's own story that this chapter is entitled 'Home Again.' And what is Naipaul's Nobel Lecture if not another return, to construct a succinct explanation of the trajectory of his life's work? 'I was born in a small country town called Chaguanas, two or three miles inland from the Gulf of Paria.'[15]

'In that he was like the rest of us.' Naipaul includes himself in the collective dilemma. Later, having introduced another character, the talented Trinidadian 'Blair' – who is to be assassinated in the African country where he went to work as an adviser to the Government – Naipaul says to the reader:

> Remember him (like me) trailing all the strands of his own complicated past, animated by that past, feeling the current running with him...and feeling (again like me) as he studied after work that he was at the most hopeful time of his life (*A Way* 1995, 27–8).

Again, having given his reading of the new black consciousness which he encountered on one return to Trinidad, his take on 'the sacrament of the square' (Woodford Square), Naipaul writes:

> Much of this feeling might have been in me – I was full of nerves on this return, for all kinds of reasons – but I believe I was only amplifying something that was true. The history of the place was known; its reminders were all around us; scratch us and we all bled (1995, 33–4).

So one may recognise in others undesirable aspects of oneself, aspects which derive from one's history and which one might instinctively wish to suppress. While the recognition bespeaks a kind of maturity, at the same time it may help to explain one's 'hang-ups.' When I contemplate Naipaul's 'put-down' of African-Caribbean people and black people in general, remembering these sentences from *The Enigma of Arrival* steadies me:

> In Puerto Rico there had been the Trinidad Negro in a tight jacket on his way to Harlem. Here was a man from Harlem or black America on his way to Germany. In each case there were aspects of myself. But, with my Asiatic background, I resisted the comparison... (*Enigma* 1988, 126–7).

Might it be that the similarity of shaping experience is so uncomfortably strong that it provokes a countervailing compulsion to establish distance between the two subjects, for fear of taint, loss of self, and, to use Naipaul's term, 'racial diminution'?

If Leonard Side does not 'understand his nature' because he does not know his history, Naipaul also concedes that full self-knowledge may be an impossibility, as is anyone's knowledge of another, including the writer's knowledge of his characters:

> ...I cannot really explain the mystery of Leonard Side's inheritance. Most of us know the parents and grandparents we come from. But we go back and back, forever; we go back all of us to the very beginning; in our blood and bone and brain we carry the memories of thousands of beings. I might say that an ancestor of Leonard Side's came from the dancing groups of Lucknow, the lewd men who painted their faces and tried to live like women. But that would only be a fragment of his inheritance, a fragment of the truth. We cannot understand all the traits we have inherited. Sometimes we can be strangers to ourselves (*A Way* 1995, 11).

That is as poignant and as resonant a chord as one will hear in all of Naipaul. Here is the acclaimed truth-sayer telling us that the truth is fragments.

'Few of us,' writes Naipaul, 'are without the feeling that we are incomplete' (128). So we must, as it were, invent complete selves in order to make some purposeful way in the world. Indeed, in order to live we must construct our worlds – to each person, each generation, each culture, each civilisation its own: 'We all inhabit "constructs" of a world. Ancient people had their own. Our grandparents had their own; we cannot absolutely enter into their constructs. Every culture has its own: men are infinitely malleable' (159).

Ultimately, in the journey that is his writing, a writing that repeatedly returns to his past as he moves forward in the present, Naipaul seeks to construct a complete, inviolable self which can report with authority and dispassion on the fragmented, uneasy selves that he sees through his writer's eye. As Michael Gorra remarked:

> Virtually all his work since the 1994 'Prologue to an Autobiography' has burnished the shield of his own myth, revisiting the scenes of his earlier travels, recapitulating the story of how he stepped from colonized Trinidad into the history of English literature.[16]

Or again, this from John Bayley:

> Naipaul thoroughly understands the romance of himself – what the novelist John Cowper Powys called his life illusion – the inner saga of himself and his destiny which each person secretly carries alongside the physical circumstances of his existence.[17]

This self-in-performance, this 'life illusion,' which is not really all that secret, is built, one might say simplified, around a few key characteristics.

To try to draw together the different threads that go to make the discovered or constructed self is to see how Naipaul's books play off against, speak to and with one another. It is to understand all the better his own summary of himself, that is, the self-realised in the writing: 'I will say I am the sum of my books. Each book, intuitively sensed and, in the case of the fiction, intuitively worked out, stands on what has gone before, and grows out of it' ('Postscript' 2004, 182–3). So, for instance, as James Wood remarks, 'Many of the elements in [Naipaul's] memoir *Finding the Centre* are repeated in the novel *Half a Life*,' and in the latter 'Naipaul seems to be writing a very dark variation on his own circumstances.'[18] Similarly, *A House for Mr Biswas* is subsumed in *The Enigma of Arrival*, and the two are mutually illuminating. *A House for Mr Naipaul* would have been a not-inappropriate title for the latter.

In 1993, when V.S. Naipaul became the first recipient of the David Cohen Prize, Britain's then newest and biggest literary prize, I wrote a small piece for the *Jamaica Observer* to mark the achievement. In it I said, among other things:

> Naipaul is quoted as having remarked, on hearing of his latest award, 'It is the British Literature Prize and I like that, because this writing career of mine has been conducted here.' This sounds like a perfectly decent and reasonable gesture of thanks, but it is also the sort of Naipaul statement that is likely to set some of us off again, on the tedious argument about whether Naipaul has betrayed the West Indies, let the side down, gone over to the colonizer.[19]

That was eight years before Naipaul won the Nobel Prize, and we all remember how true to form he was in his first public statement on being told that he had won, and the shock, disappointment, hurt, and even outrage with which his failure to acknowledge Trinidad was greeted. At this point I have to insert an aside, citing a new item that appeared in the *Daily Express* on Tuesday,

April 17, 2007 under the heading 'I'm to blame, not my husband.' Yet even this story burnishes the Naipaul myth. Here is the first part of the sentence that begins Lady Naipaul's explanation: 'When he got the Nobel, we were completely taken aback and my husband went to sleep.' Who else, having heard that they had won the Nobel Prize, would have been so completely taken aback they went to sleep?

Anyway, one relic of that moment in 2001 is a letter to the editor of the *Trinidad Guardian*. The letter, by M.F. Rahman of Woodbrook, reads like a letter which a character in a Naipaul novel may well have written. I quote most of it:

> Despite his disavowal of the land of his birth, the world knows the fatherland of Sir Vidia is Trinidad and Tobago. T & T, therefore, has no need to rush to embrace a churlish son who spurns the land of his formative and impressionable youth whence flowed all of his insights that conceived his literary works. / The loss is Sir Vidia's...by his own hand he is orphaned from his land. / We bestowed upon him, in proper time, our highest honour before his latest crowning prize, and at that time he yet retained some filial gratitude now vanished with the years. / It ill becomes our land to slight this son, ungrateful though he may be, for we cannot disown him in return. Yet we also should not rush unseemingly to grasp a share of his recent glory and seek to bask grinningly in his selfish fame. A fatherland deserves more seemly consideration. / So honour him we must, for generations will forget his ego and wonder how we could have been so shallow as to deny him some sort of name. / Yet we must make it plain to all that sons of our soil should better comport themselves on the global stage or face paternal censure.[20]

There we have life, Trinidad and Tobago life, imitating Naipaul.

I like to think that there is a nice irony in the theme of this symposium, since the phrase 'created in the West Indies' occurs in Naipaul's notorious statement in *The Middle Passage* that 'nothing was created in the West Indies.'[21] So set beside that the conference theme: 'V.S. Naipaul: Created in the West Indies.'

Notes

1. V.S. Naipaul, *The Enigma of Arrival* (1987; repr., New York: Vintage, 1988), 52; *Half a Life* (New York: Alfred A. Knopf, 2001); *A Way in the World* (1994; repr., New York: Vintage, 1995).
2. Naipaul, 'London,' *Times Literary Supplement,* August 15, 1958, 4; reprinted in *The Overcrowded Barracoon.*
3. Charles Michener, 'The Dark Visions of V.S. Naipaul,' *Newsweek,* November 16, 1981, 108.
4. For Naipaul's reference to his 'social comedies,' see *The Overcrowded Barracoon and Other Articles.*
5. Gloria Escoffrey, 'Reflections on the Rain,' *Daily Gleaner,* August 25, 1981, 3.
6. Naipaul, *The Overcrowded Barracoon* (Harmondsworth: Penguin, 1976), 16–7.
7. William Wordsworth, 'Lines Composed a Few Miles Above Tintern Abbey,' in *The Oxford Anthology of English Literature,* eds. Frank Kermode and John Hollander, vol. 2 (New York, London, Toronto: Oxford University Press, 1973), 146–50.
8. Recorded in Elizabeth Hardwick, 'Meeting V.S. Naipaul,' *New York Times Book Review,* May 13, 1979, 36.
9. Mervyn Morris, 'Sir Vidia and the Prize,' *World Literature Today* 76, (Spring 2002): 12.
10. J. Hearne, Review of *The Middle Passage, Caribbean Quarterly* 8, no. 4 (December 1962): 66.
11. Raoul Pantin, 'V.S. Naipaul,' *Express,* December 14, 1984, 8.
12. Frank Kermode, 'In the Garden of the Oppressor,' *New York Times Book Review,* March 22, 1987, 11.
13. Margaria Fitchner, 'V.S. Naipaul's Way in the World,' *Miami Herald* (International Edition), May 29, 1994: 2D.
14. Naipaul, *In a Free State* (1971; repr., Harmondsworth: Penguin, 1973).
15. Naipaul, 'Postscript: Two Worlds' (The Nobel Lecture), *Literary Occasions* (London: Picador, 2004), 183.
16. Michael Gorra, 'Postcolonial Studies,' *New York Times Book Review,* October 28, 2001, 9.
17. John Bayley, 'Country Life,' *New York Review of Books,* April 9, 1987, 3.
18. James Wood, 'Damage [rev. *Half a Life*],' *New Republic,* November 5, 2001, 34.
19. Edward Baugh, 'Let Us Praise Naipaul,' *Jamaica Observer,* April 4, 1993, 49.
20. M.F. Rahman, Letter to the Editor, *Trinidad Guardian,* October 31, 2001.
21. Naipaul, *The Middle Passage,* (1962; repr., Harmondsworth, Middlesex: Penguin, 1969), 29.

2

NAIPAUL'S LEGACY:
Made in the West Indies – for Export

Evelyn O'Callaghan

What can be said about the work of V.S. Naipaul that hasn't been said already? So many books, so many *kinds* of writing, so many critical responses; where to begin? Predictably, by referencing the (in)famous quotation from *The Middle Passage*: 'The history of the islands can never be satisfactorily told. Brutality is not the only difficulty. History is built around achievement and creation; and nothing was created in the West Indies.'[1] This is the statement that clearly – and ironically? – informs the theme of this symposium: 'Nothing was created in the West Indies.' What might 'created in the West Indies' mean now? What did it mean in 1962 when *The Middle Passage* was published? In this paper, I explore a possible hypothesis: that in certain cases, being 'created in the West Indies' is, for many artists, both the fulcrum of their work and the cause of their exile or multiple location.

I cannot recall ever seeing any product labelled, 'Made in the West Indies.' Yet the brand name is familiar to all who follow cricket, and to most in the world of literature. True, we might quibble about whether the correct term is 'West Indian' or 'Caribbean,' or whether we need to qualify it with linguistic or ethnic prefixes. However, in 2007 there is no question that there exists an internationally recognised corpus of writing, and a body of writers, created in the West Indies and/or by West Indians. We teach it, our students read it, histories are written about its development, and theoretical works expand the reaches of its nomenclature beyond national and regional boundaries to include diaspora, postcolonial and whatever other new categories of writing may emerge. There is even a West Indian literary *canon*, contested these days, but nonetheless consistent in most literary histories, anthologies and critical studies. The work of V.S. Naipaul is very much a part of that canon. Not without controversy, however.

Currently, the work of Jean Rhys generally makes the canon too. Yet there was a period when the inclusion of *Wide Sargasso Sea* in a West Indian literature syllabus was hotly debated in regional literary journals, and questions raised about the racial, residential or political qualifications required for conferment of the West Indian stamp of approval upon a text or a writer. Similarly suspicious critical reactions attached to another 'outsider' with unfashionable, even 'reactionary' political views, whose fictions focused on the colonial damage to, and complex affiliations of, a (then) marginal group in West Indian literature, those of Indo-Caribbean origin. Naipaul was denounced as a colonial; an English, as opposed to a West Indian, writer; a traitor; a 'postcolonial mandarin' who mocked Caribbean society. Peter Webb, in a *Newsweek* feature of 1980, records the reaction of local critics to Naipaul's literary awards: 'they dismissed him as "a cold and sneering prophet" who dealt only in "castrated satire."'[2] Surveying Naipaul's literary career, Caryl Phillips notes that,

> it has often appeared as though, in order to distinguish himself as separate and apart, Naipaul has decided to be hypercritical of and at times extraordinarily insensitive to the human condition as it appears in, what he would term, less civilized parts of the world than the West, including of course his native Trinidad.[3]

That was then. In the context of the political climate of the 1960s, Naipaul's caustic take on his birthplace was understandably resented. Can we *now* engage with a new 'critical moment' (Alison Donnell's term)[4] when such evaluations of Naipaul's early writing might legitimately be revisited, and some of his critiques of Caribbean society scrutinised for current relevance? Have we now matured to the extent that our writers have the right to criticise us?

For when we look back over some 50 years of West Indian literature, Naipaul's early works – the West Indian phase of his writing, on which I focus here – still have something to tell us about our situation. His fictions feature characters who increasingly see their social and economic reality as restrictive; who inhabit 'outsider' status *at home* in the Caribbean; who have internalised a colonially determined, outward directed consciousness; and who crave 'export,' escape from the parochial limitations of their environment. This condition is discernible, if differently configured, in recent West Indian fiction and the result is the same: displacement. Naipaul's characters, like those of Caribbean diaspora writers, are always in motion (physically or psychologically): they migrate to another part of the island, of the region, to the 'Mother Country' or North America, the new imperial centre. Why the common motif: constriction and the desire for escape? This is because alienation was part of what it meant to be 'created in the West Indies,' and this has been a pervasive theme in Naipaul's writing.

As John Thieme has commented, the vast majority of Naipaul's work, fiction and non-fiction, 'has been concerned with the human consequences of imperialism in colonial and postcolonial societies.'[5] In *The Middle Passage*, for example, Naipaul articulates this colonial conditioning:

> Trinidad was too unimportant and we could never be convinced of the value of reading the history of a place which was, as everyone said, only a dot on the map of the world. Our interest lay all in the world outside, the remoter the better (1996, 36).

Hence the contempt for 'colonial smallness' and the desire articulated in his Nobel lecture, for the 'bigger world' outside.[6] To be *modern*, for Naipaul, was 'to ignore local products and to use those advertised in American magazines' (40), to mimic imported manners and values, to style oneself on foreign film stars. He also accurately pinpoints the source of this self-denigration, this mimicry, this need for external validation. In 2007 it seems obvious, but in 1962 Naipaul's vilification of the legacy of colonial history was unusual:

> This was the greatest damage done to the Negro by slavery. It taught him self-contempt. It set him the ideals of white civilization and made him despise every other (62).

> Again and again one comes back to the main, degrading fact of the colonial society; it never required efficiency, it never required quality, and these things, because unrequired, became undesirable (53).

Naipaul's contempt for 'colonial smallness' was not unique. Kenneth Ramchand, writing on Naipaul's slightly younger contemporary, Peter Minshall, explains that as a young man he was profoundly influenced by

Trinidadian Carnival culture, but *also* sought 'to go away and be an artist in the real world where art was made: in London, in New York, in Paris.'[7] A generation later, Ramchand himself recalls his *own* younger self as 'the boy with a sound colonial education….He had been prepared. His destiny was elsewhere' (Ramchand 2007, 33).

Like Naipaul, the fictions of George Lamming, Austin Clarke and Merle Hodge indict the cost of this 'sound colonial education' with its dual – and dysfunctional – worldview. *The Mimic Men* sketches with devastating insight the school as a breeding ground for mimicry. 'My first memory of school,' Ralph recalls, 'is of taking an apple to the teacher. This puzzles me. We had no apples on Isabella. It must have been an orange; yet my memory insists on the apple.'[8] No wonder. His indoctrination into the fantasy of Englishness ('the coronation of the English king and the weight of his crown, so heavy he can wear it only a few seconds', Naipaul, *Mimic Men* 1969, 90) trains Ralph to view his Caribbean reality through the prism of a storybook fantasy: 'calendar pictures of English gardens superimposed on our Isabellan villages of mud and grass' (89). Real life lies elsewhere for such colonial subjects. Schooled in mimicry, steeped in colonial insecurity and alienation, Naipaul's characters seek to find themselves elsewhere.

Reinforcing the desire for escape is Naipaul's representation of the colonial Caribbean as a place where difference is rarely tolerated. In *The Middle Passage*, for example, he observes of Trinidad that ambition, excellence, the desire to achieve are regarded with suspicion:

> It was...a place where a recurring word of abuse was 'conceited,' an expression of the resentment felt of anyone who possessed unusual skills. Such skills were not required by a society which produced nothing, never had to prove its worth, and was never called upon to be efficient. And such people had to be cut down to size or, to use the Trinidad expression, be made to 'boil down' (1996, 35).

Gordon Rohlehr comments on the painful scene in *Biswas,* where Shama smashes her daughter's doll's house, an extravagant gift from Mr Biswas, because in the communal world of Hanuman House it is unacceptable to single out one child for such distinction: 'Anything which manifests individuality and difference causes dread, envy and hostility in Hanuman House,' Rohlehr notes.[9] Hanuman House serves as a microcosm of the closed Indo-Trindidadian world of the time, and since Mr Biswas insists on asserting his individuality, Rohlehr argues, he has to leave the communal space, face the void, the unknown outside world. Always the need to escape, to leave behind conformity to the mediocre norm and find a space where alternative subject positions can be explored. Wherever he finds himself in the extensive Tulsi empire, Mr Biswas insists that '[r]eal life was to begin for them soon, and elsewhere'; the temporary sojourns are but 'a pause, a preparation.'[10] Interestingly, Rohlehr connects the need of Mr Biswas and the narrator of *Miguel Street* to flee such constriction, with the escape of Naipaul the author:

> Rejecting Hanuman House and Miguel Street as two sides of the greater nightmare of being an Indian in Trinidad, he [Naipaul] seeks the freedom of the independent personality, and makes the difficult choice of exile and dispossession (1968, 138).

I would like to suggest that the exposure of Caribbean intolerance for certain forms of difference – and the apparently concomitant alternative of exile and displacement for such 'outsiders' – is part of Naipaul's legacy. Very generally, his early work speaks to the desire of those with aspirations (to make something, to write, to become artists, to become educated); the desire to escape what is demonstrably a materialistic, semi-literate colonial society obsessed with race and class, one that demands that literature is writing for 'my people' first. Speaking equally generally, one can argue that Jamaica Kincaid's early works detail the desire of women who wish to inhabit subject positions other than the traditional female role expected of them: again, the desire to escape, in this case, a conservative, patriarchal colonial Caribbean society.

María Cristina Rodríguez maintains that one important consequence of migration by women involves 'rejecting or reorganizing negative gender assumptions: a woman's "place" in island society as sex object, a faithful, passive and subservient wife, or the sacrificing mother of baby boys.'[11] Rodríguez suggests that nostalgia for 'what women lose' in migrating is consistently tempered by memories of problematic situations left behind: 'kinship abuse, gender oppression, sexual repression, violence...repressive and controlling fathers and mothers, abusing husbands...the burden of domestic work, the absence of male breadwinners...and gender fixity' (Rodriguéz 2005, 19–20). Certainly, it is 'gender fixity' that the eponymous protagonists of *Annie John* and *Lucy* categorically reject and cite as their motive for escaping their island society. A motive which Kincaid the writer shares? The 1960s Naipaul would definitely share Kincaid's assertion in 1997: 'I could not have become a writer while living among the people I knew best.'[12]

In the contemporary literary scene, I posit that Naipaul's construction of alienation and trauma at home for those who are 'different,' and the possibility of fulfilment abroad for these 'others,' finds resonance in the work of another Trinidadian writer of Indian ethnic origin, Shani Mootoo. Mootoo's three fictional works, like Naipaul's, deal with those who feel themselves to be outsiders at home and who come to see the migrant condition as the only viable alternative. The writing of these and other West Indian writers – almost always resident abroad – expand the horizons of literary history by acknowledging and critiquing a regrettable reality: that Caribbean societies create certain kinds of subjects who, by virtue of their unacceptable difference, are 'made for export.'

Jamaica Kincaid: The Right to Criticise

Bruce Bawer notes that Naipaul, in his Nobel Prize speech, described his purpose as a writer: 'to tell the truth about the world, however much that truth may confound ideology.'[13] Jamaica Kincaid also seeks this elusive clarity, and her construction of Caribbean colonial society is equally unflattering; Geoffrey Wheatcroft's pithy phrase 'Vidia Naipaul doesn't do nice,'[14] may equally apply to Kincaid. Indeed, her non-fictional writing shares Naipaul's disgust for the (unconscious) complicity of her countrymen in what he repeatedly terms the worst consequences of slavery and colonialism: self contempt; the devaluation of the local in favour of blind mimicry of the imported; the normalisation of mediocrity; and picaresque 'ginnalship' (Anansi tactics) at all levels. Jane King's excellent, if caustic, analysis of Kincaid's *A Small Place* (1988), acknowledges that

> [t]here is a conservatism about small places that is unnerving and the...fear of stasis, which may or may not be stagnation. Stimulation is different to come by in such places and Kincaid the writer does well perhaps to fear that lack. It leads to a variety of manifestations and one is the lifestyle that killed her youngest brother – a relentless search for sexual stimulation to fill the void created by the lack of any other kind.[15]

King goes on to observe that those who leave, like Kincaid, tend subsequently to look back at their societies with concern if not repugnance: 'Kincaid's attitude to the people of Antigua suggests that she believes that living in a small place coarsens both the understanding and the feelings' (890). Shades of Naipaul! Astutely, King questions why Naipaul was roundly attacked 'for his supposed demeaning of things Caribbean' while Walcott, who mocks and repudiates the political ideologies embraced by West Indian critics, politicians or writers, is tolerated. This is because Walcott lived and worked in the region 'and as a Caribbean person was deemed to have the right to comment [negatively] on Caribbean people' (891–92). Naipaul, on the other hand, forfeited that right by migrating. Yet, she points out, Kincaid, who left the region at about the same age as Naipaul, attracts critical approbation even as she searingly indicts her birthplace. Why is *her* critique deemed acceptable? For King demonstrates that, like Naipaul's, Kincaid's 'travel writing' situates the narrator 'in a unique position able to understand the tourist and the Antiguan and despise both while identifying with neither' (895).

'The Antiguans are so corrupt and money-grubbing,' King paraphrases Kincaid, 'because that is what they learned from the corrupt and money-grubbing English colonisers. The English were terrible, but the Antiguans learned from them to be worse' (897). This is essentially the same point Naipaul makes about Trinidad in *The Middle Passage*. Yet Kincaid, in an interview with Frank Birbalsingh, attacks Naipaul for learning 'to loathe where he came from, and to look at it in an untruthful way.'[16] Birbalsingh bravely responds that Kincaid's *A Small Place*

> ...seems to reproduce many of the insights of *The Middle Passage* which is still considered to be a destructive book...in the sense that both...describe a small country which had been despoiled by centuries of colonial exploitation, with the result that it's left with a people who now exploit themselves (140).

I would suggest that we may now have reached a 'critical moment' where we can more dispassionately respond to writing that characterises flaws in Caribbean social constructs. In *The Middle Passage*, Naipaul critiques West Indian writers for subsuming their work to the reflection and flattery of 'the prejudices of their race or colour groups' (1996, 64). Donnell rightly points out that this tendency has a long shelf life. That is, Caribbean critical reception has tended to favour writing that portrays the heroic resistance and survival of oppressed groups and individuals, while there is some distaste for texts which demonstrate profound limitations and insecurities among such groups and individuals. As the Bajan saying goes, 'God don't like ugly,' and neither do many West Indian readers and critics. Perhaps now, however, we can look at ugly more closely.

For if, as Alison Donnell argues, 'it is a general precept of postcolonial literary criticism that reading literature can bring us to an understanding of the conditions of being in such a way as to increase the possibility of positively reshaping those conditions' (2006, 232), then Kincaid's and Mootoo's writing now, like Naipaul's early work, highlights issues that urgently demand our attention. Caryl Phillips asks, with King, '[w]hy somebody who lives so comfortably outside thinks she has the right to criticise those who have to live inside?' (2002, 145). He answers his own question; because 'only somebody with her heart in Antigua could have written with such ferocity of purpose and self-revelatory hurt. Quite simply, she has the right to criticise because, irrespective of residence or nationality, she belongs' (146). While I would argue that exactly the same can be said of Naipaul, the wider point is that Caribbean critics can now *ask* such questions, can revisit notions of which authors have the right to offer such critiques, and why. This is a part, I propose, of Naipaul's legacy.

Shani Mootoo: 'Novels of Migritude'

Kincaid's Lucy migrates in order to escape her mother's internalised systems of patriarchal control. As Donnell explains, Lucy needs 'to be free from her mother's low expectations for her future and high hopes for her sexual morality; free, that is, from the conventional scripting of Antiguan femininity' (2006, 197). Like Kincaid, Shani Mootoo also constructs the West Indian home space as a place where traditional gender roles are still rigidly policed and transgression of 'proper' female sexual conduct results in dysfunctional generational and gender relations, and sometimes in horrific domestic and sexual violence. By contrast, the metropolitan centre seems a more positive location for the 'freeing up' of alternative sexual subject positions. Certainly, Naipaul's depiction of Indo-Caribbean women's socialisation into obedience, loyalty to caste and patriarchy at the cost of their own agency, is pursued in Mootoo's three fictions. Also, like Naipaul's early work, Mootoo's fictions vividly demonstrate the quotidian employment of violence against women who transgress. In her latest novel, *He Drown She in the Sea*, the female protagonist who crosses moral and class boundaries has to flee her island home to escape the murderous jealousy of her husband. In several of the stories in *Out on Main Street*, Indo-Trinidadian women are subservient and decorous, fearful of brutality or abandonment at the hands of their male partners:

> *...you drive me to want to beat the shit out of you*....In his mind he can see the dark purple, green and navy blue bruises on Tanya's shoulder blade. A curious satisfaction, pride of possession, comes over him when he watches them turn colour.[17]

Donnette Francis calls attention to developments in West Indian writing that, as critics, we must take into account. Specifically, she refers to the 'unspeakability' of this kind of intimate violence committed against women which is finally being addressed by 'third wave' Caribbean women's writing. Such writing is the 'transnational' product of authors like Edwidge Danticat, Patricia Powell, Elizabeth Nunez, Oonya Kempadoo and Shani Mootoo, all of whom have lived and written for extensive periods *outside* the Caribbean. Francis valorises these crucial interventions into the 'hushed up' stories of Caribbean sexual subordination and abuse 'at home,' literary texts which openly challenge 'sexual values in the region' and 'reveal the violent inner workings of dominant sexual ideologies.'[18] I want to suggest that the connection between Naipaul's construction of alienation and trauma at home and the possibility of fulfilment abroad, is echoed in the fictions of Shani Mootoo. Specifically, several of Mootoo's novels and short stories, like those of Naipaul and Kincaid, focus on characters who are constructed as outsiders at home and who come to see the migrant condition as the only viable alternative. In Mootoo's case the mark of 'difference' is not the desire for artistic achievement, or for freedom from gender inequality, but the desire for same-sex love.

In *Cereus Blooms at Night*, the lesbian lovers have no option but to escape – once again – a jealous husband's murderous rage and a society's opprobrium, leaving girl children behind to face a perverse punishment for their mother's 'difference.' Also in several of the stories in *Out on Main Street*, 'abroad' (in this case, Canada) is portrayed as far more homely because more tolerant of difference, less imbricated in powerful patriarchal and heterosexist norms. As Otoh's mother explains to her transgendered child in *Cereus*, 'you don't realize almost everybody in this place wish they could be somebody or something else?'[19] The fulfilment of that desire is not permitted 'in this place.' One is reminded of Naipaul's remark in *The Middle Passage* about the fear of nonconformity in Trinidadian society, the need for everyone to 'boil down.' In *Cereus*, difference is punished and the collusion of the community in male abuse is forcibly highlighted: the serial rape of his daughter is referred to as the father's having 'mistaken Mala for his wife.' After all, Mala's mother 'had mistaken another woman for her husband' (1999, 197). The implication is that the daughter is enduring what a wife *normally* endures; invoking the respectable marital institution masks the actual horror of violent incest. The silencing of such perversion, the inability/failure to name it, and the link between the unnatural sexual behaviour of the father with that of the (lesbian) mother, implicitly indicts the deeply conservative nature of Caribbean morality, of intolerant and repressive attitudes to sexual desire and sexual difference.

Reviewing *Cereus*, Jane Bryce notes that Mootoo's text pushes back categories of gender and sexual orientation and attends to the silenced stories of homosexuality in the West Indies. Significantly, it is writers like Mootoo who have *left*, who are based in North America or Europe, that dare to treat with such issues in their work.[20] Faith Smith, in her preface to a special issue of *Small Axe* ('Genders and Sexualities'), observes that in both legal and popular discourse, male homosexuality is viewed as a transgression of the 'moral fabric of society' which threatens 'the image of the virile, straight, Caribbean man,' and is publicly denounced as an infection from abroad.[21] Witness one (there are many such) letter in the local Barbadian press, 'Take the high road on moral values' by Angelo Lascelles. The writer castigates talk 'about decriminalising homosexuality (which is very nasty) and prostitution, to ruin our Constitution' linking

> ...these two acts [sic], which are based on no morals whatsoever and which by The Bible are deemed as fornication, [and] would be basically giving these two classes of people license to parade up and down our streets displaying what they do in their spare time.[22]

Such folly sends the wrong message to future generations: 'If God made man for man, he would not have made Adam and Eve. And if God made women to exploit themselves...he would not have instituted marriage'

(Lascelles 2005, 10). The fear of and hostility towards expressions of female sexuality and male homosexuality are the common stuff of such male-authored letters.

In the 1960s, Naipaul (significantly, located outside of the region) highlighted the traumatic consequences of colonial alienation, self-contempt and mimicry. In the 1990s, Kincaid (significantly, located outside of the region) turned an equally angry eye on the traumatic consequences of internalised colonial patriarchy in the West Indies and its enforced policing of gender roles and sexual double standards. In the twenty-first century, Mootoo (significantly, located outside of the region) exposes the 'trauma, damage and loss that are caused by the denial of sexual self-determination and by the violent enforcement of female purity' (Donnell 2006, 208–9). We are talking here about *real* trauma. The kind of trauma reported on February 15, 2007 in the *Jamaica Observer*:

> Three men branded as homosexuals were yesterday rescued by police from an angry mob outside a pharmacy in Tropical Plaza, where they had been holed up for almost an hour....The approximately 2,000 people gathered outside the Kingston pharmacy hurled insults at the three men, with some calling for them to be killed...the three men and the staff inside the pharmacy were visibly terrified as the mob demanded that they be sent out so they could administer their brand of justice....The cops were forced to disperse the large mob by dispensing tear gas....[23]

Jennifer Rahim, referring to the 'discourse of [the] unspeakable' in Caribbean writing, underlines the mapping of the local space as one in which the particular kinds of sexual difference alluded to above cannot be accommodated: 'Whether denial is expressed as physical violence, indifference or polite deference, it seems that the terms of existence prescribed by the heterosexual status quo for same-sex oriented persons is mandatory invisibility.'[24] The poignant title of Dionne Brand's *In Another Place, Not Here* (2000) reflects the vain search of Caribbean lesbians for a place in the region where their right to love is recognised. At a West Indian literature conference, held in Trinidad in 2006, Shani Mootoo attracted some hostile reactions when she admitted that, for her, Trinidad could no longer be home: her sexual preference and her self-constitution as a woman who refuses traditional gender roles, constructed her – in 2006 – as much of an outsider as Naipaul felt himself to be in the 1960s. Like him, Mootoo is created in the

West Indies, but for export. Donnell calls for critics of Caribbean literature to address the inscription of diverse sexual identities in their theorisations of difference (2006, 181), referring to Mootoo's fiction as prioritising the troubling consequences of the heterosexual imperatives that operate in the Caribbean. Indeed, Donnell suggests that such writing of difference makes the case for a new kind of 'social contract through which sexual difference can be mapped onto the identity matrix of Caribbeanness' (9). For her, Mootoo's work – rather like Naipaul's – has a 'diagnostic' function: that is, the 'airing of prejudices, traditions and social practices that disempower through the policing of rigid sexual and racialised identities' (208). Regardless of Naipaul's personal views about such 'difference,' Mootoo's work reconfigures his legacy for the current generation.

Postscript: Naipaul's Legacy - 'Created in the West Indies'

> Why were we born under the star of rhyme
> Among a displaced people lost on islands...?
> Here we are architects with no tradition,
> Are hapless builders upon no foundation. [25]

This paper proposes consideration of a model of Caribbean literary history that, following Pius Adesanmi, seeks 'connections between things' rather than emphasising discontinuities and ruptures.[26] Increasingly, students at the University of the West Indies, when exposed to a range of early and recent West Indian writing, make unexpected links; when the focus is on rigidly stratified periods or schools, they tend to overlook connections. I have argued that part of Naipaul's legacy lies in exposing the consequences of certain norms and expectations in West Indian society which marginalise difference and exceptionality, and construct such marginalised subjects as fit only for export. However, his influence can *also* be observed in the less controversial area of style.

Laurence Breiner, writing on Eric Roach, refers to 'the dilemma of his generation' (2006, 33) outlined in the epigraph from Roach, above: that is, the dilemma of staying at home and – usually – achieving little acclaim, or going abroad in order to get published, reach an audience and concomitantly be adjudged successful at home. As Bawer reflects, Naipaul (like Ralph Singh in *The Mimic Men)* 'is haunted by the question: What *does* a gifted, ambitious person from a place like Trinidad do with his life....Is such a person fated to end his life in exile, a lonely émigré?' (2002, 374). Roach, Naipaul and other early West Indian writers express concern about the lack of local models and authorial traditions. Yet out of this 'void' and out of the anguish and vain mimicry that constituted the colonial condition, out of a society that mocked the very profession of writer, Naipaul's father Seepersad *did* produce and publish his stories. The story of how he came to his writing is now a classic of West Indian literature, *A House for Mr Biswas.* After Seepersad, Sam Selvon's *The Lonely Londoners* (1956) and Naipaul's first three fictions (written and published within a year or two of Selvon's) as well as *A House for Mr Biswas* and *The Middle Passage,* furthered the incorporation of Trinidadian vernacular and the insertion of the marginal, 'exotic' Indo-Caribbean subject into highly crafted literary genres like the short story, the comic novel, the *bildungsroman,* and the travel journal. Nothing was created in the West Indies? In an interview with Alastair Niven (2004), Naipaul acknowledges his early awareness that he couldn't simply mimic the traditional English novel with the added input of 'pouring our own experiences into it. This meant that we were really writing other people's books and falsifying experience, because experience had to find its own form.'[27] His creative work has, I maintain, engaged with this task of constructing its own 'correct form' for the mixed-worlds, postcolonial reality to which he bears witness. As he put it in his Nobel lecture, 'I had to do the books I did because there were no books about these subjects to give me what I wanted' (2001).

Further, Naipaul acknowledges to Niven that 'I write for the voice' (2004, 106), thereby locating his work in relation to the Caribbean oral tradition. Selvon's use of the range of Trinidadian language varieties has been much remarked; Naipaul's less so. Yet as Ervin Beck's analysis of the story 'B. Wordsworth' demonstrates, Naipaul's use of form and language was quite revolutionary. This tale is 'his first explicit handling of the problem of literary mimicry – that is, the colonized subject responding to the English literary canon thrust upon him by colonial education.'[28] For the would-be poet's pathetic and derivative aping of this colonial literary canon is rendered in non-standard Trinidadian vernacular and 'indiginized...by using a calypso-influenced, Trinidadian form' of narrative. Indeed, Beck notes that 'snatches of lines from calypsoes appear in other stories in *Miguel Street*' and moreover, that 'each short story itself [within the collection] is calypso-like in being a gossipy, satiric sketch of a socially aberrant character' (2002, 176).

Naipaul's legacy is, I would venture, also that deliberate care for language and form that marks the work of Caryl Phillips and Jamaica Kincaid. Both share the relish for the sound and meaning of words that identifies the narrator of *Miguel Street* as a potential writer; a similar delight in terms impeccably placed and exactly used. Kincaid and Phillips are also masters of the irony and satire that have come to characterise Naipaul's tone, and share with him a discerning eye for the subtle incongruities of the postcolonial condition. Other successors have taken the experiment with form and language much, much further. They utilise all the resources of the post-Creole continuum, incorporate folklore and alternative epistemologies, manipulate genre boundaries and create mutant forms and fusions, and – as evident in the work of Kincaid and Mootoo (along with fellow Trinidadians Lawrence Scott and Robert Antoni) – appropriate elements of the magical and the gothic, as well as decentering narrative voice and reinventing Caribbean geographies. Newer writers will continue to expand the horizons of West Indian literary production; but let us give Naipaul's contribution its due.

Notes

1. V.S. Naipaul, *The Middle Passage: A Caribbean Journey* (1962; repr., London: Picador, 1996), 20.
2. Peter Webb, 'The Master of the Novel,' *Newsweek*, August 18, 1980, 34.
3. Caryl Phillips, 'V.S. Naipaul,' *A New World Order: Selected Essays* (London: Vintage, 2002), 189.
4. Alison Donnell, *Twentieth-Century Caribbean Literature: Critical Moments in Anglophone Literary History* (London: Routledge, 2006), 11, and throughout.
5. John Theime, 'V.S. Naipaul's Third World,' *Journal of Commonwealth Literature* 10, no.1 (1975).
6. Naipaul, 'Two Worlds,' The Nobel Lecture, December 7, 2001. http://nobelprize.org/nobel_prizes/literature/laureates/2001/naipaul-lecture-e.html
7. Kenneth Ramchand, 'On Minshall and the Reading of Mas,' *Caribbean Review of Books* 11 (February 2007): 33.
8. Naipaul, *The Mimic Men* (1967; repr., Harmondsworth: Penguin, 1969), 90.
9. Gordon Rohlehr, 'The Ironic Approach: The Novels of V.S. Naipaul,' in the *Islands in Between*, ed. Louis James (Oxford: Oxford University Press, 1968), 137.
10. Naipaul, *A House for Mr Biswas* (1961; repr., Harmondsworth: Penguin, 1969), 147.
11. María Cristina Rodríguez, *What Women Lose: Exile and the Construction of Imaginary Homelands in Novels by Caribbean Writers* (New York: Peter Lang, 2005), 12.
12. Jamaica Kincaid, *My Brother* (New York: Noonday Press, 1997), 162.

13. Bruce Bawer, 'Civilization and V.S. Naipaul,' *The Hudson Review* 55. no.3 (2002): 371–72.
14. Geoffrey Wheatcroft, 'A Terrifying Honesty,' *Atlantic Monthly* 289, no.2 (2002): 88–92.
15. Jane King, 'A Small Place Writes Back,' *Callaloo* 25, no.3 (2002): 885–909. One thinks immediately of 'the lifestyle' of Cliff and Ossi in Oonya Kempadoo's *Tide Running* (London: Picador, 2001) or that of the narrator in Naipaul's *Miguel Street*, who grew into the role allocated to Caribbean men: drinking, womanising, exploiting any opportunity to gain financially regardless of ethics: 'we confiscated liquor in the slightest pretext' (1967; repr., Harmondsworth: Penguin, 1969), 166. 'You getting too wild in this place,' his mother complains, 'I think is high time you leave' (166).
16. Frank Birbalsingh, 'Jamaica Kincaid: From Antigua to America,' in *Frontiers of Caribbean Literature in English*, ed. Frank Birbalsingh (London: Macmillan, 1996), 139.
17. Shani Mootoo, *Out on Main Street* (Vancouver: Press Gang Publishers, 1993), 71.
18. Donnette Francis, 'Uncovered Stories: Politicizing Sexual Histories in Third Wave Caribbean Women's Writing,' *Renaissance Noire* 6, no.1 (Fall 2004): 78.
19. Shani Mootoo, *Cereus Blooms At Night* (London: Granta Publishers, 1999), 258.
20. Jane Bryce, 'Review of Oonya Kempadoo, *Buxton Spice* and Shani Mootoo, *Cereus Blooms at Night*,' *Wasafiri* 30 (Autumn 1999): 72–3.
21. Faith Smith, Preface to 'Genders and Sexualities,' Special Issue on Genders and Sexualities *Small Axe* 7 (March 2000): v–vii.
22. Angelo Lascelles, 'Take the High Road on Morals,' *Daily Nation*, July 12, 2005, 10.
23. http://www.jamaicaobsever.com/news/html/20070214T220000_0500_119155_OBS_COPS_ SAVE_THREE_ALLEGED_HOMOSEXUALS_FROM_ANGRY_CROWD.asp
24. Jennifer Rahim, 'No Place to Go: Homosexual Space and the Discourse of Unspeakable Content in Mendes' *Black Fauns* and Kincaid's *My Brother*,' *Journal of West Indian Literature* 3, nos. 1 and 2 (2005): 119–40.
25. Eric Roach, 'Letter to Lamming,' quoted in Laurence Breiner, 'Laureate of Nowhere,' *The Caribbean Review of Books* 10 (November 2006): 32.
26. Pius Adesanmi, 'Entanglement and *Durée*: Reflections on the Francophone African Novel,' *Comparative Literature* 56, no. 3 (Summer 2004): 230.
27. V.S. Naipaul, interview by Alastair Niven, 'V.S. Naipaul,' *Writing Across Worlds: Contemporary Writers Talk*, ed. Susheila Nasta (London: Routledge, 2004), 104.
28. Ervin Beck, 'Naipaul's B. Wordsworth,' *The Explicator* 60, no.3 (Spring 2002): 175.

3

CONSORTING WITH KALI:

Migration and Identity in Naipaul's 'One Out of Many'

Paula Morgan

Above all, human beings need to belong. The quest to locate a stable entity around which to construct our identities and our sense of belonging is intensified in modern societies, in which ancient tribal and traditional certainties have been shattered. Instead, we confront myriad, ambiguous and shape-shifting identities and modes of being. Globally, mass migrations, interracial relations, hybrid and transitional identities increasingly characterise societies.

Modern migration, in its unvarnished form, can be characterised by the movement of labour to capital. The colonial enterprise, the largest such endeavour in human history, sought to erase the subjectivities of the colonised and to re-inscribe alien and alienating identities. One legacy has been a spate of mass and individual neuroses. Related to this, is the ongoing impulse within diasporic individuals and multi-cultural societies to grapple with the dilemma of 'who are we becoming' in the processes of transportation and transculturation.[1] Stuart Hall notes that identity is not in the past to be found, but in the future to be constructed.[2] Moreover, perhaps even for the majority, this grail is as such that the most desirable ethnic identification is that which may be constructed as the most pristine, original and authentic. The greater the admixture, the greater suspicion of loss, the greater the impulse to name, to classify, to interrogate, to justify; and the greater the imperative to reclaim ethnic and ancestral (un)certainties.

In 'One Out of Many,' V.S. Naipaul presents a terse, multi-faceted exploration of transcultural migration. Traversing rural, urban and metropolitan landscapes, the mild-mannered protagonist from the hill country in India touches down in Washington 'the capital of the world.'[3] Santosh (Hindi for fulfilment and peace) loses the protection of his traditional caste-defined social identity and is constrained to craft a hybrid identity against the backdrop of the American counter-cultural hippie and Civil Rights movements. The former represents youth migration away from the myth of a monolithic, idealised American dream/identity; the latter represents the outworking of forced African migration to the Americas.

The narrative raises fundamental issues. What confers ethnic identity? On what is fundamental commitment to cultural and ethnic identity based? How does the creative writer employ the ancient language of myth to explore transitions into alien worlds? This paper shies away from an essentialist view of ethnic identity. Rather, I choose to interrogate how commitment to ethnic identity changes in specific historical or personal circumstances, and to explore possible consequences of such commitment, as demonstrated in the fictional scenario.

Naipaul's immigrant Santosh represents a man in a liminal transitional state with all the ambiguity and potentiality which that implies. Victor Turner argues that all rites of passage or 'transition[s] are marked by three phases: separation, margin (or *limen*, signifying 'threshold' in Latin) and aggregation':

> The first phase of separation comprises symbolic behavior signifying the detachment of the individual or group either from an earlier fixed point in the social structure, from a set of cultural conditions (a 'state'), or from both. During the intervening 'liminal' period, the characteristics of the ritual subject (the 'passenger') are ambiguous; he passes through a cultural realm that has few or none of the attributes of the past or coming state. In the third phase (reaggregation or reincorporation) the passage is consummated.[4]

Naipaul's first-person narrator retraces his journey, speaking (presumably from a settled spatio-temporal reference point) of his meanderings as a threshold person, that is, one who 'elude[s] or slip[s] through the network of classifications that normally locate states and positions in cultural space' (Turner 1990, 147). Santosh begins his tale at its ending: 'I am now an American citizen and I live in Washington, capital of the world. Many people, both here and in India, will feel I have done well. But.' (1973, 21). The narrative undermines the opening statement by dealing with the gaping chasm underlying the 'but.' The tale told in retrospect is an act of memory, which reconstructs the process of (un)becoming.

The first phase for Santosh is separation from the crowded, warm cocoon within the servant class of Bombay pavement dwellers.[5] Santosh's sense of self is shored up on every hand by caste certainties – unambiguous communal affirmation, prestige and respect based on commonly shared, widely acknowledged markers; hierarchical social ordering with its implied enforcement of communal sanctions. The sense of 'them and us' remains intact, because not all pavement dwellers are equal: '…some of us, like the tailor's bearer and myself, were domestics who lived in the street. The others were people who came to that bit of pavement to sleep. Respectable people; we didn't encourage riff-raff' (21).

Within the relatively more stable communal environment, the I-narrator is closely intertwined with landscape as well as the community. The split between the memory of past joy and present discomfort inspires the narrator to canticles of praise so lyrical that I have taken the liberty of altering line length to emphasise their musicality:

> I liked walking beside the Arabian Sea,
> waiting for the sun to come up.
> Then the city and the ocean gleamed like gold.
> Alas for those morning walks, that sudden ocean dazzle,
> the moist salt breeze on my face, the flap of my shirt,
> that first cup of hot sweet tea from a stall,
> the taste of the first leaf-cigarette. (22)

Appeal to visual, tactile, kinetic, auditory and gustatory senses creates a highly evocative, sensual experience. The sense of soothing harmony with the landscape is enhanced by the repetition of fricatives and sibilants. The entire scene is tinged with the sepia tones of nostalgia. Observe the interplay between the innocent experiencing self and the wiser, 'westernized' narrator, displaced in time and space. Ironically, this description echoes the romanticised discourse of empire – with its resonances of the quest for eastern exotica and for gold. It resonates too with our century's travel/tourism discourse with its relentless signification of 'paradise.' Although the narrator is speaking of a time of innocent, self-erasure, there is an intense insistence on first-person interiority. In the first seven lines, the pronoun I is used seven times. The narrator and the implied author conspire in tones of gentle mockery. He muses: 'I had become a city man' (22).

The second phase sees Santosh as migrant to the United States moving into a transitional (b)order/existence.[6] Naipaul explores the responses of the individual under forces of unrelieved physical displacement and psychical disharmony. The journey itself is a humiliating, distasteful reminder of the culturally determined conditions and structures needed to sustain the most basic habits and postures of diet, dress, and defecation. Santosh undergoes extreme humiliation, as an adult male who regresses to an infantile level in these respects, even to the extent of being publicly flayed for losing control during defecation, while air borne.

'One Out of Many' represents the USA as a series of worlds that elide rather than intersect and constrains those who cross their borders into similarly truncated and suppressed postures. Mainstream American culture is never directly presented. Rather it is mediated through the television screen as a psychic space to which Santosh travels daily to observe with anthropological penetration, a field in which the natives buy and clean, and clean and buy:

> I entered the homes of the Americans…I saw them buying clothes and cleaning clothes, buying motor cars and cleaning motor cars….The effect of all this television on me was curious. If by some chance I saw an American on the street….I felt I had caught the person in an interval between his television duties. So to some extent Americans have remained to me, as people not quite real, as people temporarily absent from television (1973, 33).

The television portrayals cause Americans to become essentialised. They suffer from a form of metonymic freezing such that the single face comes to represent the whole.

How is the displaced Asiatic portrayed in the new environment? He is self-effacing, anxious to please, vulnerable and jittery.[7] Santosh's employer, a man of taste, transforms the apartment into a replica of a magazine layout 'with books and Indian paintings and Indian fabrics and pieces of sculpture and bronze statues of our gods' (32). The harried ambassador presents an Easterner's offering to the West – an exotic scene set up to conform to the latter's stereotype, to earn his regard if not his respect. Significantly, he is presented as falsely representing, even prostituting the spirituality of his people and culture.

His encounter with the American (the only one who draws near) passes judgment on the spiritual paucity of the Oriental and Occidental alike. The culture-hungry dinner guest boasting that he paid a guard $200 to hack off an entire head of an ancient god in a temple states blandly '...if I had a bottle of whisky he would have pulled down the whole temple for me' (1973, 37). The American disgraces even the televised representations by defiling the spiritual essence of another's culture, from desecrating temples and seducing guides with mammon, to decapitating gods to create souvenirs. He is shadowed though, in the nervous employer who sees this blasphemous desecration only as a personal affront on his self-importance, 'They think an official in Government is just the same as some poor guide scraping together a few rupees to keep body and soul together' (38).

Santosh's first halting steps towards the sense of individuality, which is pivotal to survival in the new society, come in response to sexual interest. A *hubshi*[8] (read black) woman finds him attractive so he goes to the mirror to find out why. The discovery of an individual identity predictably yields an intense self-preoccupation, which, arguably, is anathema within his inherited cultural framework and endemic within his host society. The discovery that he has a face – unique and handsome – coincides with the recognition that he inhabits a racialised body. This, in turn, generates a frenzy of comparison with culturally determined, ossified televised images of American beauty. The same applies to clothing. His domestic's garb, neither clean nor dirty, is an appropriate signifier of his station in the old world. In the new culture, it speaks of strangeness, filthiness and poverty. Yet to don clothes that would 'speak the right language' in the new context, would be to abandon the markers of the old order and consequently his rightness of fit in his natal land. The hastily purchased green suit is physically and psychically too big because his emerging sense of self, and self worth, has not yet grown sufficiently.

At this stage of his journey, Santosh is moving away from a communal framework of interpretation towards the formulation of individual assessments and constructs of meaning. Self-perception empowers him to perceive others with greater insight and understanding. He sees for the first time a different basis for kinship with his employer (shared age, vulnerability and anxiety) which penetrates beyond the former ritualised patterns of interaction: 'I used to tell him then that beside him I was as dirt...I was ceasing to see myself as part of my employer's presence, and beginning at the same time to see him as an outsider might see him' (1973, 36–7). Does greater understanding create greater intimacy in interpersonal interactions? At this stage, the nascent self becomes a vulnerable preserve to be defended. For Santosh, and presumably for the employer, this basis for more intimate interaction never comes to fruition; rather it creates the necessity for masking and subterfuge.

The recurrent motifs of Santosh's psychical displacement are helplessness and claustrophobia. As he gradually becomes acquainted with the metropolitan maze, he hovers in what Turner terms an ambiguous threshold state. In his nightmarish wanderings, he vacillates between humility, nothingness and a sense of tentative potentiality to become and even perchance to belong. Santosh who has not been homeless on a Bombay pavement now is cast adrift seeking a context within which to locate himself. He learns painfully that identity is first mirrored by community and only subsequently appropriated by an individual. His caste sensibility imparts the fear of contamination that hinders him from making contact with the other.

Santosh wanders in and out of potential sub-cultural communities; mainstream culture remains hermetically sealed behind the television screen. His initial encounter is with a friendly *hubshi* cashier who teaches him his first English words: 'Me black and beautiful.' The pronominal reference is ambiguous but one can infer from this an invitation to locate himself as a 'soul brother.' The second phrase invites him to adopt a stance that is oppositional and adversarial to the dominant authority structure. The entire formula is 'Me black and beautiful....He pig' (34). He wanders into cafés without shoes only to be rejected as a hippie; in the hippie cafés he is welcomed but atavistically sniffed because he carries the pervasive odour of hashish. Eligibility for access to each potential community is cast in negatives – he is not black like the *hubshi*; not a soul brother because he cannot identify with their struggle; not non-conformist like the barefooted, weed smoking hippies; not disguised (externally) like the Mexican waiters dressed to provide Indian authenticity at the restaurant.

None of these ambiguous states of identity is as compelling and repulsive as that of the Hari Krishna sect, forever sealed in 'in-betweenity.' They appear as ludicrous examples of cultural syncretism, dancing somewhat like Red Indians in a cowboy movie, while chanting Sanskrit words in praise of Lord Krishna:

> I was very pleased. But then a disturbing thought came to me. It might have been because of the half-caste appearance of the dancers; it might have been their bad Sanskrit pronunciation and their accent. I thought that these people were now strangers, but that perhaps once upon a time they had been like me. Perhaps,

> as in some story, they had been brought here among the *hubshi* as captives a long time ago and had become a lost people, like our own wandering gipsy folk, and had forgotten who they were. When I thought that, I lost my pleasure in the dancing; and I felt for the dancers the sort of distaste we feel when we are faced with something that should be kin but turns out not to be, turns out to be degraded, like a deformed man, or like a leper, who from a distance looks whole (1973, 30).

He is perceptive enough to accurately assess that, even within India, syncretic hybridity is the legacy of the travellers, but his rigidity and fear of contamination lead him to reject the pleasure of kinship and potential for community which they offer. Syncretisim and hybridity bring risk, not enrichment.

What are the lessons to be learnt? Multiple identities can be evoked in multiple scenarios. Categories of ethnic identities are not without ambiguity. Rather they are capable of being understood and appropriated in a range of ways. According to anthropologist Aisha Khan,

> ...these categories are frequently equivocal: contingent upon individual perception (though obviously not entirely) and upon varying and not always predictable emphases or combinations of attributes. Categorizations of ethnic identity that marshall a variety of historical, social, and cultural dimensions in their constructions may also encompass apparently contradictory images since traits, qualities, stereotypes, and the like are not self contained or mutually exclusive. Indeed, the very fact of combination and ambiguity foregrounds the fluidity of ethnic identity.[9]

Despite Santosh's initial revulsion, for a time the Hari Krishna spin magic because they demonstrate the intense potential for bonding which can occur within a liminal state. This bonding resembles the second of two major models of human relatedness identified by Turner. The first is of 'society as a structured, differentiated, and often hierarchical system of political-legal-economic positions' based on 'caste, class or rank hierarchies.' The second, which emerges in the liminal period, is 'unstructured or rudimentarily structured and relatively undifferentiated *communita*.'[10] In Western society, the latter state is manifested in groups such as the hippies and the Hari Krishnas who emphasise 'spontaneity, immediacy, and existence.' The hippies 'stress personal relationships rather than social obligations, and regard sexuality as a polymorphic instrument of immediate *communitas* rather than as the basis for an enduring, structured social tie' (Turner 1990, 153).

As much as the Hari Krishna retain their appeal even to a mature Santosh contemplating his final 'renunciation,' on a more fundamental level he cannot join them because he learns to read them for what they are: 'I had watched the people in the circle long enough to know that they were of their city; that their television life awaited them; that their renunciation was not like mine' (1973, 56). Moreover, it is the ancient community not the transient *communitas* that he craves. Unwilling and unable to renounce the old framework of interaction, he pines after the reinvention of the group into a nostalgic, gold-tinted dream of another life: an allegory of a travelling community, a village welcome and the 'sinking sun' which turns the 'dust clouds to gold' (56).

It is in his relationship with Priya that Santosh's most valid option for community emerges. Priya, who has successfully manoeuvred the bittersweet phases of transition and has attained a viable hybrid identity, emerges as a guide and model of acculturation. Blending divergent stereotypes, he retains that marvellous linguistic meandering and philosophical bent of India, astutely combined with the hard-headed business acumen of America. Moreover, Santosh names him as an individual and potentially as a friend.

Reflecting a stratified rigid, traditional framework in which a person's occupation, status and social designation are reflected from birth to death in caste designation, Santosh never names his initial employer.[11] Priya, however, is named from inception and relates to Santosh on an intimate, individual basis, until he offers to introduce him to a potentially viable community. These are Indians in Washington who meet to reaffirm community, rootedness and belonging by ritualised viewing of Indian movies. The road to the cinema takes them through the burnt out *hubshi* streets:

> ...old smoke-stained sign-boards announcing what was no longer true. Cars raced along the wide roads; there was life only on the roads. I thought I would vomit with fear.
>
> I said, 'Take me back, *sahib*.'
>
> I had used the wrong word. Once, I had used the word a hundred times daily. But then I had considered myself a small part of my employer's presence and the word as not

> servile; it was more like a name....Priya I had always called Priya; it was his wish, the American way, man to man. With Priya the word was servile. And he responded to the word....I never called him by his name again (48–9).

Santosh's anxiety is triggered here by the presence (even in absentia) of the ubiquitous *hubshi.* It manifests itself as a mild agoraphobia, that is fear of open spaces. Again he signals his rejection of his emerging individuality and new patterns of interaction with the verbal marker that restores the time worn but increasingly irrelevant hierarchies.

His perception of his racial difference and his horror of being defiled by contact produces his obsession with the African-American whom he signifies as *hubshi* (Hindi for Abyssinian). Underlying this obsession is the strong sense of sexual fascination/revulsion which steadily accumulates. It is not surprising then that an overpowering female figure surfaces in the African-American woman with whom he eventually defiles himself through sexual union. Santosh's fear of violation with the *hubshi* is based on the belief in karma and transmigration:[12]

> It is written in our books, both holy and not so holy, that it is indecent and wrong for a man of our blood to embrace the *hubshi* woman. To be dishonoured in this life, to be born a cat or a monkey or a *hubshi* in the next! (34–5)

With the growing recognition of individuality and freedom to act comes an imperative to accept responsibility for action. It is here that the Santosh's involvement with the *hubshi* woman (whom he constructs as Kali) as a consort takes on dual significance.

What then is the significance of evoking the myth and symbol of Kali? A grim and terrifying mother goddess of death and destruction, Kali is particularly prominent in the Tantric Hindu tradition.[13] Physically, she is revolting.[14] Emotionally, she is cruel and brutal, excessive, always demanding, never satisfied. Symbolically she is associated with disorder, chaos, blood, battle and vengeance. Moreover, Kali is intoxicated and she is mad:

> She is dark as a great cloud, clad in dark clothes. Her tongue is poised as if to lick. She has fearful teeth, sunken eyes, and is smiling. She wears a necklace of snakes, the half-moon rests on her

> forehead, she has matted hair, and is engaged in licking a corpse. Her sacred thread is a snake, and she lies on a bed of snakes. She holds a garland of fifty heads. She has a large belly, and on her head is Ananta with a thousand heads. On all sides she is surrounded by snakes…[she] has corpses for ear ornaments.[15]

Given that the tribe creates myths, as a means of explaining threatening reality and ordering chaotic experiences, it is not surprising that Santosh, newly ejected and meandering through formless, disrupted worlds should invest his mating with the *hubshi* woman with mythic significance. In fighting temptation, Santosh had prayed to the bronze gods, installed as living room ornaments, that he would not be dishonoured. However, in their designation to ornamental status they have been rendered powerless and are overturned by a flesh and blood incarnation of the mother archetype in Hindu culture.

There is much to support an interpretation that his sexual union with the *hubshi* betrays his basic inability to move into individuality and responsibility. The incident is narrated with subtle shifts in voice that reveal how Santosh rejects responsibility for the act:

> The *hubshi* woman came in, moving among my employer's ornaments like a bull. I was greatly provoked. The smell was too much; so was the sight of her armpits. I fell. She dragged me down on the couch….I saw the moment, helplessly, as one of dishonour. I saw her as Kali, goddess of death and destruction, coal-black, with a red tongue and white eyeballs and many powerful arms. I expected her to be wild and fierce but she added insult to injury by being very playful, as though, because I was small and strange, the act was not real. She laughed all the time. I would have liked to withdraw, but the act took over and completed itself. And then I felt dreadful (1973, 38).

The sex act is presented as a reversal of the male aggressor, female receiver mould. The woman becomes a horny bull (male gender) who attacks, mauls and humiliates Santosh (the small, defiled, feminised, recipient of the sexually aggressive act) as less than a man. The impetus for the sex act comes not from the dictates of his appetites, the thrusts of his loins, but rather from the strength of her many powerful arms that drag him to destruction. At each stage he is governed, if not by the power of the woman, then by the compulsiveness of the act.

Since Santosh has not chosen, he has simply perceived and then fallen; the encounter can be seen as Kali's victory over impotent, ornamental gods. The powerful destructive mother goddess sucks the male into the womb. It is a rejection of manliness and exertion of individual will. His subsequent attempts at re-establishing contact with the bronze gods consist of dissipating guilt in a heightened emotionalism by theatrical austerities; rubbing his penis with a lemon, rolling naked on the floor and howling; donning a *dhoti* and seeking to meditate, and fasting. The insincerity surfaces the moment he gets an audience to impress with his super spirituality. These rituals of reintegration prove ineffective. Symbolically, he attains freer identification and release through the burning of the city in rebellion against social injustice, inequity and pernicious racism as an act of civil unrest. Here too he longs for the fire started by the *hubshi* (a parallel of the fiery passion triggered by the woman) to annihilate him: 'I wanted everything in the city, even the apartment block, even the apartment, even myself, to be destroyed and consumed....I wanted the very idea of escape to become absurd' (1973, 40). He longs for the fire of purification to become the fire of consumption, an engulfment that ends individual choice and moral responsibility.

The *hubshi* woman bears the symbolic weight of Santosh's fear and resistance to the Indo-American hybrid identity that is inexorably emerging. Yet there is an even deeper denial. According to Turner, in the liminal state, norms that govern structured relationships are transgressed or dissolved. Underlying anomie is latent potential for new and creative bonding that holds tremendous potency:

> *Communitas* breaks in through the interstices of structure, in liminality; at the edge of structure, in marginality; and from beneath structure, in inferiority....Liminality, marginality, and structural inferiority are conditions in which are frequently generated myths, symbols, rituals, philosophical systems and works of art. These cultural forms provide men with...periodical reclassifications of reality and man's relationship to society, nature, and culture. But they are more than classifications, since they incite men to action as well as to thought (1990, 153).

It is within this context that the dual significance of Kali myth and symbolism poses another alternative. Santosh's caste sensibility imparts virulent, deep-rooted fear of despoliation and pollution. His small stature and the *hubshi's* sheer bulk generate a desperate and extreme vulnerability.

Yet to gain citizenship, Santosh eventually marries the *hubshi*. The question remains: is legal standing all that he stands to gain?

In yielding to the black woman's flesh, Santosh is saying yes to death; death of the old self. Yet tacitly, he is acknowledging, as all migrants must, the possibility of rebirth of a new hybrid self. On the physical plane, his union can potentially say yes to life, to sensuality, to procreation and to the other face of the dark goddess:

> Kali's dark, voluptuous, bloody presence is similarly 'wet'. Immodest in her nudity and aggressive in her sexuality, she represents the ever fertile womb from which springs the eternal throb of life...the throb of life gone out of control... (Kinsley 1975, 155).

He is caught in a maelstrom of change, unable to return, afraid to proceed. Santosh's mating with Kali/the *hubshi* represents the potential to take to his bosom 'the forbidden thing' which encapsulates all his fears – loss of self, language, order, framework of meaning, caste and ritual pollution.[16] Encoded in his representation of the *hubshi* as Kali is the possibility to adopt the pathway of the transgressive Tantric hero for whom the 'forbidden is not to be propitiated, feared, ignored, or avoided. Kali is to be confronted boldly...and thereby assimilated, overcome and transformed into a vehicle of salvation' (Kinsley 1975, 112). Here is the opportunity to transcend the polarities inherent in consciousness and identity, self and other, chaos and order, past and present. This allows Kali/*hubshi* to become 'an agent of transformation and renewal, fostering his unfolding and integration within the community.'[17] This is at the root of his obsessive fascination/revulsion. It is this that beckons from the moment the *hubshi* gives him his first words of English, his first glimpse of self in the mirror. It is this specter/possibility that hangs over the burnt out street. Ultimately, it is this latent possibility that he also denies.

In making this decision, Santosh reassesses his entire history: 'I hadn't escaped; I had never been free. I had been abandoned. I was like nothing; I had made myself nothing. And I couldn't turn back' (1973, 53). The emptiness he feels at the core, having been ejected from the warmth of comfortable society, he now falsely reinterprets as the calm of renunciation: 'To be empty is to be calm, it is to renounce' (55). His union becomes his formal renunciation to Kali only as the goddess of death and destruction. It is his rejection of Kali as chaos and disorder on the brink of being contained. He enters into a stage of quiescence, permanently trapped in the borderline state, a threshold person unable to die and powerless to be born. Ironically, within the communal gaze he achieves his Karma, entering into his next incarnation as a *hubshi*:

> ...and then the dark house in which I now live.
> Its smells are strange, everything in it is strange. But my strength in this house is that I am a stranger. I have closed my mind and heart to the English language...to the pictures of *hubshi* runners and boxers and musicians on the wall. I do not want to understand or learn anymore (1973, 57).

Yet migration with its attendant diseases – trauma, displacement, depression, despair and acculturation – has given birth to the narrator in exile. Santosh is after all the working class, uneducated immigrant. His is the voice that is usually silenced in the travel narratives – the voice of the helper, the servant, the Sherpa, the invisible sidekick to the authentic hero.[18] In this sense, Santosh gives face to the faceless and voice to the silenced.

His voice testifies from the no-man's-land of cultural liminality – grim experiential knowledge of multiple sites of dislocation and non-belonging. He aslo constructs a subtle, deeply intuitive, complex narrative of self in an alien tongue which he refuses to speak, claiming: 'I have closed my mind and heart to the English language' (1973, 57). Instead, he hones the language to relate the trauma of excoriating his native tongue, and climbs into an alien language/skin. From this position, he breaks the seal of representation to speak back to the American mainstream culture about other Americas they would perhaps prefer not to acknowledge. He sends a solemn warning to naive and complacent would-be immigrants. It is from this position that he enters into fruitful discourse with us.

Naipaul's characterisation of Santosh invites us to interrogate Homi Bhabha's rationale for shifting the issue of identity from a concern with the 'persuasions of personhood' to 'a question of historical and geographical location...shifting the question of identity from the ontological and epistemological imperative – What is identity? To face the ethical and political prerogative – What are identities for?'[19] This is a useful proposition perhaps, but is it viable? Santosh's deep-seated inability to release a sense of self which condemns him to a state of living death, implies that for this first generation migrant and perhaps for many others who have walked in his shoes such a shift may well nigh be impossible.

Consider an alternative. The progeny of ex-slaves, ex-indentees, ex-colonials will, of necessity, pursue reconnection with erased, submerged, defaced ancestral identities. However, they can only be the bedrock, not the substance of the imperative to locate something fixed around which to construct a usable identity. In the beginning, I explored Santosh's 'westernized' narrative of 'authentic' origin. I end with the words of Stuart Hall:

> Identity is not only a story, a narrative which we tell ourselves about ourselves, [they are] stories which change with historical circumstances....[Identities] are the way in which we are recognized and then come into step into the place of recognition which others give us (1991, 6).

Such a formulation could conceivably grant if not Santosh, then his progeny, the power to 're-aggregate' or even the power to return.

Notes

1. In relation to modern Europe and North America, Werner Sollors argues that ethnicity and ethnocentrism may be described as Europe and North America's most successful export items: 'The processes of modernization and urbanization which weakened specific forms of familial, vocational and local belonging strengthened the commitment to more abstract forms of generalizing identifications such as ethnic and national ones.' Sollers, 'Ethnicity,' in *Critical Terms for Literary Study*, eds. Frank Lentricchia and Thomas McLaughlin (Chicago: University of Chicago Press, 1995), 289.
2. Stuart Hall, 'Cultural Identity and the Diaspora' In *Colonial Discourse and Postcolonial Theory: A Realer*, 401–402, eds. Patrick Williams and Laura Chrisman. (London: Harvester Wheatsheaf, 1993).
3. V.S. Naipaul, *In a Free State* (1971; repr., Harmondsworth: Penguin Books, 1973), 21, 58.
4. Victor Turner, 'Liminality and Community,' in *Culture and Society Contemporary Debates*, eds. Jeffrey C. Alexander and Steven Seidman (Cambridge: Cambridge University Press, 1990), 147. Turner describes reaggregation as reincorporation into a relatively stable state in within which the individual has 'rights and obligations vis-à-vis others of a clearly defined and "structural" type.'
5. In 1962, Naipaul visited his ancestral homeland India for the first time. He wrote in *India: A Wounded Civilization* of rural urban migration into Bombay. 'It is said that every day 1500 more people, about 350 families, arrive in Bombay to live. They come mainly from the countryside and they have very little; and in Bombay there isn't room

for them.... By day the streets are clogged; at night the pavements are full of sleepers.... One report says that 100,000 people sleep on the pavements of Bombay; but this figure seems low. And the beggars: are there only 20,000 in Bombay, as one newspaper article says, or are there 70,000, the figure given on another day' (Harmondsworth: Penguin Books, 1997), 57–8.

6. Significantly, of the thirteen-part short narrative, the first deals with Santosh's life in Bombay and the last, with the stage of quiescence into which he settles; eleven parts deal with what I have classified (with reference to Turner) as a liminal state.
7. Naipaul carefully sketches his Indian males as the passive, mother-centred, insular men who have grave difficulty adjusting to Western culture and society. When I encounter criticism of this now stereotypical view of the Asian migrant, I contemplate (albeit briefly) the power of representation and the age-old mystery of the chicken and the egg.
8. Hindi for Abyssinian; the term is used by Santosh as a signifier for African-Americans.
9. 'What is "a Spanish"? Ambiguity and "Mixed" Ethnicity in Trinidad,' *Trinidad Ethnicity*, ed. Kelvin Yelvington (London: The Macmillan Press, 1993), 180.
10. Turner prefers this Latin term *communitas* instead of the English word 'community' to distinguish this 'modality of social relationship' from 'an area of common living' (1990, 148).
11. Similarly, he never names his wife even as an African-American, far less with a personal name reflective of her unique, individual identity.
12. Belief in Karma does not necessarily constitute a deterrent to the performance of bad deeds in the present incarnation. Indeed it has the potential to do the opposite. The very deeds which would lead to a negative repercussion in future life may be interpreted as having been decided by evil deeds in a past life, and hence accepted as the present Karma.
13. Drawing reference to famous Bengali literary figures such as Rabindranath Tagore and Bankim Chatterjee, David R. Kinsley indicates that Kali is both extremely popular and extremely maligned by Hindu and non Hindu alike in *The Sword and the Flute: Kali and Querns Dark Visions of the Terrible and the Sublime in Hindu Mythology* (Berkeley: University Press of California, 1975), 81.
14. This statement must be qualified by a point made by Julius Lipner that to the devotees both of the more socially acceptable and the more transgressive forms of Kali worship, she is not revolting. See *Hindus: Their Religious Beliefs and Practices* (London: Routledge, 1994). Rather devotees even tenderly plead in relation to her more shameful attributes: '*Oh Kali! Why dost Thou roam about nude?/Art thou not ashamed Mother?*' From Sinha, Jadunath, *Rama Prasada's Devotional Songs: The Cult of Shakti* (Calcutta: Sinha Publishing House Pvt. Ltd, 1966).
15. Quoted in Kinsley (1975, 81), from the *dhyana mantra of guhya-kali* from Krsnananda Agamavagisa's *Tantrasara* 1:326.
16. Kinsley writes: 'The figure of Kali conveys the image of death, destruction, fear, terror, the all-consuming aspect of reality. As such she is also "a forbidden thing" or the forbidden par excellence for she is death itself' (1975), 112.

17. Stephanos Stephanides, *Translating Kali's Feast: The Goddess in Indo-Caribbean Ritual and Fiction* (Amsterdam: Rodopi, 2000), 235.
18. The authentic hero is traditionally constructed in travel narratives as the individual with means and agency to travel. Even (or maybe even especially) in great tales of discovery, the contribution of the guide, the helper, the servant, is erased.
19. Editor's Introduction to 'Minority Manoeuvres and Unsettled Negotiations,' *Critical Inquiry* 23 no.3 (1997): 434.

4

CONSUMING THE SELF:

V.S. Naipaul, C.L.R. James and A Way in the World

Rhonda Cobham-Sander

If today, the Caribbean men and women who began to publish their work in the 1950s are considered the first cohort of internationally recognised Caribbean writers, then those of us born in that decade can count ourselves among the first generation of Caribbean readers, that is, the first generation of Caribbean children to grow up taking the existence of Caribbean literature as a given. By the time I entered secondary school in Trinidad in the 1960s, independence had washed over the 'islands of the bluuuee Caribbean sea,' as we sang of them in our new national anthem, and books by local authors were beginning to find their way into libraries, literary soirees, and middle class homes. Unlike our parents, we took it for granted that West Indians *could* give birth to books, although, since practically none of these writers still lived in the islands, we were not quite sure where or how this literary conception happened.

The silence in our school curriculum on the subject of Caribbean writers raised additional doubts about the literary merit of such works as well as the moral standing of their authors, so we tended to talk about them, like the uncle who had fled to Venezuela to escape a little problem with the police, in the past tense, or the subjunctive. To make matters worse, the snippets of Caribbean poems and stories we heard recited at special events at the Public Library downtown or at the USIS Library children's hour, we considered embarrassingly folksy, not to say vulgar. Like students subjected to today's politically correct educational agendas, we quickly worked out that many of the adults around us considered such events an uncomfortable duty, not nearly as appealing as attendance at the latest British Council evening of operatic arias. Public readings of West Indian literature were a bit like sex education – an attempt to make something we all knew was perverted sound straightforward and unremarkable.

Deviance delivers its own pleasures, however. Lacking the official seal of approval of the Cambridge School Certificate examination board, Caribbean books were free to pervert us rather than to uplift. Samuel Selvon's *Turn Again Tiger* and Edgar Mittelholzer's *Children of Kaywana* were the first 'dirty' books I remember having read. I found Selvon's tucked away in the back of a bookcase in my grandmother's house. My older sister bought the cheap paperback edition of Mittelholzer's *Kaywana Trilogy* with her own money and waved it inches away from my nose as a book that was 'too old' for me. Of course I had to read it. It did not disappoint.

Even more than illicit sex these novels were about racial transgression. It was not just that they showed Caribbean people of different races in relationships of appalling intimacy with each other. Their stories presented non-white characters in ways that transgressed the conventions of the nineteenth-century English and twentieth-century American novels we usually read. Indians did not just skulk around in exotic, Kiplingesque settings, charming snakes and sleeping on nails. Blacks did not merely cower and croon. Chinamen were not sages whose pigtails always hung behind them. They were teachers, bakers, shoemakers, schoolchildren, cane farmers, laundresses, insurance salesmen and saga boys. Some were enterprising, others lackadaisical, still others downright evil but, at least in Mittelholzer, in a savvy, complex fashion. The whites were not all missionaries or Governors General doing time in the tropics either. Many were bored housewives or struggling clerks, who had never been to the Mother Country, and who lived in backwaters like Berbice, British Guiana, or on sugar estates in Tacarigua, Trinidad, or in crumbling family villas along Old Hope Road in Jamaica.

We knew all these people. Some were our playmates, some, friends of our parents, others, relatives. Some were just people whose mango trees we lusted after. However, until now they had not existed for us with the certainty with which we *knew* that Miss Havisham in *Great Expectations* existed. I devoured those books, furtively, defiantly, and obsessively. In return, they delivered up those pleasures that Freud assures us are part of the process by which shame becomes bound up with the erotic, and desire with art.

The Caribbean books we read may have been transgressive, but that did not mean that they were politically 'progressive.' Many of these early writers valued the colonial legacies they attacked. Today it has become fashionable to see early Caribbean writers who failed to abjure their relationship to the colonising power as somehow unliberated, or lacking in self-assurance. Nonetheless their ambivalence bequeathed to my generation of readers something the writers themselves had never had: a vast new library of words and images – some borrowed, some cloyingly folksy, some illuminating, some downright embarrassing – with which to begin to name *all* our worlds; a language through which to express *all* our desires, however politically retrograde some of them may now appear. They allowed us to see our world clearly for the first time through the prism of art, which afforded us the luxuries of self-deception – as well as the promise of self-fabrication.

And indeed, we laughed hardest where we most refused to recognise ourselves. Movies, dances, and football games were off-limits for Mrs Cobham's daughters, so most of our teenage suitors had to make do with the blue wicker couch on the front gallery. I no longer remember whose copy of *Miguel Street* we found wedged between the cushions, but I remember one suitor looking at the title and saying with an air of self importance, 'That's Luis Street, you know,' which was the street at the other end of Woodbrook where he lived. We read Naipaul's stories out loud to each other. I remember laughing till I cried at Man Man on the cross, urging the onlookers to 'stone me, brethren, stone me!' and screaming with delight at the idea of his dog leaving symmetrical piles of droppings on the stools in the Café at the corner of Alberto Street where we regularly stopped for sweet drinks. Of course we were convinced that Man Man really must have been Mr Assee, whose endless chalked sentences on the pavement of Damien Road we were careful to circumvent when we took the short cut from the Avenue to Roxy Roundabout. It never occurred to us that we also might have been the subjects of Naipaul's satire: Mrs Cobham's daughter, hedged in by all the elaborate protocols of black middle class respectability, but longing to play out a grand passion before the cinema audiences of which she could not be a part. The suitor, somebody's well behaved boy child masquerading as a Black Panther under his Afro and knitted beret, reading short stories on the blue couch when he really wanted to do something else.

'The first sentence was true. The second was invention,' Naipaul says in *Finding the Centre* of the famous opening exchange in *Miguel Street*:

> Every morning when he got up Hat would sit on the banister of his back verandah and shout across, 'What happening there, Bogart?' Bogart would turn in his bed and mumble softly, so that no one heard, 'What happening there, Hat?'[1]

That claim itself may be a writer's fiction but it captures something of our first response to *Miguel Street*. We saw but did not see our world in the pages of Naipaul's novel. We imagined that our own lives were not *that* sordid or petty and yet we knew that we had heard all the words, seen all the sights Naipaul described a hundred times before. The second sentence was always fiction; the first, already fact. Naipaul's sleight of hand convinced us that our experience as readers of his text – of any text – was as authentic as that of any other reader. He allowed us to gaze at our lives without feeling ourselves to be merely the diminished object of that gaze. For Naipaul framed our lives with art and art is always distancing and oblique.

My essay examines the meaning of this achievement in the work of a writer whose accomplishments over the past 50 years have been sustained and celebrated. That achievement has allowed Naipaul in recent years to experiment with forms which, in the work of writers of lesser repute, might have been considered too eccentric for serious consideration. It has given him a protected space to face up to issues that earlier he may have been too insecure or too inexperienced to confront, even as it leaves him open to the temptations of narcissism and isolation such license conceals. Naipaul knows that his work will outlive him, and in this later writing he is fighting for the right to influence the way in which that legacy will be read. The readings I offer here from Naipaul's *A Way in the World* demonstrate how the project of writing one's critical legacy can be understood as an overriding thematic concern as well as an important source of stylistic innovation.

In *A Way in the World*, Naipaul uses a character named Lebrun to talk about his fellow countryman, the political activist and intellectual, C.L.R. James.[2] By basing Lebrun's character on James, Naipaul finds a way to examine the problems of co-optation that come with fame – problems with which both he and James have had to struggle. I will focus on his descriptions of two meals that Naipaul's semi-autobiographical narrator shares – the first with Lebrun, the second with Lebrun's Manhattan friends. Naipaul challenges readers who have seen him and James as representing diametrically opposed positions in Caribbean intellectual thought to acknowledge the angst and insecurity, the refusals and accommodations that must of necessity have lain behind James's poised public persona. Without an understanding of this angst, he contends, we cannot fully appreciate either the greatness of a figure like James or the limits of his vision. At the same time, this reading of James through the fictional character Lebrun offers us strategies for understanding the fictional persona Naipaul has created for himself in his writing.

Reviewers of *A Way in the World* note as a matter of course that Naipaul models the figure of Lebrun on the historical figure C.L.R. James, a fellow Trinidadian who, as Naipaul has done, achieved international renown as a thinker and writer during his lifetime. Naipaul includes several such characters, based on thinly disguised public figures, in his novel. Foster Morris, for example, the minor British writer whom the young narrator at first envies because he seems debonair and once wrote a 'serious' book about Trinidad politics called *Shadowed Livery*, is based on the English novelist, Arthur Calder-Marshall, whose documentary, *Glory Dead* (1939), provides a detailed account of the political background to the 1930s oilfield riots in Trinidad. Naipaul's method depends on readers 'in the know' being able to pick up on these factual details, enhancing our sense that what we are reading is fact. However, Naipaul does not change the names of all of his loosely historical characters: Sir Walter Raleigh and the Spanish adventurer Miranda remain Raleigh and Miranda. Henry Swanzy, the producer of 'Caribbean Voices Programme' and an associate of Calder-Marshall, remains Henry Swanzy. On the whole it seems that only the characters whose lives he must manipulate in order to produce the effects he needs are given new names.

It is difficult, though, to decide what we are to make of Lebrun, as the few facts of Naipaul's acquaintance with C.L.R. James seem identical with his representation of the relationship between his narrator and Lebrun. Moreover, such deviations as there are between his description of Lebrun's career and the received record of James's life can be documented easily by reference to the numerous volumes by and about James that have become available since his death in 1989.[3] James is such a well-known public figure in Leftist and Caribbean circles that altering his name seems to be as futile a gesture as it would have been for Naipaul to alter Raleigh's name in his chapter on the explorer. Naipaul's insistence on distinguishing Lebrun from James, therefore, seems to be his way of signalling his interest in imagining the private life of a public figure; to recreate through fiction the most intimate motivations of someone *like* James (or like himself), rather than to put on record an accurate historical estimate of the political contribution of C.L.R. James, the man. Thus, Naipaul can use Lebrun, the writer and intellectual, as a foil and mirror for himself, in ways he could not have done with the specific historical figure of C.L.R. James, even as he draws on the public record of the life of his fellow countryman to create the illusion of fact.

James is one of the few Caribbean intellectuals, certainly the only other Trinidadian, to have attained an international reputation equal to Naipaul's as a consequence of his writing. In spite of significant political differences between them, Naipaul clearly respects this distinguished graduate of his alma mater, Queen's Royal College, and his precursor on the British and American intellectual scenes. James had also anticipated many of Naipaul's themes in his own publications as he and Naipaul share an interest in the history of the Caribbean and Latin America and in Trinidad's role within that history. Indeed, Naipaul's awareness of James's achievement probably goes further back than he discusses in this novel. James was the co-founder of the early Trinidad literary magazine, the *Beacon*, with whose extended circle of literati, Naipaul tells us elsewhere, his father, Seepersad Naipaul, interacted.[4] Naipaul himself was probably directly influenced by the stories of the *Beacon* group. He refers in the essay 'Jasmine' to a handful of local short stories he encountered as a child through which he

> ...began to appreciate the distorting, distilling power of the writer's art. Where I had seen a drab haphazardness they found order; where I would have attempted to romanticize, to render my subject equal with what I had read, they accepted. They provided a starting-point for further observation; they did not trigger off fantasy.[5]

Seen through these connections to Naipaul's father, Naipaul's school, Naipaul's intellectual interests, and the international literary scene, the historical James was probably an early role model for Naipaul, as the younger writer acknowledges in his review of James's *Beyond a Boundary*:

> To me, who thirty years later followed in his path almost step by step – but I only watched cricket, and I won the scholarship – Mr James's career is of particular interest. Our backgrounds were dissimilar. His was Negro, Puritan, fearful of lower-class contamination; mine was Hindu, restricted, enclosed. But we have ended speaking the same language; and though England is

> not perhaps the country we thought it was, we have both charmed ourselves away from Trinidad. 'For the inner self,' as Mr James writes, 'the die was cast' (1963, 75).

James had to struggle with the limitations of a colonial society not that much different from Naipaul's, if anything it was, as Naipaul notes, a world much harsher than his own in its racial divisions. Yet James had made a way for himself in the world. He had become known through his writing, in all the ways that Naipaul as a literary novice in the 1950s, must have aspired to be known.

Perhaps the most important aspect of Naipaul's relationship to James is his unfeigned respect for James as a fellow craftsman of words. This is one of the qualities Naipaul gives to his fictional Lebrun, who publishes a review article about the narrator's work in 'one of the Russian "thick magazines"' – not unlike the early review of *A House for Mr Biswas* that James wrote:

> The article seemed to me a miraculous piece of writing. It stuck closely to what I had actually written, but was about so much more. Reading the article, I thought I understood why as a child I felt that history had been burnt away in the place where I was born. I found myself constantly thinking, 'Yes, yes. That's true. It was like that' (1994, 114).

The words 'seemed,' in the first sentence quoted, and 'I thought I understood,' later on, prepare the reader for the painstaking deconstruction of Lebrun's reading that follows this passage. Yet the tone of the narrator's response communicates an intuitive recognition of a fellow mind – a fellow *something* – which the figure of Lebrun represents for Naipaul at this moment in the story.

Lebrun's essay evinces the attention to surfaces capable of excavating the writer's hidden meanings, which Naipaul tells us elsewhere in *A Way in the World* is the essence of good close reading. Indeed, the intensity of Lebrun's critical engagement with the narrator's novel returns to the author a satisfying assurance of having been seen and heard. Naipaul even displaces onto Lebrun's reading insights that originate in his own writing. Most of Naipaul's critics are familiar with his pronouncement in *The Middle Passage* that '[h]istory is built around achievement and creation; and nothing was created in the West Indies.'[6] In this rendering of his ideal reader, however, it is Lebrun who provides the narrator with the language through which to articulate a half understood childhood notion that 'history had been burnt away in the place where I was born' (1994, 114). By converting his written dismissal of Caribbean history into a thought that comes unbidden to his narrator as a child, and which the respected public oracle, Lebrun, is able to divine, Naipaul anticipates the absolution he hopes history will give his political pronouncements. He displaces his harshest judgments onto his reader via Lebrun, but in a form benign enough to suggest insight and acceptance, rather than what some have seen as the defensiveness of Naipaul's original formulation or, of the critical responses to it. 'Look,' he seems to say, 'Lebrun can see what I mean. He has a wonderfully expansive intellect that is not afraid of the truth. He has borne witness to what many others can see but are afraid to acknowledge in their readings of my work. He has anticipated what the world may only come to understand about my aesthetic vision in retrospect many decades from now'.

When the narrator finally meets Lebrun, he characterises his conversation as being,

> like Ruskin's on the printed page, in its fluency and elaborateness, the words wonderfully chosen, often unexpected, bubbling up from some ever-running spring of sensibility. The thought-connections – as with Ruskin – were not always clear; but you assumed they were there. As with the poetry of Blake (or, within a smaller compass, Auden), you held on, believing there was a worked-out argument (1994, 117).

Never mind the tongue in cheek, the Naipaulesque insinuation, too mischievous to let pass, that there may indeed have been no worked-out argument beneath the elegantly formulated rhetoric. Naipaul is comparing Lebrun here with the literary models that dominated his colonial education and subsequent literary initiation at Oxford. His association of Lebrun with the mercurial genius of Blake, the perfect poise of Ruskin, and the contemporaneous glamour of Auden, whose plays and poetry were much in vogue at Oxford in the 1950s, allows Naipaul to mark the narrator's enthusiasm as an initiate's naive response to a specific notion of literary greatness that he has been taught to admire. At the same time, however, Naipaul makes the point that in terms of what at that moment it was possible to imagine oneself as a colonial striving to attain through language, Lebrun had achieved it all.

Naipaul's representation of the relationship between his semi-autobiographical narrator and the public oracle, Lebrun, as opposed to a simple account of the relationship between V.S. Naipaul and C.L.R. James, allows him to foreground a number of similarities between himself and a historical figure who many consider his nemesis. For contemporary Caribbean aficionados, James epitomises a tradition of committed black intellectual thought associated with such figures as George Padmore, Frantz Fanon, and Eric Williams, to name a few. It is a tradition from which Naipaul often has been accused of distancing himself. This perspective on the opposition between Naipaul and James sits well on both sides of the literary and ideological divide, where Naipaul is ostracised, by one camp, as a betrayer of the Third World and lionised, by the other, as the consummate aesthete and man of conscience – embodying all the essential purities Kripalsingh projects onto his Aryan ancestors in *The Mimic Men.*[7] For both kinds of readers, the essential Naipaul is a man divorced from his Caribbean roots: the purist made nauseous by filth and flesh, or the racist who has 'forgotten' his own family's sojourn in the cane fields of the New World.

Naipaul signifies on both the purist and racist readings of his work in his description of two meals, one of coo-coo, with Lebrun and other West Indians in London, and one of gefilte fish, with Lebrun's influential American friends in Manhattan. The meal with Lebrun takes place in a Maida Vale flat in London, filled with overstuffed furniture. Naipaul describes those present with the kind of meticulous attention to racial nuance we West Indians invoke as a matter of course when describing ourselves. Thus, the host is described as Lebanese Trinidadian, his wife as a Creole who could pass for white but is from one of the smaller islands. Lebrun himself, though fairly dark in complexion, has a dash of Amerindian that gives his skin a reddish tinge. Only Lebrun's woman friend, described as a Polish or Czech woman, is given no ethnic specificity at this point.

Their meal, which Naipaul, somewhat inexactly, calls coo-coo, is described in even greater detail:

> A heavy glistening mound was placed on my own plate. I probed it: boiled yams and green bananas and possibly other tubers mashed together with peppers, the whole mixture slimy from the yams and – the Lebanese touch – olive oil. Below the pepper it had almost no taste, except one of a tart rawness (from the green bananas), and I thought it awful, the texture, the slipperiness. I

> didn't think I would be able to keep it down. I let it be on my plate. No one noticed.
>
> While Lebrun ate, and his dutiful woman friend ate, and the smell of meat and oil became high in the squashed sitting room with the old upholstered chairs, and people asked the Lebanese where they had got the yams and green bananas from, I (feeling that I was betraying them all, and separating myself from the good mood of the evening) remembered my aunt twenty years before, fanning her coal pot on the concrete back steps of our house in Port of Spain, and talking about Grenadians boiling their 'pitch-oil tin' of ground provisions once a week.[8]

Naipaul sets up this moment of excruciating embarrassment and gross satire very carefully. The cosmopolitan mix of the company around the table is set off by the crude peasant meal of coo-coo they make a point of eating; their stuffed mouths and the high smell of the food in the cramped room, against the elevated intellectual conversation Lebrun proceeds to initiate. Furthermore Naipaul draws into this moment, through the reference to his narrator's aunt, the ramifications attached to this meal for him in its original Caribbean setting. Naipaul associates the ingredients of the meal with the Grenadian and Vincentian labourers he describes earlier in the chapter, who flocked to the Trinidad of his colonial childhood in search of work.[9] In the course of this earlier description, the narrator first introduces the satirical portrait of his aunt – now 'an alert, generous, elegant woman' (1994, 80), resident in Canada but then a somewhat garrulous character, fanning a coal pot on the back steps of the Port of Spain house, filled with recently relocated migrants from the countryside. Her derogatory reference to small islanders and their pitch oil tins of ground provisions indicates some of the consequences for the status of Indo-Trinidadians that this 'small island' invasion produced.

Before the influx of immigrants, the Indo-Trinidadian peasant population of Trinidad was considered by many to occupy one of the lowest rungs on the very complex ladder of Trinidad social status. Further down in colour hierarchy than the other indentured labourers of Chinese and Portuguese origin, less urbane and cosmopolitan than the black and mixed race Creoles of the city, Indo-Trinidadians who began to make the transition from country to town in the interwar years, may well have seized the opportunity to revise the public image of their community as backward and foreign when a new group, with even less prestige, arrived in the island after the Second World War.[10] Thus, the narrator's aunt does not need to acknowledge the squalor of her coal pot on the back steps if the living and cooking arrangements of the small islanders can be represented as even more primitive. At the same time, any provincial unease with the cosmopolitan foods and customs of Port of Spain she may have felt can be transformed into disgust, when redirected at the foods and customs of the new immigrants.

All the words through which Naipaul makes the coo-coo seem revolting can be associated with the ramifications Naipaul brings to its description from other moments in the novel, especially from his earlier presentation of small island squalor and East Indian social angst. The way the elements of the meal are mashed together recalls the overcrowded Port of Spain house both the narrator and his aunt have since fled, even as it explains the need to enhance their social standing that dictated the distance Indo-Trinidadians struggled to maintain between themselves and the bodies of the unassimilated small islanders. The emphasis on the meal's indiscriminate mixing of African, Indian, even Lebanese ingredients, which the narrator's probing fork uncovers, also signifies on the racial mixture – not to say sexual promiscuity – associated with Trinidad Creole culture that the narrator, like a reader of pornography, approaches with a mixture of curiosity and revulsion. The narrator's characterisation of the taste and texture of the meal, as that of 'tart rawness' overlaying blandness and of 'slipperiness,' has obvious sexual overtones, as do the visual images associated with tubers and green bananas. These are further codified for the Caribbean reader through the popular association in Trinidad calypso between dried salt fish – the side dish usually served with coo-coo – and the female genitalia. Finally, the meal's sexual connotations are reinforced by the narrator's mildly envious allusions to Lebrun's reputation as a successful womaniser, repeated throughout the chapter, but conveyed in the passage quoted here through the narrator's uncomfortable awareness of the devotional attitude of the Polish or Czech woman friend at Lebrun's side, dutifully consuming the slimy meal.

Naipaul's emphasis on the racial and sexual connotations associated with coo-coo highlights cultural distinctions that still persist in the Trinidad popular imagination between the island's Indo-Trinidadian population, with its supposedly homogenous social contours, and the much vaunted cultural hybridity of the wider Creole society. One of the reasons why the narrator cannot quite bring himself to eat this 'mushed-up' meal with the gusto and aplomb of the other middle class West Indians at the dinner party – for some of whom it *also* is an exotic dish – is that his relationship to cultural mixture, to culinary slumming if you like, is complicated by the conservative notions of cultural separateness that the others associate with the uncreolised aspects of Indo-Trinidadian culture. Thus, when the narrator notes parenthetically, in the passage quoted, that he feels as if he is betraying them all, he is expressing both an ironic distance from what he perceives as their staged indulgence in the culture of a class of people to which no one at the dinner party (including Lebrun) belongs – poor, uneducated, black, small island labourers – and a genuine sense of the limits placed on his Creole identity. His feelings of isolation are exacerbated by the way in which his Indianness in this self-consciously Creole context is never quite fully assimilated, even (especially!) when it is overlooked.

Critics in the 'Naipaul as purist' cultural camp will be quick to celebrate the narrator's squeamishness as evidence of Brahmin sensibility, which Naipaul codes here through his references to the high smell of meat (actually another inexactitude, since if the meal *had* been coo-coo it would have been served with salt fish or flying fish). On the other hand, critics of the 'Naipaul as cultural betrayer' camp will want to claim his over refined expressions of disgust as one more piece of evidence for his distaste of all things associated with black West Indians. Yet Naipaul's position at this stage in his narrative is a lot more complex. Earlier in the chapter on Lebrun, Naipaul makes a point of noting the influence of George Lamming's first novel on his literary development. Lamming's successful use of comedy in *In the Castle of My Skin* affirmed for Naipaul something he had been unable to acknowledge until then in his attempts to write; that 'comedy, the preserver we in Trinidad had always known, was close to me, a double inheritance, from my storytelling Hindu family, and from the Creole street life of Port of Spain' (1994, 89). Naipaul thus uses his connection to a black Caribbean writer to underwrite his literary sensibility as deriving from both Creole and Hindu cultural influences. Similarly, Lebrun's Creole urbanity is one of the features Naipaul allows his narrator to admire in his fictional rewriting of James, whose 1936 'barrack yard' novel, *Minty Alley*, is one of the clearest precursors of Naipaul's urbane satirical style in Trinidadian fiction. Within Creole culture, no racial or ethnic trait exists beyond co-optation. A Lebanese Trinidadian may integrate coo-coo into her cuisine with the same matter-of-factness that an Indo-Trinidadian writer can emulate the satirical conventions of the calypsos he hears on the streets of his neighbourhood, or of the folk tales he absorbs via Caribbean writers of African *and* Indian descent.

The problem with Creole appropriation, however, is that it inevitably involves a loss of ethnic specificity. All Trinidadians constantly negotiate the tension between their specific ethnic and racial origins and their sense of belonging to a multiracial Creole culture. In fact, it is the elegance with which these contradictions are finessed that constitutes the hallmark of Creole cultural hybridity. However, once this hybridity is perceived in terms of loss, rather than opportunity, it is possible to read the Creolisation process as a denial of difference, a form of cultural erasure. This is the defensive sentiment that fuelled in part the Black Power reassertion of African roots in the Caribbean during the 1960s and 1970s. It is also the fear that constrains Naipaul's narrator: the minority sensibility that rewrites the inclusive gestures of Lebrun's dinner party as a denial of the specificity of his Indo-Caribbean background, including his embarrassing private insecurities about consuming or being consumed by small island food.

Naipaul's naming of coo-coo as the meal his narrator cannot consume obliquely indicates the limits of the Creole identity that the narrator (at one level) seems so anxious to claim. Naipaul's choice of the word coo-coo as the name of the meal he describes enables a second intertexual reference to George Lamming's *In the Castle of My Skin.*[11] The closing chapter of Lamming's first novel contains a famous passage describing how G-'s mother prepares a final meal of coo-coo for him before he leaves Barbados for Trinidad. In his essay, 'Cuckoo [sic] and Culture,' the critic Edward Baugh reads this passage as marking the moment at which the boy G- affirms and accepts the African/ peasant roots of his culture, 'so that every movement of his mother's hands, every ingredient that is added to the meal, becomes a kind of last sacrament and celebration of a culture which the boy G-, until this moment, has experienced with deep ambivalence.'[12] Paradoxically, this insight comes at a point in the novel when the narration shifts from the third person, in which the boy is signified by the anonymous 'G-,' to a first person, 'I,' narrator, through whose agency the boy finally becomes an independent speaking subject. Separated from his mother and insulated from her culture, he can now reify each, as madonna and sacrament.

The meal of coo-coo in Lamming's text is thus both a gesture of embrace and a sign of the process of individuation that disrupts the connection between mother and son. The narrating, 'I,' who reifies the folk, is less enmeshed in the folk culture than the boy, 'G-.' By highlighting the difficulties his Indo-Caribbean narrator experiences when invited to participate in the same sacramental rite of consuming coo-coo, Naipaul helps us understand how Lamming's gesture could be read as an aggressive act of cultural appropriation, similar to the culinary slumming for which his narrator indicts the Caribbean intellectuals at Lebrun's dinner party. He also may be making the point that the limits to cultural and literary convergence between himself and Lamming, or himself and James, are imposed ultimately by the different relationships to power reflected in their respective social histories. Lamming's narrator's ability to simultaneously claim and distance his mother's dish of coo-coo does not liberate Naipaul's narrator automatically from the complexly different socio-cultural anxieties he brings to a similar meal.

Read in relation to the response of Lamming's 'G-,' however, Naipaul's narrator's refusal to eat may also signal a failure of the maturation process: an inability on the part of this narrating 'I' to free himself of primal anxieties around status and identity embedded in his unconscious. Thus, the flashback to his garrulous aunt and his recourse to her language of 'ground provisions' and 'pitch oil tins' may be a way of signalling his failure – and everyone else's struggle – to complete the process of separation from an infantile identification with an imaginary mother culture. The impressionable child, who has never quite freed himself from the half articulated fears and dreams of his maternal community, resurfaces in the hysterical man, gagging inexplicably when faced with a meal that triggers the feelings of suffocation, vulnerability, and inarticulateness that also assault the boy, 'G-,' but which Lamming resolves in his novel by creating an independent speaking subject.

In Lamming's resolution, to be Creole is to be mature, that is, to be capable of choosing for oneself those aspects of one's own cultural heritage, as well as the cultures of others, which one wishes to celebrate or reject. To be mature is also to perform an identity one writes for oneself, rather than to live out an identity provided by others. This is the notion of identity that the Caribbean group at James's dinner party seems to celebrate when its ethnically diverse members self-consciously reclaim the humble small island meal of coo-coo as part of their shared culture. It is also a perspective on personal choice that Naipaul supports, or at least sees as an inevitable condition of modernity, in his emphasis on the personal rewritings of the self in all of the stories in this novel. Yet, in this story about Lebrun, Naipaul reminds us that the borrowed cultural practices in which these 'new men' (and women) clothe themselves coexist at all times with more deeply held, primal patterns of belonging, from which none of us is ever fully liberated. Moreover, these new identities may threaten or erase the subjectivity of others – the black small island labourers represented only by their coo-coo at Lebrun's cosmopolitan dinner; the Indo-Trinidadian whose induction into the Creole cultural circle around the table conceals a threat or promise far more fraught than that associated with the inclusion of Lebrun's completely foreign Polish or Czech woman friend.

Naipaul uses the fear of cultural appropriation his narrator's inability to participate in the ritual meal of coo-coo intimates to reflect on the threat of cultural appropriation implicit in Lebrun's consummate ability to read his work. 'The man want to take you over' (1994, 127), the chief minister says of Lebrun in the course of another significant meeting and meal. Trinidad historian and former Prime Minister Eric Williams, the model for this character, was one of the most famous of James's protégés to later part company with his mentor.[13] Through him, the narrator comes to realise that what at first seemed to be an ideal interpretation of his writerly intent in Lebrun's article may have concealed a gesture of political co-optation that relegates the narrator's specific vision to a niche within Lebrun's elegantly formulated materialist reading of global culture. From that perspective, there is something sinister about a globalising impulse that can cheerfully exoticise the narrator's racial difference, while at the same time insisting that the narrator demonstrate his successful assimilation by consuming Creole food.

When Lebrun, between mouthfuls of coo-coo, launches into a consideration of the debate between 'Lenin and the Indian delegate, Roy, at the Second Congress of the Comintern in 1920' (1994, 120), the narrator feels even more like the token outsider among the guests at the meal. In the end, he concludes that the price he must pay for his inclusion in Lebrun's vision of international solidarity is simply too high. It demands that he trivialise his aunt's deep-seated fear of poverty and squalor, expressed in her casual jab at small island culture. It calls upon him to fit his complex understanding of himself as Indo-Trinidadian into the broad generalisations about 'Indians' that structure the debate between Lenin and Roy. From Naipaul's perspective such generalisations merely exoticise his narrator's racial specificity, by reducing it to one more instance of local colour, divorced from its original setting like the now harmlessly fashionable meal of coo-coo served up in a Maida Vale flat.

But perhaps ultimately race, or cultural difference, is not the point. There is a real distinction – one might say, a *disciplinary* distinction – between Naipaul's narrator's position on co-optation and that of Lebrun that has everything and nothing to do with race. A writer like James, who approaches the representation of experience by formulating a theoretical position and then attempting to read the world around him in terms of that theoretical claim, is doing something quite different from a writer who works, as Naipaul does, empirically; that is, from a specific gesture, an observable trait, an emotional insight, *towards* a reading of his world. That is not to say that both writers do not start off with certain – perhaps identical – framing assumptions about the worlds they inhabit, or that both writers are not ultimately dependent on the power of the specific images their words evoke for credibility and rhetorical force. Indeed, the two approaches to reading the world can be viewed as complementing each other.

This is why at a certain level James remains Naipaul's ideal reader. He can use his theoretically honed vision to excavate layers of meaning below the surface of Naipaul's text that the creative writer can only indicate through anecdote and elision. As a theoretician, James is not bound by the limits of the world he can see or reproduce imaginatively. This freedom allows him to extrapolate layers of meaning from Naipaul's work so that he can explain the process by which the writer constructs the world in a certain fashion. Yet the theoretician's paradigms also can generate speculative universes, which operate according to the laws enumerated by his theories but which bear no relationship to reality as experienced by any human society. Divorced from their empirical grounding, such theories can abstract human experience to the point where they obscure rather than elucidate the truths they purport to apprehend. By manipulating logic and language, they can substitute concepts for each other that in the 'real' world may have been diametrically opposed, thus achieving a theoretical or political resolution where a lived contradiction may remain.

Between Lebrun and Naipaul's narrator, these disciplinary differences acquire additional nuances when race and culture become part of their concern. For Naipaul, racial attitudes and cultural perceptions have their origins in a plethora of factors affecting his characters, which his fictions can never pretend to exhaust. For his stories to work, he cannot merely summarise his racial situation, as part of an Indo-Trinidadian minority in a culture shaped by the early confrontations and accommodations between Africans and Europeans, in the categorical terms I am using in this sentence. We can read his garrulous aunt as expressing a racist stereotype when she dismisses small islanders and their pitch-oil tins of ground provisions but, in the context of a fiction, she merely may be articulating her desire to escape the heat of her own coal pot, or repeating a catchy phrase she has picked up from her Creole neighbour, or invoking a barely remembered culinary taboo from her own forgotten cultural antecedents. Or maybe she is just a cantankerous old curmudgeon. There is, after all, something quite splendid about her theatrical dismissiveness that compels our attention as readers of fiction, the more so as the narrator tempts us to fantasize about how these qualities are subsumed into the facade of her later incarnation as a sedate, conventionally generous dowager living in Canada.

The successful fiction must find a way to leave all of these possibilities open. It must move beyond literary cliché or theoretical paradigm even as it appropriates this one characteristic impression of the aunt to convey the multiple associations Naipaul imposes upon her words in the context of Lebrun's dinner party. Indeed, the writer of fiction is never quite in control of how his readers will interpret his characters – as my earlier reading of this moment in conjunction with Lamming's novel as a hysterical failure of the narrator's voice demonstrates. Naipaul acknowledges this understanding of the disciplinary and stylistic boundaries that separate a writer like himself from a writer like James when his narrator says of Lebrun,

> ...we both soon got to recognize – what I felt sure we always knew – that the relationship between us was forced. We shared a background and in all kinds of unspoken ways we could understand one another; but we were on different tracks (1994, 121).

The problem of appropriation, of what from Naipaul's perspective it means to be read through someone else's intellectual assumptions, whether it be through the transplanted Creole norms of Caribbean immigrant culture or the intellectual paradigms of Lebrun's essay, is crucial to an understanding of what is at stake in Naipaul's reading of the meal of gefilte fish that he shares in Manhattan with Lebrun's powerful friends. Through the second meal, the narrator comes to realise that Lebrun, too, has been the victim of co-optation; that what Lebrun describes as the 'political resolution' through which he comes to terms with the humiliations of his racial history is in part a form of spiritual capitulation to the meanings others have assigned to his body and his writing. During the Maida Vale meal, Lebrun recounts his humiliation at realising that his great-uncle's stories of being treated like a guest in the kitchens of London Great Houses in the mid-nineteenth century were fantasies nurtured to deny the realities of colonialism and racism. The narrator uses this story to anchor his imaginative insights into Lebrun's inner life. Lebrun claims that he is only released from the shame he connects with his own participation in his great-uncle's self delusion when he can tell this story in public to others. However, he also maintains that, 'every black man has a memory like that. Every educated black man is eaten away quietly by a memory like that' (1994, 119). Indeed, the narrator remains unconvinced that the shameful desire for approval, which fuels the great-uncle's fantasies of equality with white servants, is not still eating away at Lebrun. Thus, as Lebrun approaches senility, his compulsive need to repeat his great-uncle's story marks the persistence of the trauma caused by this early childhood memory, just as the narrator remains unable to move beyond the range of his aunt's invective when confronted with small island food.

Naipaul invites us to read the second meal of gefilte fish from the perspective of the shame surrounding this painful legacy of gratitude to one's oppressors, which Lebrun's great-uncle bequeaths his nephew. At first, the narrator is horrified to realise that the sophisticated Manhattan intellectuals into whose company he has been admitted by virtue of Lebrun's introduction can see him only through the paradigms offered by Lebrun's article in the 'thick' Russian magazine. All their vaunted knowledge of the islands has been siphoned off second-hand from their readings of Lebrun and other Left wing theoreticians. They seem to him to have no feeling for the nuances of cruelty, betrayal, indifference and joy that separate and connect different regimes and racial groups within the region with which they claim solidarity. Where Lebrun offers the narrator coo-coo but is at least willing to overlook the fact that he cannot eat it, Lebrun's Manhattan friends appear to treat the narrator's refusal of their meal of gefilte fish as a kind of betrayal. Like the contrived global paradigms through which Caribbean societies often are read in metropolitan intellectual circles, the worked over, indeterminate mass of gefilte fish is offered to the narrator as a token of the automatic solidarity between oppressed Jewish and Caribbean peoples:

> The idea of something pounded to paste, then spiced or oiled, worked on by fingers, brought to mind thoughts of hand lotions and other things. I became fearful of smelling it. I couldn't eat it. With the coo-coo or the foo-foo in the Maida Vale flat I had been able to hide what I did to the things on my plate. That couldn't be

> done here: everyone knew that the gefilte fish had been specially prepared for Lebrun's friend from London (1994, 128).

Naipaul never names Lebrun's friends directly as left wing Jewish intellectuals, just as he never gets further than identifying Lebrun's woman friend as Polish or Czech. For his narrator, the ramifications of all their racial and ethnic histories remain opaque. He can see no organic link between the affluence and sophistication of his New York hosts and the social limitations of his Caribbean childhood, just as someone from the outside who did not know his aunt before she became a gracious Canadian lady would have had difficulty associating her with the shrieking harridan fanning a coal pot on the back steps of an overcrowded Port of Spain house. Or, as someone who had not read the novel's earlier descriptions of Leonard Side, the Trinidadian descendant of Lucknow's Shia Muslim dancing transvestites, whose long perfumed fingers iced cakes and laid out dead bodies at Parry's Corner, might miss the necrophilic associations Naipaul brings to the description of the way his narrator imagines gefilte fish is prepared. The narrator concedes in his story of Leonard Side that 'we go back all of us to the very beginning; in our blood and bone and brain we carry the memories of thousands of beings' (1994, 11). Yet he sees that legacy as expressing only 'a fragment of the truth' we understand about our racial inheritances. He distrusts his hosts' insistence that he equate their history of oppression with what they imagine is his own; that coo-coo is somehow equivalent to gefilte fish and that the consumption of such meals confer on their eaters a badge of authenticity as representatives of the oppressed. For him, the distinctions in social status between himself and his hosts of which he remains most acutely aware have less to do with the coincidences of oppression within their respective histories than with the ease with which they now assume they can read him. They take it for granted that they can co-opt and categorise his experience, even as they prescribe how they expect him to read their own.

As he struggles with the social ostracism to which he imagines his refusal of the meal of gefilte fish exposes him, Naipaul's fictional double begins to reflect on the difficult line someone like Lebrun must constantly walk among such powerful patrons; the extent to which his global paradigms can be read as an attempt to protect himself from the appropriative power of his mentors, even as they seduce him into simplifying the stubborn contradictions of his specific history. He speculates that Lebrun's consummate rhetoric and his air of having transcended the legacies of slavery and racial oppression may in fact conceal a sense of incompleteness, a desire to be accepted, like that of his nineteenth-century great-uncle, that betrays him into the false securities of unequal alliances.

Naipaul's speculations about the private motivations behind Lebrun's 'political resolutions' produce one of the novel's most direct autobiographical statements and one of the few moments in the text when he seems to distance his narrator completely from Lebrun. The narrator is able to refuse the form of solidarity he imagines he has been offered over the meal of gefilte fish because he values his personal integrity as a writer above his hosts' approval. By contrast, Naipaul reads Lebrun's consent to the appropriation of his ideas by people, who neither acknowledge the moral ambiguities nor understand the personal humiliations out of which his political resolutions arise, as evidence of Lebrun's feelings of incompleteness:

> Few of us are without the feeling that we are incomplete. But my feelings of incompleteness were not like Lebrun's. In the things I felt myself incomplete Lebrun was – as I thought – abundantly served: physical attractiveness, love, sexual fulfilment. But there were other yearnings that no shedding of skin could have assuaged: my own earned security, a wish for my writing gift to last and grow, a dream of working at yet unknown books, accumulations of fruitful days, achievement. These yearnings could be assuaged only in the self I knew (1994, 128).

There is a double subterfuge at work in this passage. In the first place, Naipaul structures his observation in such a way that Lebrun's gifts and insecurities are reduced to those that Naipaul's narrator can read through his own limitations. So, in a way, he is asking us to read Lebrun through his narrator's limited paradigms – in exactly the way he accuses the Manhattan crowd of reading his work exclusively through Lebrun's paradigms. It is also difficult to avoid the impression that Naipaul is protesting too loudly. His distancing of his narrator from a particular reading of Lebrun's capitulation masks a defence of Naipaul *himself* from similar charges of having 'sold out' to the influential champions of his work within the literary mainstream.

Naipaul uses the representation of his narrator as perversely difficult, as someone who refuses to make the kinds of compromises Lebrun has made and for whom the excellence and integrity of his work as a writer is paramount, to counteract the image of himself as the Third World writer who has made a fortune saying the derogatory things the First World wants to hear about his world. Thus, just as his writing seems most clear, most forthright, most free of elision, Naipaul conceals between the lines a passionate defence of himself from a criticism of his work that remains unformulated as such within his text.

Perhaps, in the end, this is the point of Naipaul's estimate of James and himself through the character of Lebrun. For Naipaul, Lebrun is always most interesting when his facade of consummate urbanity cracks; when his naked sexual envy in relation to the writer Foster Morris flashes out, just as Naipaul's narrator's literary vanity is piqued by this same man; when his bitterness about a personal dilemma betrays him in Africa, as it has at times betrayed Naipaul in other settings, into vicious or reckless political pronouncements which others then proceed to take seriously; when the old hurt and humiliation associated with his great-uncle's gratitude over being allowed to take tea with the servants in an English Great House betrays his pain at having to accept the way his ideas are co-opted by his powerful patrons – just as Naipaul's have been.

Through Lebrun, Naipaul sees men like himself and James as 'men on the run.' Both writers have relinquished membership in the communities of their birth in order to pursue fame through their writing, thus gambling with the possibility of their co-optation by more powerful communities on a global stage. Both have claimed for themselves the license, as Naipaul notes of Lebrun, to critique anything and anybody wherever they find themselves but neither has stayed long enough anywhere to have had to live with the consequences of their pronouncements (1994, 160). The difference between them from Naipaul's perspective is that his narrator claims to be aware of the dangers and limitations inherent in his way of reading the world, whereas a public figure like Lebrun, whose work has been politically appropriated by others, is constantly shielded from the consequences of the 'real world' limitations of his vision by those who lionise him. Thus, while Naipaul's narrator must constantly revise his reading of himself in the face of relentless criticism, Lebrun remains 'oddly pure' (160) because the ideals of revolution and African redemption that he espouses have become fashionable 'progressive' clichés whose inherent contradictions no one cares to expose.

Naipaul's novel builds on the anecdotal. It incorporates into the character of Lebrun recognisable traits of C.L.R. James as well as observations Naipaul has made over time of other writers and colonial impresarios of James's generation. Naipaul offers us little concrete evidence that James ever evinced the fears or responses the narrator imputes to Lebrun.[14] Yet, Naipaul's autobiographical narrators have often evinced just such forms of personal angst. They know what it means, as the narrator says in his final estimate of Lebrun, to have one's 'intellectual growth…at every stage…accompanied by a growing rawness of sensibility,' to face the realisation that '[one's] political resolutions, expressing the wish not to go mad, [have] been in the nature of spiritual struggles, occurring in the depth of [one's] being' (1994, 160–1).

Through the ambiguous gesture of generosity and co-optation contained in this epitaph, Naipaul imputes to James, via his construction of the character of Lebrun, all the real and imagined fears of appropriation he has experienced as a writer. He challenges readers who have seen him and James as representing diametrically opposed strands in Caribbean intellectual thought to acknowledge the anguish and insecurity, even the petty viciousness, that must of necessity have lain behind James's perfectly poised public persona. Without an understanding of this angst, Naipaul contends, we cannot fully appreciate either the greatness of a man like James or the limits of his vision. At the same time, Naipaul presents himself, through his narrator's words, as having been able to refuse most of the accommodations someone like James in his opinion has had to accept. He claims he is able to do so, on account of the accidents of history that brought him into the literary world at a less brutal moment than James. These include the changes in the politics of racial patronage that separate a Caribbean intellectual impresario of the 1930s from a Caribbean Oxford graduate of the 1950s, as well as Naipaul's understanding of himself as a creative writer rather than a political theoretician. Finally, Naipaul sees the double dispossessions of his Indo-Trinidadian racial heritage as making him less susceptible to the myths of racial affirmation that in his opinion have created the dissonance between the themes of global transcendence and cultural nationalism in James's political pronouncements.

One of my colleagues a well-known literary reviewer, sent me a copy of his review of *A Way in the World* before I read the book, by way of acknowledging the help I had given him in identifying some of the autobiographical references in the novel. In his review, my colleague quoted the passage about coo-coo around which this essay is built as an example of everything he considered superfluous, even self-indulgent, in the book. I had scarcely read more than a line of this excerpt when I was overcome by a memory that I had completely repressed. It was of my grandmother, who had visited us from Barbados when

I was a child, bringing with her a biscuit tin, in which, wrapped in oily paper and held together by twine, lay a glistening mass of coo-coo.

Reading Naipaul's description I registered as if for the first time how horrified and disgusted I had felt on seeing that glistening mound, in much the same way that Naipaul's narrator feels. It was not just because of its unfamiliar texture, but because somehow, at the age of six, I already had divined that this was 'small island food;' something that Trinidadians like my family, who lived in the city and considered themselves cultured and urbane, did not readily admit to eating. As I read on, all the ambivalence and confusion of that childhood moment returned. Those feelings persisted, even after I realised that the meal he was describing was not actually what I thought of when I thought of coo-coo. Before I had read another sentence in the novel, I thought I understood what Naipaul was trying to do with this description and why it was so crucial to the story he needed to tell about how he had made his way in the world.

Naipaul's language in that moment put me in touch with feelings I had not even allowed myself to think I had ever had. These were not feelings of nostalgia. They did not take me back to a childhood place that was wholesome, or affirming, or political or correct but, rather, to a place that I knew was emotionally true, whatever the interpretation I had given to that emotion in the interceding decades. I should add that I love coo-coo now and would probably have been wolfing it down in that Maida Vale flat with Lebrun and his partners, had I been there, and acting as if my relationship to the meal was somehow less complicated than that of Naipaul's narrators.

Any gifted writer can make us feel good about ourselves. It is Naipaul's capacity to pick away at the scabs we all carry in our hearts, the insecurities and wounds and uncertainties and failures we all fear most when no one else is looking, that makes him truly great – that draws me back to his words year after year, decade after decade. Sometimes, I find beneath the scab a clean clear growth of new skin that is fresh and optimistic and filled with possibility. At other times I find only a pus-filled abscess. Yet this is writing that always gets under my skin.

Notes

1. V.S. Naipaul, 'Prologue to an Autobiography,' in *Finding the Centre* (1984; repr., Harmondsworth: Penguin, 1985), 19; *Miguel Street* (1959; repr., Harmondsworth: Penguin, 1971), 9.

2. Naipaul, *A Way in the World* (New York: Alfred A. Knopf, 1994).
3. Several volumes of James's *Selected Works* were reissued in the 1980s and new editions of *The Black Jacobins* and *Beyond a Boundary* are also now widely available. The James Archive maintained in New York by Charles Murray has been partially indexed by Anna Grimshaw *in The C.L.R. James Archive: A Reader's Guide* (New York: C.L.R. James Institute, 1991). Grimshaw also has edited James's love letters, *Special Delivery: The Letters of C.L.R. James to Constance Webb 1939–1984* (Oxford: Blackwell, 1996). A collection of James's newspaper columns appeared in 1997, called *C.L.R. James on the Negro Question*, edited by Scott McLemee (Mississippi: University of Mississippi Press, 1997). The James Institute supports a C.L.R. James Society and publishes *The C.L.R. James Journal.* Other recent publications include Kent Worcester's *C.L.R. James: A Political Biography* (New York: SUNY, 1996), several books of essays on James's legacy, including Paul Buhle's *C.L.R. James: His Life and Work* (London: Allison & Busby, 1986), and Grant Farred's anthology *Rethinking C.L.R. James* (Oxford: Blackwell, 1995). Most of these anthologies refer, in passing or in detail, to the correspondence or interaction between Naipaul and James. Although I was unable to consult it in preparing this version of my essay, the original correspondence between James and Naipaul is now housed in the West Indian Special Collection at the University of the West Indies, St Augustine campus. See Naipaul's assessment in 'Sporting Life *Beyond a Boundary*,' *Encounter* 21 (1963): 73–5.
4. See V.S. Naipaul's Foreword to *The Adventures of Gurudeva and Other Stories* by Seepersad Naipaul (London: André Deutsch, 1976), 9.
5. Naipaul, *The Overcrowded Barracoon and Other Articles* (Harmondsworth: Penguin, 1976), 24–31.
6. Naipaul, *The Middle Passage* (1962; repr., London: Penguin Books, 1988), 29.
7. Naipaul, *The Mimic Men* (1967; repr., London: Picador, 2002). For examples of Naipaul as betrayer see Selwyn Cudjoe, *V.S. Naipaul: A Materialist Reading* (Amherst: University of Massachusetts Press, 1988), especially his introduction, where he explicitly compares Naipaul's take on the Caribbean to that of James (33–4) and Rob Nixon's 'London Calling: V.S. Naipaul and the License of Exile,' *The South Atlantic Quarterly* Vol. 87, no. 1 (Winter 1988). The best known of these attacks is probably Achebe's essay on *A Bend in the River*, 'Viewpoint,' *Times Literary Supplement* (February 1, 1989): 71, 271, in which he dismisses the book without having read it, and Edward Said's critical remarks in 'The Post-Colonial Intellectual: A Discussion with Conor Cruise O'Brien, Edward Said and John Lukacs,' *Salmagundi* 70–71 (Spring–Summer 1986): 65–81. O'Brien and Lukacs argued for Naipaul. Other examples of what Nixon calls 'Naipaul worship' include Eugene Goodheart, 'V.S. Naipaul's Mandarin Sensibility,' in *Partisan Review* 50 (1983): 224–56, and Joseph Epstein's 'A Cottage for Mr Naipaul' *New Criterion* (October 1987): 6–15.
8. Naipaul, *A Way in the World*, (1994), 120. Although the meal Naipaul describes looks like coo-coo, the ingredients he ascribes to it seem more like those of a dish known as 'rundown' in Jamaica, made with yams, eddoes, and green bananas in a coconut milk sauce. The small island equivalent is known in the Eastern Caribbean as 'bluefood,'

or 'oildown' usually made without coconut milk. Naipaul may not have been aware of the differences between these meals, or he may purposely have 'smushed' them together. The sleight of hand allows him to draw on his aunt's memorable phrase, clearly a reference to oildown, to produce that wonderfully gross description of the meal's contents, without sacrificing the many folk and literary references associated with coo-coo that I describe in the course of my reading of the meal.

9. For an earlier version of Naipaul's response to the small island presence in Trinidad see the chapter on Trinidad in *The Middle Passage* (47–8). His indignant response to a Trinidadian customs officer's callous treatment of 'small island' children on the ship achieves greater resonance when we keep in mind that Indo-Trinidadian children were routinely treated in a similar fashion by other Trinidadians at the time.

10. Ramabai Espinet's essay 'Indian Cuisine,' in *The Massachusetts Review* 35, 3–4 (Autumn–Winter, 1994): 563–73, provides independent corroboration of my hunch here that eating coo-coo has a special set of sexual connotations associated with Creole promiscuity among Indo-Trinidadians. Describing her own first attempts at making coo-coo in her Indo-Trinidadian home, she recounts the revulsion with which most of her family greeted it, as well as her mother's consternation when she realises that her father is eating it with the practiced gusto of a long time connoisseur: 'I heard the hiss in her voice, "Yuh know bout coo-coo? Where yuh know bout coo-coo?" I was still doing home-work on the big table outside and listened attentively. I had heard a neighbour whispering to Muddie that Da-Da had a Creole woman and that it wasn't really the gambling job that took up so much time' (570).

11. George Lamming, *In the Castle of My Skin* (New York: Macmillan, 1970).

12. Edward Baugh, 'Cuckoo and Culture: *In the Castle of My Skin,*' *ARIEL* 8.3 (1977): 23–33.

13. Most commentators concede that Williams's understanding of the class dimension of his economic study of the roots of abolition were a result of James's influence on him. Williams himself acknowledges that the idea for *Capitalism and Slavery* was an elaboration of the thesis about the economic motivations of 'The Owners' put forward in Chapter 2 of James's *The Black Jacobins* (see Robert Hill, 'In England: 1932–38' in Paul Buhle, *C.L.R. James: His Life and Work*, 79). The break between the two men occurred during the period 1958–62 when James worked as editor of *The Nation*, the official organ of Williams's PNM party in Trinidad. The two men differed on the question of the party's willingness to compromise with the US Government over the matter of ownership of the Chaguaramas Naval Base in Trinidad. Williams offers a summary of his version of their political falling out in his autobiography, *Inward Hunger: The Education of a Prime Minister* (London: André Deutsch, 1969), 267–8, but does not mention James's earlier influence on his intellectual development. For a summary of James's explanation of the split, see Kent Worcester's comments in *C.L.R. James: A Political Biography* (153–4).

14. Worcester, *C.L.R. James: A Political Biography,* takes exception to Naipaul's portrayal of James/Lebrun as an insecure intellectual:

> ...to the degree that Lebrun is intended to represent James, the idea that he actively repressed an underlying madness is completely at odds with all other portrayals of a proud and dignified rhetorician. A closer approximation of the truth would be to say that James – 'in the depth of his being' – had a pacific temperament, coated by a pride in achievement and aptitude. *Pace* Naipaul, James was never a Stalinist hack, nor was he in 'anguish.' James did not 'become a child again...looking only for peace' in his old age. Instead, he remained a sane old man, waiting to be liberated from a sick body, committed to basic socialist principles (1996, 175).

Yet Naipaul's point here is precisely that, as a writer of *fiction*, he needs to be able to imagine the inner life and tensions of such a man as James. Moreover, he remains persuaded that to the extent that James, like every other colonised West Indian, shares the humiliations of Naipaul's own colonial socialisation, there *must* be a level at which he remains traumatised by that experience. In fairness to both views it must be said that James, for all his charm and conviviality, remained for most people a distant person who seldom allowed others to see him 'out of control.' So it is really anyone's guess, Worcester's as well as Naipaul's, as to what really lay behind that carefully cultivated urbanity.

Section Two

Form Matters

5

THE CONFESSIONAL ELEMENT IN NAIPAUL'S FICTION

Gordon Rohlehr

Confession has always assumed the confessant's consciousness of a body of rules or ideals, a prevailing moral and spiritual order against which he or she has transgressed. The process of confession involves acknowledgement of error or crime and taking personal responsibility for having sinned in thought, word and deed. Ideally, the confessant feels sorrow, shame, guilt, remorse of conscience. The confessant bears a heavy burden of guilt from which he seeks relief. Or he may think of himself as soiled and of confession as the prelude to a cleansing and a renewal of spirit. Confession, sometimes conducted in public before an entire congregation or in private before a single confessor, is meant to be a laying bare, a coming clean.

Among Christians, the doctrine of original sin makes a person responsible for Adam's transgression; though the Incarnation of Christ, a second Adam has absolved humankind of what the seventeenth-century Anglo-Catholic poet John Donne complained was 'that sin where I begun/Which was my sin, though it were done before.'[1] In West Indian literature, the history of discovery, conquest, genocide, enslavement, violation, destruction and erasure has become a type of original sin, a karmic burden that has demanded of Wilson Harris's protagonists cycles of rebirth and anguished reparation. A need to atone and take responsibility for the past, or alternatively to forget, wipe out and lay the past to rest, has surfaced in the work of several writers and is implicit in the writing of even those writers who seek to deny the relevance of the past.

The persistence of criminal violence and horrible atrocities in several Caribbean societies has led to the thesis that the postcolonial Caribbean is, like the colonial Caribbean, a civilisation in trauma. George Lamming's suggestion over forty years ago was that the former colonisers and the neo-colonised needed to confront each other in a Haitian-type Ceremony of Souls:[2] a cleansing dialogue that would involve not only confession of past transgression, but also release, a laying to rest of the burdensome past towards what Kamau Brathwaite calls a refashioning of the future.[3]

When apartheid-ridden South Africa, that ultimate colony and prison-camp, emerged from the shadow of its oppressive police state, it sought national healing through the Truth and Reconciliation Commission. This is a concrete example of the possibility of Lamming's Ceremony of Souls. The Truth and Reconciliation Commission is driven by the institution of confession, and some such Commission might well be necessary in places such as Guyana, Haiti, Jamaica with their recent post Independence history of politically-sanctioned internecine violence, and Trinidad and Tobago where its contesting ethnicities pursue separate and equally fruitless monologues over rights of predation.

V.S. Naipaul is as much concerned as any other West Indian writer, with issues of aboriginal terror, the question of the past and its legacy of crime, guilt and dereliction, and the near impossible ordeal of restructuring and rebuilding what he has termed these 'half-made,' 'haphazard,' 'crazy' societies, places which though termed new he regards as having already exhausted their possibilities. Naipaul's Africa of 'In a Free State' and *A Bend in the River* bleeds cyclically with the effort of reconciling the bush, a place that is 'not yet part of the present,' with such postmodern civilisation as is characterised on the one hand by the prefabricated Big Burger joint and on the other by the advanced machinery of mass murder. When Salim, seeking a new life, first arrives at the unnamed town at the bend in the river after a drive 'from the east coast right through to the centre,' his first reaction as he encounters the equatorial forest is: 'But this is madness. I am going in the wrong direction. There can't be a new life at the end of this.'[4]

'Confession' in Naipaul has been concerned with the dilemma of constructing identities, defining commitment to or negotiating escape from these dreadful places where green beginnings are strangely identical with dead ends. Such confession has been both direct – as in his interviews, essays, travelogues and other non-fiction – and indirect as in his fiction, where the protagonists function as complex and manipulable masks for their creator: Naipaul, the author. This essay will pursue a chronological pathway through Naipaul's writings from the 1960s to the late 1970s, when the issues of confession were most clearly manifest in his work. These issues include that of the writer's responsibility to the country of his origin; the necessity for escape and exile and the consequent ordeal of alienation; the quest for personal independence and the fortitude necessary for existence unsupported by the props of nation, ideology or easily accessible guidelines; the impossibility of illumination in an ever-darkening private and public landscape; the irony of intervention and committed action in situations that seem to be historically predetermined to end in disaster.

Both Naipaul and his fictional masks have consistently wrestled with these concerns and, as I hope to illustrate, have found themselves entangled in the processes of confession: self-accusation, condemnation of self, Other, and social milieu; paradoxes of disclosure and concealment, honesty and self-deception, self-judgment and self-exoneration. Naipaul from the very start perceived his haphazard society as being peopled by survivalists, tricksters, picaroons and a whole theatre of amoral hustlers living by the grace of their wits. The trickster, with his ethic of survival by any means necessary, is a Machiavellian character who cannot afford to listen to the cry of conscience or the remorse central to confession. Naipaul's primary assumption, stated in *The Middle Passage* and elsewhere, was that Trinidad society lacked moral and spiritual values, order, solidity or firmly lived ideals. Thus Naipaul's rogues, frauds and self-propelling mediocrities are genuinely unaware of error as they pragmatically measure their gains and losses on the compelling and chaotic stage of life. Characters such as Ganesh or Harbans quite naturally shun the depths of self into which confessional self-assessment would lead them. Like their society, they lack a moral centre and thus greet their success with self-congratulation, rather than the self-recrimination of the confessant.

The first truly confessional protagonist in Naipaul's fiction is Randolph (formerly Choonilal), the narrator of 'A Christmas Story.' Choonilal, an aspiring schoolteacher, has converted from Hinduism, a religion he had practised throughout his boyhood and until age 18 had seen as consisting of 'meaningless and shameful rites,' to Christianity, a religion that he associates with manners, enlightenment, civilisation and education. He stresses that he has in no way been coerced into conversion but has freely chosen Presbyterianism as a superior and civilised religion, over the darkness of Hinduism 'with its animistic rites, its idolatry, its emphasis on mango leaf, banana leaf and – the truth is the truth – cowdung.'[5] To symbolise the irreversible nature of his choice, Choonilal accepts the new and aristocratic English name 'Randolph,' and can become violently angry if anyone regresses and calls him by his old barbarian name, Choonilal.

'A Christmas Story,' like 'One Out of Many' or 'Tell Me Who To Kill' almost one decade later, raises certain pertinent questions such as: Where is the author located with respect to Choonilal's self-contempt? Does part of Naipaul, the Indo-Saxon element in him, partake of the self-contempt that he, using Choonilal/Randolph or Ganesh Ramsumair/G. Ramsey Muir as masks, holds up to ironic scrutiny and laughter? Is he employing the narrator to articulate and interrogate his own cultural and aesthetic choice as a self-confessed refugee from what he has termed his barbarous background towards the sterilised sanity of M'Lady's timeworn boarding house? Or does he simply present Choonilal as an extreme example of what has happened throughout the New World since Columbus's arrival, namely: cultural erasure, the aesthetic rejection of ancestral names, languages and customs; the eventually willing choice of the more acceptable culture of the ruling class as superior; the unquestioning acceptance of colonialism's binaries of 'civilization' and 'barbarism'?

Half of the charm of the confessional mode, as here employed by Naipaul, is that we can only speculate about the answers to these questions. Choonilal's confession reveals guilt and shame, but for the wrong reasons. Naïve in the midst of his laboriously acquired education, he is incapable of questioning his choice of cultures. Yet he envies his successful Hindu cousin, a relatively uneducated but highly practical businessman, and twice admits his nostalgia for the family life and ethnic lifestyle from which he has chosen to isolate himself. His self-exposure via confession reveals a pettiness of spirit that he deceives himself is magnanimity, a sense of shame at only his own failure, and an anguished recognition that every apparent gain is accompanied by a correspondent loss: the Mohun Biswas epiphany.

Choonilal confesses (note he employs the phrase 'I must confess' five times altogether on pages 33, 35, 36 twice, and 51) that his deepest shame has been his failure to achieve prestige and significance proportionate to his years of hard work, his spectacular manifestations of religious piety, or his febrile efforts at pulling strings. It takes him ten years to get into Training College and more than twenty to find a proper wife: one that is as civilised as he is. It is a degrading and demeaning struggle, one that requires much manoeuvring for him to wriggle his way to the position of Headmaster, a few years before he reaches the age of retirement.

As Headmaster, though, he relishes the respect he is now given by folk, the uncivilised 'others,' who used to mock at his change of name and his strenuous efforts to acquire culture. He values in particular the joy of castigation and shares out weekly doses of licks to pupils and pupil-teachers alike every Friday afternoon. He is especially proud when teachers throughout the island adopt his disciplinary system, even though he seems not to have been accorded the full recognition due to him as a trendsetter in education.

As Headmaster he is also able to augment his starvation teacher's wages by monopolising the giving of lessons to scholarship pupils. The additional income enables him to marry and support a wife and son; but he soon loses the ability to do so when he retires and has to revert to a pupil teacher's salary. Strategic string-pulling by his father-in-law, a school inspector, results in Choonilal Randolph's appointment to the even more prestigious sinecure of school manager. While the normal agenda of the school manager allows for the exercise of considerable power without the real grinding responsibility of being a Headmaster, Randolph sets his sights on higher things. He undertakes supervision of the construction of a new school, a job for which he hasn't the slightest qualification. At this point he joins Ganesh, Harbans and Biswas as representative trickster/survivalist types, whose common talent lies in an ability to adapt to whatever any new situation requires.

'Ability' is, however, a misnomer in Randolph's case. He mismanages the project, overspends his budget and produces a shoddily built atrocity months after the stipulated time. Randolph now lives in dread that his crowning failure will be revealed two days after Christmas when the inspectors from the Church Board are due to visit the building site. To protect himself from this final disgrace, the climax of a life that he describes as 'taking one step forward and one step back' ('A Chistmas Story' 1967, 44). Randolph decides to burn down the school, pleading that: 'The burning down of a school is an unforgiveable thing, but surely there are occasions when it can be condoned, when it is the only way out' (50).

It is condonation that he seeks, sympathetic understanding of why the crime had to be committed: exoneration from guilt. This is what triggers his confession, the apparent 'frankness' of his self-disclosure (46). '[T]he time has come for frankness,' he declares, as after the fashion of Albert Camus's Jean-

Baptiste Clamence, he tries to convince the reader that he is telling the whole truth; laying bare everything, however shameful, however embarrassing. Yet it is not judgment he seeks, but condonation. His motives for the crime he is about to commit, he tries to convince the reader, are not only honourable, but also altruistic. He is torching the school and destroying evidence of his failure 'not only for my sake, but for the sake of all those, villagers included, whose fates were involved with mine' (51).

In other words, if Randolph (respected god and culture-hero for the illiterate villagers and their example of self-emancipation from barbarism) were to fall into disgrace – such is his spiel – the whole village will fall with him and suffer his shame. Thus, hilariously, the reader savours the confessant's attempt to delude both himself and the judgmental audience. The act of burning the school, he argues, must not be construed as an act of depriving the children of the poor of education, but one of saving the poor from the anguish of feeling a sympathetic embarrassment at the disgrace of their god and role model. This is rich comedy, particularly since Randolph has already confessed that at every stage of his evolution from Hinduism into Indo-Saxondom, he has been overtly and covertly mocked by 'the others,' the ordinary folk of the village. True, they respect him when he becomes headmaster and school manager; but that is only because of the fearsome power he wields over their children's destiny. Disrespect and ridicule are never far away, and it is the fear of this ridicule, rather than any altruistic concern for the good name of the village, that drives Randolph – against his conscience, he tells us – to devise the plan of arson that will conceal his errors.

The denouement of the plot is also fabulous. Randolph decides not to burn the school, but to accept his fate with a final saint-like fortitude. His wife and son, who angrily abandon him just before Christmas, interpret this decision as cowardice. Yet the school is set afire, by whom Randolph never discloses, though it could only have been by his wife and son who were privy to the original plot, and who return soon afterwards to his grateful embrace. Randolph is therefore 'innocent' (since he can claim that he neither burnt nor witnessed the burning of the school). Randolph has also outwitted the fate that had determined that his every success had to be counterpointed and negated by failure. The 'fear, self-reproach, self-disgust,' 'the days passed in sorrow, in nightly frenzies of prayer and self-castigation' the '[r]egret for what might have been' and 'for what was to come' that he feels before the school burns, all disappear after the school burns (51). For all the Christian moral and spiritual values that Randolph has claimed, throughout his narrative, to have rigorously upheld, he emerges as a pragmatic and amoral, if thoroughly incompetent trickster, who somehow finally manages to rejoice simultaneously in iniquity and in partial, self-deluding truth.

After this light-hearted yet painful anatomy of the confessional trickster, that contradiction in terms, Naipaul progresses by distinct stages towards the darker and more harrowing grotesquerie of the Dostoevskian and Camusian types of confessional anti-hero. The world of Choonilal/Randolph whose schizophrenia is more comical than sinister because the man is more Fool than Knave, is replaced by the darkening landscapes of 'A Flag on the Island' (1965), *The Mimic Men* (1967), *Guerillas* (1975), *In a Free State* (1971) and *A Bend in the River* (1978). Located at the vestibule of all of these descents into the Inferno is Naipaul's personal descent into his own central and decentering darkness, *An Area of Darkness* (1964).[6]

'A Flag on the Island' is less obviously confessional than 'A Christmas Story,' yet it does represent a distinctive stage in Naipaul's experimentation with the confessional mode, the anti-hero, and the marginalised, nauseated, melancholic, malcontent whose grey voice has pervaded confessional fiction from Dostoevsky's *Notes from Underground* to Camus's *The Fall*, Ellison's *Invisible Man*, Denis Williams's *Other Leopards*, John Stewart's *Last Cool Days* or Saul Bellow's *Dangling Man* and *Herzog*. 'A Flag on the Island' is narrated by Frank, a former marine who during the Second World War used to be stationed on the American Base that was at the time planted on Chaguaramas Bay, Trinidad. As in *Guerillas* a few years later, Naipaul never gives Frank's island a name; his aim being, perhaps, to indicate the facelessness, the unformed features and the indistinctness of the island's emerging post-Independence identity.

Frank, whose name suggests honesty, is in fact a morally neutered yet judgmental anti-hero. During the War, he ran a 'racket' in which he supplied a small local clientele with items ranging from canned foods to uniforms smuggled out of the American Base. His greatest success is in the theft of a truck that, somehow, the filthy rich Americans never miss. They have so many more like that truck. This story, I should warn you, is subtitled 'A Fantasy.'

In return for the access he provides to all of this largesse, Frank is granted a privileged place in the city's seedy, semi-rustic underworld, where he has his choice of *wahbeens* and the best of the city's rankly flowering nightlife. The craftiest and most resourceful of the locals grow with Frank's sponsorship, expanding their business from quaint folksiness to plastic petty bourgeois fakery and false sophistication. Frank himself probably grows rich, though he never tells us this, as he modestly excludes himself from his narrative.

The time present of Frank's story is the early 1960s, when he fortuitously returns to the island on a tourist ship seeking refuge from an imminent hurricane. It is about 16 years since he left at the end of the War. The country has become independent and the changes initiated by Frank and the ten thousand other Americans during the War have made the country into the sort of 'crazy tourist place' that Naipaul constantly deplored during the 1960s, ceasing only when the weight of years made him tired, and the lucrative rewards he received for his books in the American market softened somewhat his opinion of Americans and Americanisation. Frank serves as a mask behind which Naipaul condemns neo-colonial Trinidad for what he sees as a loss in autonomy, due to a persistent self-contempt, a failure to cherish genuine aspects of the past, and a consequent surrender to Americanisation and modernity. Frank narrates as judge, not as penitent. He never makes the connection between the folksy paradise that he helped corrupt, and the fallen and unreal city that he rediscovers on his return.

Frank shares with the post-Dostoevskian confessant a recoil from the emptiness and mediocrity of the fabricated city. Naipaul signals this through one of his most repeated tropes: the association of eating with nausea. Trying to decide whether to remain on board in the antiseptic cabin of the tourist ship or to indulge in the nostalgia of a return to old familiar pleasure spots, Frank anticipates the pleasure of consuming plates of local oysters, but then remembers that oysters also used to make him nauseous. When Frank goes ashore he consumes a plate of one hundred oysters and views the city through the ensuing nausea and delirium.

Like Sartre's Roquentin, Dennis Williams's Lionel Froad of *Other Leopards* or Naipaul's Kripalsingh of *The Mimic Men*, Frank experiences a nausea that is simultaneously physical and existential. He is repelled by what seems most to attract him. The act of eating, a pleasurable pastime in most persons, always seems to produce a shudder of recoil in the Naipaul protagonist. Sometimes, as in *A Bend in the River* or *An Area of Darkness* where the protagonist is Naipaul himself, food and faeces are presented as the twinned metaphors not only of life in those ancestral places, but of the protagonist's depth response, his attraction to and repulsion by existence itself. Nausea, I think, is Naipaul's peculiar way of signalling his simultaneous relish for and recoil from the substance of life. Physical nausea both masks and signals existential recoil.

This ambivalence of attraction and recoil, of attraction to what the individual knows will repel him, might be seen in Kripalsingh's anticipated relish of the adventure of hunting (his word) prostitutes, which is always contradicted by his self-loathing and the violation he feels during and after performance of what he disdainfully terms 'the act required' (*Mimic Men* 1967, 30). It is also visible in the attraction that both Naipaul the author and many of his creatures feel towards countries, cultures, landscapes and situations that repel them: situations such as the recurrent image of a festering, stinking, perpetually smoking rubbish heap in *Guerillas*, a symbol of Dante's inferno of concentric circles. The image is indulged in, relished almost, long after the horror it signifies has been communicated to the reader.

The confessant protagonist emerges out of this sensecape, this psychic state of fascinated desire and nauseated recoil. In *An Area of Darkness*, Naipaul's desire to experience at last the landscape of his ancestors is succeeded by a revulsion that centres on the image of overwhelming faeces and a Conradian recollection of the journey to the central station as being a nightmare. Naipaul one time dismissed his critics with the reply that he did not invent defecation and that only six pages of the book were devoted to that particular image and function.

In *A Bend in the River*, Salim masks his deeply traumatised sensibility under the flat grey monotone with which he narrates even shameful scenes of personal humiliation; but like all other Naipaul confessants he is sensitive to the link between food and faeces; the Big Burger palace that signals progress Western style, twinned with the prevailing stench that envelops it; or the native Africans' attraction to toilet bowls because they have proven useful for storing cassava.

The confessant, faced with the paradox of faeces festooning the precincts of the Taj Mahal, naturally grows depressed and recognises his placelessness. Yet he equally becomes fascinated by the very extremity of the paradox and may even grow, like Dostoevsky's Underground Man, or Swift's Gulliver in Laputa to relish it. A harsh, mad laughter informs Naipaul's parody of Churchill's 'We will fight them on the beaches' speech in that startling passage of *An Area of Darkness* that begins: 'Indians defecate everywhere. They defecate, mostly, beside the railway tracks. But they also defecate on the beaches; they defecate on the hills; they defecate on the river banks; they defecate on the streets; they never look for cover' (1964, 74). This grotesque laughter one recognises as that of the confessional anti-hero. Overexposure to the food/faeces attraction/ repulsion paradox leads naturally to a sense of the Absurd, humour of the grotesque, a relish for caricature, parody and distortion, and a savouring of ugliness. Kripalsingh, secretly devastated by the breakdown of his bizarre marriage to Sandra, becomes attracted to Wendy Deschampsneufs, Sandra's former girlfriend and possibly her lover, because Wendy is so 'engagingly ugly' (*Mimic Men* 1967, 202). This is clearly the humour of the Underground Man, rooted in ugliness and a relishing of whatever nauseates.

Kripalsingh begins his memoirs after living for 18 months in 'the anaesthetizing order of life in this hotel' until 'despair and emptiness had burnt themselves out' (291). Kripal's beginning as an Absurd confessional writer involves a recognition of 'the formlessness of my experiences and their irrelevance to the setting in which I proposed to recount them' (292). Writing, this encounter with an attempt to impose order and pattern on formlessness, commences with a feeling of nausea. Kripal recalls that in 'the faded light' of 'late afternoon,' 'my stomach, head and eyes united in a dead sensation of sickness' (292). This nausea, I have argued, is a Naipaul trope that signals the author's violent recoil from self and life. Kripal's sickness of the stomach, head and eyes suggests an equation of writing with pregnancy and childbirth. Senses, reason and vision, major elements in the creation process, are all united in this single sensation of nausea and deadness. Memory grows out of this flat grey deadness.

It is how it happens with Dostoevsky's absurd confessional narrator who begins his narration with the warning that: 'I am a sick man....I am a spiteful man. I am an unattractive man.'[7] Kripalsingh shares in this sickness and resembles the Underground Man in several particulars. He is petty bourgeois, 40 years old, an outsider, who resides on the outskirts of a great city: London in the case of Kripal, St Petersburgh in the case of Dostoevsky's confessant. Both men exist on small precarious incomes; both have withdrawn from active engagement in life; both are full of overweening pride and its opposite, a crippling sense of inferiority. Both live within their heads, relish ugliness, are given to fantasy, self-exposure and self-deception. Kripal confesses to flippancy but is frequently overwhelmed by deep melancholy; the Underground Man speaks of his strange sense of humour as 'grinning between clenched teeth.'

Both anti-heroes have been oddities at school, weaklings aware at all times of their nonentity. The process of education increases their alienation.

Their friendships with schoolmates are painful and lack candour. If the Underground Man develops a kind of universal scorn, Kripalsingh develops nausea and disgust which begin as self-disgust and shame for his eccentric, depressed father. Both fear intimacy, and locked up in their narcissistic selves, both are incapable of the commitment and self-surrender that love demands. Both cherish isolation, but also feel the need to confess, perhaps to themselves, perhaps to an imaginary but hoped-for audience of confessors and judges. Yet neither can really endure judgment and what they seek through confession, while not quite absolution, is an unburdening and a release which Kripal calls 'the final emptiness' (*Mimic Men* 1967, 7).

One of the qualities shared by Mimic Man and Underground Man is that of a lack of will or inner motivation; a disinclination to choose to act, surrender to the pointlessness of things. Almost none of Kripal's engagements with life spring from an autonomous desire to act or perform. Every role he plays, even as a boy, is a reaction to someone else's idea of how he should represent himself. He eventually arrives at the conclusion that: 'We become what we see of ourselves in the eyes of others' (*Mimic Men* 1967, 25). Here, the confessant seems to valorise and celebrate his lack of will or autonomy. Identity, which in England becomes 'spectral, disintegrating, pointless, fluid' (*Mimic Men* 1967, 61), generally lacks solidity or substance. Salim will confess this as well in *A Bend in the River* and will raise the issue of whether a secure sense of self can ever be achieved in a context of constant political crisis and societal disintegration that is the common situation of those wretched former colonies that have come under Naipaul's withering gaze. Identity for Kripalsingh becomes a series of roles which are always modelled on an admired or envied Other or on some improbable fictional Hero.

Kripal is Camus's gallery of Absurd types: Actor, Dandy, Lover, Warrior, Conqueror and Writer; men who seek fulfilment and completeness via insistent role-playing, desperate carnality, pointless violence, unending conquest and the imposition of linguistic order on the formless chaos of experience. What Kripal lacks is the energy or drivenness of any of these archetypes as Camus envisaged them. He is too far gone in deadness for that. However, before he discovers the 'sickness' and consolation of writing, it is the actor archetype that (encouraged by one or other of his acquaintances) he seeks most strenuously to fulfil.

Thus the text is littered with terms pertaining to acting: drama, theatre, comedy, fantasy, role, role-playing, game, scene, character, playacting, illusion, minstrel, clown, timing, licensed fool, joker, parody, performance. The impression conveyed by all these references to theatre and role-playing is that life itself, especially life on haphazard anarchic Isabella, is one vast clown show, a day-to-day serial of variety acts. The greatest actors are those hollow men who seek and gain powerless power: people like Kripalsingh the cripple and Browne the clown in *The Mimic Men,* or Meredith in *Guerillas.* Naipaul adds the postcolonial politician to Camus's list of absurd archetypes. The most driven, the most obsessed actors are those bearing, like Kripal, the deepest psychic wounds and those with the greatest deficiencies of character.

The link to Camus's *The Myth of Sisyphus* and Sartre's *Nausea* is established by the frequency with which terms like 'absurd' and others suggesting revulsion and recoil, appear in the text. In Camus, the Absurd is most immediately typified by cyclic, tedious, repeated unfulfilling activity; meaningless routine and the ennui of a hollow life consumed by such routine. Kripalsingh is no more absurd than when he settles into the routine of his hollow antiseptic life in the bleak English boardinghouse where he now ekes out his days. It is typical of the self-deception of the confessional anti-hero that Kripal should seek to misrepresent this non-achievement as a strange sort of fulfilment: the closure of a cycle of existence in which, acting in accordance with the dictates of his Aryan ancestors, he has been 'student, householder and man of affairs, recluse' (*Mimic Men* 1967, 300). This bland, self-aggrandising summary of a life in which there has been no willed choice of any of these roles, has itself been mimicked from the widow's sentimental interpretation of the phases of Kripal's father's life (153). Kripal is dishonestly appropriating to his own life, meaning that has, previously been imposed on his father's madness.

Kripal's absurdity is linked to the themes of void, non-meaning, emptiness, silence, and notions of the futile and the ridiculous that surround his every action. The absurd is conveyed through a design for anti-climax that informs the structuring of Kripal's narrative, where we know of the failure of all of his schemes and his final exile before we are told about the sequence of incidents that resulted in this exile. Anti-climax marks and mars Kripal's every achievement. For example, the fulfilment and perfection of his youthful sexual desire is marred by the fact that his soulmate is his aunt Sally, and that the dreadful narcissistic 'purity' of his incestuous embrace of what he terms almost his own flesh, destroys forever the possibility of a healthy reciprocal love-relationship with any other woman in the future (186–90). What he says he feels after he and Sally are discovered is total blankness: 'no shame, no guilt, no anxiety' (190). There is seemingly, nothing to confess, yet this escapade damages Kripal forever. It is, in fact, the central trauma of Kripal's life, one that he needs to evade and deny, even years afterwards in his supposedly frank confession. Kripal's method of coping with the trauma of lost, incestuous love is to deny and suppress any future feeling. He will eventually confess that he frequently lies to himself by underplaying and undervaluing his own emotional reactions to events (220).

Anti-climax also marks the crowning achievement of the Roman House that Kripal builds to herald his remarkable success as a land-developer and business magnate. Kripalsingh's wife and muse, the decentered, displaced dropout Sandra, a recurrent object of his mocking caricature, leaves him on the very day of the bizarre house-warming party which ends when the guests in an ecstasy of envy and malice begin to smash crockery, furniture and glass windows, and Kripalsingh in a paroxysm of rage – the first genuine emotion he has felt for well over a decade since his return to Isabella – drives them out of his house. Climax is anti-climax, and anti-climax is built even into the structuring of paragraphs that, if they begin in hope are almost certain to end in flatness, 'the gold of imagination giving way to the lead of reality' (13).

The Camus Absurd is illustrated by the recurrent themes of chaos, disorder, disturbance and formlessness. Kripal speaks of 'this absurd disorder of placelessness' (184). Camus ends *The Rebel* with the statement that humanity needs ceaselessly to pit its lucidity against 'the savage formless movement of history.'[8] While there is little of the energy of Camus's assertion in Kripal's conclusions about his own existential or artistic commitment, he does regard the completion of his memoirs as both an imposition of order on a chaotic jumble of events and feelings, and a prelude to fresh encounter with life: 'I have cleared the decks, as it were, and prepared myself for fresh action. It will be action of a free man' (300).

Whether Kripal will be capable of fresh action beyond his now paralysed gaze at life from the sidelines, is debatable. It was a question that worried Naipaul, who in *Guerillas* and *In a Free State* clearly questioned the value of detached voyeurism: the view from the Ridge in *Guerillas,* the detached authorial transient tourist's gaze in *In a Free State,* and in the dozen or so journalistic travelogues that, as imagination waned, he began to consider as more important than fiction.

The link to Sartre is, as we have illustrated, suggested by the term 'nausea' and its attendant concepts of sickness, blight, corruption, disease, taint and stench. We have argued that Naipaul confronts the reader with nausea as a physical phenomenon in order to convey the existential dimensions of his protagonists' and perhaps his own recoil from life. To nausea may be added Naipaul's own term: 'violation' and the attendant words such as rupture, damage, crippledom, frenzy and madness. These words are signposts in the geography of the universe within Kripalsingh's ridden skull.

Dare one speculate about the connections that may exist between Kripalsingh, the complex mask, and Naipaul who fashioned him and forced the reader to see the world through his eyes? Naipaul adopted the confessional mode and adapted the confessional narrator from templates laid down by Dostoevsky, Camus, Sartre, Ellison and Denis Williams, at the point in time when he was trying to come to terms with his own 'placelessness.' In his interviews between 1965 and 1976, that is just after *An Area of Darkness* (1964) and between *A Flag on the Island* (1967), *The Mimic Men* (1967), *The Loss of Eldorado* (1969), *In a Free State* (1971), and *Guerillas* (1975), Naipaul was constantly working out his relationship to the land and region of his birth and to the wider world of letters.

Naipaul's antipathy towards Trinidad, historical and contemporary, was openly expressed for the first time in *The Middle Passage*. He had been invited home by Premier Eric Williams who was acting on the suggestion of C.L.R. James that both the West Indies and its brilliant novelist would benefit from his return to the region. The islands would benefit from Naipaul's critical insight into their history, identity and efforts at building new nations, while Naipaul himself would be rescued from alienation through a reacquaintance with his origins. Naipaul asserted that 'the history of this West Indian futility' would not be satisfactorily told because history was about 'creation and achievement' and nothing had been created in the West Indies.[9] In so far as identity was concerned, the region lacked that as well. Ancestral identities had all been mutually eroded and violated and no new people had emerged with a character and purpose of their own. Naipaul used the return trip, not to strengthen non-existent roots, but to explain an alienation he had always felt from the land of his birth and to justify his chosen exile abroad.

As a self-justifying confessional, *The Middle Passage* provided the transition between the early Naipaul and the later dark, acerbic, melancholy, doomsday prophet that he became. His statements after *The Middle Passage* record a growing distance from his origins. In a 1965 interview with Derek Walcott, Naipaul referred to Trinidad as 'a haphazard sort of society' in contrast to

India, a society that for all its expanse and variety he saw as 'self-contained and unique. It is possible to get at the truth or appear to get at it.'[10]

Naipaul noted then that: 'I do not think one can ever abandon one's allegiance to one's community, or at any rate to the idea of one's community. This is something I feel must be said'. On the other hand, he confessed that: 'I find this place frightening. I think this is a very sinister place (Walcott 1997, 6). Naipaul's memory in *The Middle Passage* of Trinidad as a 'nightmare,' had simply been reinforced by his vision of the three-year old nation as 'a very sinister place.' 'A Flag on the Island' where a tropical island is presented through the nauseated eyes of a decadent American, is Naipaul's first attempt to write about this sinister place. *The Mimic Men* is his second and quite comprehensive effort at Absurdist confessional. One notes that Naipaul's uncle, Rudranath Capildeo, one of the possible prototypes for Kripalsingh, was at the time caught up in Trinidad's racially polarised and darkening politics.

The holocaust of Guyana 1962–65 with its riots, burnings, deaths and thousands of injuries had cast a shadow over the politics of post-Independence Trinidad and Tobago whose population of Afro-Creoles, Indo-Creoles and a substantial group of Caucasians, mixed races, Syrian-Lebanese and Chinese was sufficiently similar to Guyana's to make sensitive Trinidadians take note of the warning. Naipaul registered alarm at the growing manifestations of racialism in Trinidadian politics. He also told Derek Walcott that 'the culture has changed' and 'that aspiration has been dropped, that the manners of the proletariat have infiltrated the values of the rest of the society' (6–7).

As Sparrow's narrator was even then declaring in 'Solomon Out' (1965), 'This place too damn democratic.' Oddly emerging as spokesperson for the upper and middle class elites, groups he had dismissed in *The Middle Passage*, Naipaul complained that the trouble with both colony and metropole was that 'Political views are now being imposed on the top from below. And fashions. And entertainments' (Walcott 1997, 7). Naipaul was firmly against popular politics and popular culture, manifestations that he considered hostile and threatening to what his work represented. Thus while Naipaul asserted *a priori* that one cannot 'abandon allegiance to one's community' and declared: 'I have...grown out of Trinidad and in a way I am grateful to the Trinidad I knew as a boy for making me what I am' (7), the Trinidad to which he was grateful no longer existed. The distressing proletariat were on the move not only in the crumbling ex-colonies playing at independence, but alarmingly in England, Australia, New Zealand and South Africa.

Five years later in an interview with Israel Shenker of the *New York Times Magazine*, Naipaul no longer felt he had to acknowledge his place of origin, or show allegiance or gratitude to any community. He explained that:

> The society I came from was colonial, and was originally a slave society to which, later, people like myself, from Asia, went. There was a double inferiority about it: the slave society which created nothing, which depended for everything on the master society, and the Asiatic living in this closed society of myth.[11]

Naipaul had gone back to the absolute and uncompromising position of *The Middle Passage*. Such a place deserved no one's allegiance or gratitude. And what about 'the values of the rest of the society' (Walcott 1997, 6), for whose deterioration he had in his 1965 interview with Walcott blamed the proletariat. Naipaul had this to say in 1971 about the aspiring colonials of his youthful years:

> The people I saw were little people who were mimicking upper-class respectability. They had been slaves, and you can't write about that in the way that Tolstoy wrote about even his backward society – for his society was whole and the one I knew was not (see Shenker, 49).

So writing about a fragmented, haphazard society required models quite different from ones that could be found in Indian or Russian literatures, the literatures of 'whole' societies. Discovering the existentialists, Naipaul discovered modern European models that were not fashioned out of the notion of a 'whole' culture, but out of Ezra Pound's 'botched civilization' and 'an old bitch gone at the teeth'[12] and T. S. Eliot's 'stony rubbish' and 'heap of broken images.'[13] The opening chapter of Naipaul's *The Mimic Men* is strongly reminiscent of Eliot's 'Preludes' and 'The Waste Land.' Existentialist ideas, particularly those of Camus's *The Myth of Sisyphus* provided Naipaul with the theoretical base for writing about his own uncreated and uncreative society.

The modernists' redefinition of Europe had been taking place for at least seven decades before *The Mimic Men*. It inspired him to write *The Mimic Men*, in which Kripalsingh, the confessional protagonist, abandons any notions of allegiance or gratitude to his corrupt little island located in its 'tainted encircling sea' (1967, 179) and lives the rest of his life as a mixture of refugee and guest in the refurbished once-fine, now-tawdry and tasteless aristocratic castle that symbolises what Olde England has become for this Indo-Saxon colonial.

One cannot but compare Naipaul, who says that as a colonial he had emerged from 'a great vacuum' and that he really had no society with which he could be in dialogue, with Kripalsingh, who is in fact living in a great vacuum, but who weeps with gratitude when his presence as 'our overseas guest' is acknowledged by the hierarchy of the English great house. Throughout the 1960s, Naipaul's burden was that his talent remained unrecognised; that he did not have 'an audience' in England, the land he had run to, nor did he have 'political backing' from his own society, the people from whom he had escaped. He was now a man in permanent transition. He lamented to Mel Gussow:

> The writers who get the attention belong to recognized cultures and societies and countries. That keeps you warm. I thought that my writing would make its way by itself, but there are other things that are needed – a kind of political backing.[14]

Trinidad had not supplied him, could not supply him, with the backing or recognition he needed to find 'a way into another world.'[15] The place was a cultural desert and, 'the writer has no living cultural world about him, and has to make his way into another world, one which is entirely alien to him' (Rowe-Evans 1971, 57). So Naipaul set out to discover and speak his own truths, to make his own space, and to establish his independence of people, nations, and external support of any kind:

> I come from a small society; I was aware that I had no influence in the world; I was apart from it. And then I belonged to a minority group, I moved away, became a foreigner, became a writer (Rowe-Evans 1971, 59).

Writing out of this exile that was at once imposed on and chosen by him, Naipaul like Kripalsingh, became definable not via his origins, ethnicity or the colony-become-nation-become-neo-colony from which he came, but solely through his writing: 'I was confined to a smaller world than I had ever known. I became my flat, my desk, my name' (Gussow 1976, 17). This chosen path led to isolation, freedom and non-involvement with people, ideologies or causes. Naipaul declared with pride in 1971:

> I have never had to work for hire; I made a vow at an early age never to work, never to become involved with people in that way. That has given me a freedom from people, from entanglements, from rivalries, from competition. I have no enemies, no rivals, no masters; I fear no one (Rowe-Evans, 59).

In spite of this bold batonnier's litany of pride and defiance, Naipaul also said that he 'began with this very romantic vision of the writer as a free, gifted, talented, creative, admired person' but soon grew to recognise writing as an ordeal: 'In fact writing is just a sort of disease, a sickness. It is a form of incompleteness, it's a form of anguish, it's despair' (Shenker 1977, 51). Here, far more than in their common and confessed pursuit of au pair girls and prostitutes lies the link between Naipaul and his mask, Kripalsingh. Both are examples of the writer as Absurd man, seeking completeness and fulfilment of the spirit through the organisation of chaotic experience into meaning via the shaping and arrangement of words. Both are examples of men driven to write as if life and sanity depended on it. Both affirm writing as sickness and therapy, as the imposition of order on outward and inner chaos.

Naipaul feels 'despair, desperation, panic.' 'All my work begins in panic,' Naipaul confesses to Adrian Rowe-Evans:

> It is a feeling you can't communicate, explain to other people; you can assuage it only by starting to write, even though your mind is as blank as the next man's; you have no consciousness of anything you want to say. And then, given the panic, the next thing you need is a certain fortitude, a tenacity, to carry on through all the ups and downs. They are very painful, these downs that can hit you even when the work is quite advanced, and you have been practicing for a long time. They can last for years, literally; and the only cure is to lever yourself out of it, bodily, by sheer work. And sheer luck – you need luck all the time (Rowe-Evans 1971, 61).

What lies at the end of all this agony? The writer's, the confessant's, the writer as confessant, the confessant as writer? Clarification, perhaps; absolution and catharsis, maybe. Yet clarification, absolution, and catharsis are gifts that emerge out of having lived and worked through the ordeal with fortitude, and not as bequests from any agency outside of the writer as straitened subject. Whatever the confessant's concern with the community he has been forced to abandon, such absolution as he achieves is private and cannot be transferred to that already doomed world.

Naipaul's Ferdinand, named after the young duke in *The Tempest* whose marriage to admired Miranda signals the birth of a 'brave new world' purged of the sins of the fathers, is the least hopeless and most evolved African portrayed in *A Bend in the River*. Yet, his final prognosis is bitterly pessimistic:

> Nobody's going anywhere. We're all going to hell, and every man knows this in his bones. We're being killed. Nothing has any meaning. That is why everyone is so frantic. Everyone wants to make his money and run away. But where? That is what is driving people mad. They feel they are losing the place they can run back to (*A Bend* 1979, 272).

This place of imagined refuge is, for Ferdinand, not Kripalsingh's defunct European castle in the countryside, but the tribal village in the bush of his childhood. However, the village too is being systematically destroyed by the multinational mining companies, and there will be no future in what used to be the world of Ferdinand's past.

The confessional mode has provided Naipaul with a relatively safe vantage point from which to observe these grim scenarios in which dead-ends are already inherent in green beginnings. Such bitter irony is meat and drink for the nauseated confessant, be he underground or mimic man. Confession offers not only the possibility of a partial personal catharsis, but the opportunity to deliver the severest condemnation on both colonial history and the ruined societies it has left and continues to leave in its wake. It is, finally, the Trickster's triumph that Naipaul seeks: the privilege of becoming at one and the same time confessant and confessor; of achieving simultaneously the postures of self-exposure, self-diagnosis, self-healing and the flagellant's self-righteous joy in excoriating the hide of an already doomed old new world.

Notes

1. 'A Hymne to God the Father' in *The Poems of John Donne*, ed. Sir Herbert Grierson, (London: Oxford University Press, 1937), 337–8.

2. George Lamming, *Season of Adventure (*London: Michael Joseph, 1960); see also George Kent, 'A Conversation with George Lamming,' *Black World* 22, no. 5 (March 1973): 4–15; 88–97.
3. Kamau Brathwaite, *The Arrivants* (London: Oxford University Press, 1973), 224.
4. V.S. Naipaul, *A Bend in the River* (1979; repr., New York: Vintage Books, 1980), 4.
5. Naipual, *A Flag on the Island* (London: André Deutsch, 1967), 33. See also 'One Out of Many,' *In a Free State* (Harmondsworth: Penguin, 1973), 21–58; 'Tell Me Who to Kill,' *In a Free State* (Harmondsworth: Penguin, 1973), 59–102.
6. Naipaul, 'A Flag on the Island,' in *A Flag on the Island* (London: André Deutsch, 1967), 147–235; *The Mimic Men* (London: André Deutsch, 1967); *Guerillas* (London: André Deutsch, 1975); *In a Free State* (London: André Deutsch, 1971); *An Area of Darkness* (Harmondsworth: Penguin Books, 1964); *A Bend in the River* (1979; repr., New York: Vintage Books, 1980).
7. Fydor Dostoevsky. *Notes from Underground.* Translated by Richard Pevear and Larissa Volokhonsky. First Vintage Classics Edition. (New York: Random House, 1993).
8. Albert Camus, *The Rebel,* Trans. Anthony Bower (London: Penguin Books, 1962), 265.
9. Naipaul, *The Middle Passage* (1962; repr., London: Picador, 2001), 20.
10. 'Interview with V.S. Naipaul' (1965), *Conversations with V.S. Naipaul,* ed. Feroza Jussawalla (Jackson: University Press of Mississippi, 1997), 6.
11. Israel Shenker, 'V.S. Naipaul: Man Without a Society' (1971), *Critical Perspectives on V.S. Naipaul,* ed. Robert D. Hammer (Washington D.C.: Three Continents Press, 1977), 49.
12. 'E. P. Ode Pour L'Election de Son Sepulcre,' in *Ezra Pound: Selected Poems* (New York: New Directions, 1957), 64.
13. T.S. Eliot, 'The Wasteland,' *Collected Poems 1909–1962* (San Diego: Harcourt Brace Jovanovich, 1998), 176, 53.
14. Mel Gussow, 'Writer Without Roots,' *The New York Times Magazine,* December 26, 1976, 19.
15. Adrian Rowe-Evans, 'V.S. Naipaul,' *Transition* 40 (December 1971): 57.

6

SIGNIFYING NOTHING:
Writing about Not Writing in The Mystic Masseur

Barbara Lalla

This essay is about *nothing* and the way in which it can be created, and, in particular, about V.S. Naipaul's presentation in *The Mystic Masseur* of how nothingness can be discursively constructed. On one level, *The Mystic Masseur* is about the lack of signification. Observations of what are presented as curious facts lead to absence of information, cryptic utterances beneath which gapes meaninglessness, rituals of lost significance, fake honours and letters behind the name that attest to nothing. Titles like *teacher* or *Lord* lack authenticity; directives like RSVP 'don't mean nothing' but 'is nice to have,' all 'pretty wordings' empty of any signification beyond their niceness.[1] Equally, the discourse contains endlessly undermined commentary, such as, 'Later this was to be seen as important,' when it was not. On this level, then, the novel conveys that there is not anything created. Yet on another level the novel seems actually to construct nothingness and the narrator to confer significance falsely on this void. How is the signification of *nothing* inscribed in both senses, that is, both reflected and discursively constructed, and to what end?

In the first place the text draws on various narrative techniques that evoke in the reader an evaluation of falsity. The most obvious of these techniques is the selection of form associated with biography. The narrative adopts the pose of biography grounded on an autobiography, Ganesh's *The Years of Guilt* – assessed by its writer's mysterious admirers as 'a spiritual thriller and metaphysical whodunit' (1978, 119). The critical acclaim of this autobiography is never grounded by reference to named critics, and this fictive autobiography and fictive criticism are framed within a larger fictive non-fiction – the biographical form adopted in the narration that they support. This use of the 'false document' technique, that is, the explicit projection of the narrative as a record of fact, backed up by repeated reference to other records – all of these records being patently fictitious – this false document technique implicitly undermines the normal authenticating function of records and discredits the value of written discourse that is valorised throughout the action of the novel.

Another explicit technique closely related to the autobiographical is the engagement with history. The narrator's claim that the Ganesh story is a 'history of our times' sweepingly asserts universal significance. As his life must therefore be of wide interest, the narrator acts, from time to time, as audience surrogate, implicating the reader's inevitable eagerness for each shining detail about Ganesh whose claim to fame is, of course, negated by actual (and deserved) obscurity.

Similarly the roaming narrator who dips into the text, disappears and travels to Britain parallel to Ganesh's nebulous quest, but this roaming narrator delivers his report in such a way as to include widely separated eyewitness accounts. The interrupted eyewitness of the traveller's account suggests the dignified witness of the correspondent, and the account indeed projects a nineteenth-century approach to literary discourse as a record of experience, as an observation of objective reality that demands social commentary by a superior consciousness qualified to make judgments. The narrator adopts such a professional reporter's voice for the biography.

However, these setups of narratorial reliability (biographer, historian, reporter and the like) frame various less esteemed discourse types – the gossiping, twittering, parroting discourses of characters moving within the text. Also, within the text, parallel to this mindless dialogue, occurs the epiphany of Ganesh's self-realisation as a potential writer, one with something significant to inscribe but, in addition, as a consciousness (himself a text) designed to unfold. In narrative as elsewhere, epiphany (a manifestation of power, illumination or insight of divine brilliance) is triggered suddenly by some object or situation that is essentially ordinary, and the experience vastly disproportionate to its ordinary stimulus.[2] Epiphany, however, as in the actual revelation of the mystic in Ganesh, is complemented by revelation of Ganesh's insignificance; and the revelation of the writer in Ganesh is complemented by the revelation of the *nothing* that he writes. In this way epiphany defers its central irony of disconnection between mundane situations and extraordinary response, to a disconnection between the extraordinary response of the narrator and the mundane reality of his stimulus.

One of the things that prepares us for the negation of significance in one dim epiphany after the other is a dispersal of truth-value. Truth-value is dispersed through the undermining of non-fictionality and indeed the melting of boundaries between the fictional and non-fictional, an interrogation and subversion of the distinction between fact and fiction (or panfictionality).[3] Events unfold simultaneously with narrative interpretation of these events, and the events belie this interpretation, further eroding the fact/fiction boundary. This is one way in which the author contrives an undermining of narrative reliability by dispersing truth-value in these statements.

Foregrounding of falsity is further achieved by manipulating narrative perspective, which is a crucial dimension in constructing the speaker – that fictional self from whose angle events are presented. Perspective or point of view substantially affects readers' sympathy and/or identification with characters, and shifting perspective can enable ambivalence.[4] In the case of *The Mystic Masseur*, the narrator repeatedly embraces the observations of Ganesh's wider audience – that is, Ganesh's immediate associates, the general public in Trinidad, the colonial office and, of course, the international forum to which the reader belongs. The reader, however, draws quite different conclusions to those expressed by the narrator, who draws his conclusion through loose references to a circle of admirers – references that remain unsubstantiated. What this discrepancy foregrounds is authorial attention not so much to Ganesh's nonsense as to the nonsense of social commentary and to critical void, lack of substance in what William Labov identifies as Evaluation, a component of narrative structure.[5] I would argue that the holes in the narrative implicate an authorial position.

To examine the effect of narrative perspective more closely, I would point out that *The Mystic Masseur* presents a retrospective account of Ganesh's progress, in that the narrator recounts what *has* taken place, but also a prospective account in that he follows his subject from the remote to more recent past – the most usual of narrative patterns. Yet at particular points in the more remote past, the narrator pauses to point forward to the future (a future in the past, a point in the speaker's more recent past to which his account has not yet arrived), a 'prophetic' technique often associated with omniscience. The narrator's view along the way therefore alternates between his perceptions of Ganesh in the remote past, his perceptions of him in the recent past (*both* within *story time*), and his evaluations current in *speaker time*, or the time of narration. As his experience of Ganesh begins in childhood, the narrator's perceptions include those from varied stages of maturity. So *The Mystic Masseur* conveys a narrative view that shifts from child to adult vision and from the innocent to the educated, suggesting prolonged and maturing experience. Nevertheless, whatever the depth of *perceptual* perspective (the view based on physical orientation in space or time), *conceptual* perspective (mental orientation) remains stagnant and shallow. The narrator's view of Ganesh remains credulous and uncritical however omniscient a stance he may from time to time adopt.

Commentators on perspective have noted that perspective may sometimes be revealed *after* an event, suggesting or enabling re-appraisal or recontextualisation. Catherine Emmot suggests that a text 'may force a reader to reinterpret a stretch of narrative or to hold two different interpretations simultaneously.'[6] In *The Mystic Masseur*, however, no development of conceptual perspective produces narrative revelation. The narrator's claim to insight, associated with public recognition of Ganesh, remains hitched to Ganesh's own epiphanies. The fragmented nature of the narrator's actual connection with Ganesh, and his dependence on scattered and inexact testimony produce loosely re-membered rather than coherently remembered events. Ganesh's life is indeed not memorable but highly forgettable, one on which larger significance can only be artificially imposed – unless one's narrator, though a successful product of the Caribbean, is of an intellectual capacity to be unable to identify failure when he sees it or is operating in a moral vacuum.

Apart from narrative technique, narrative structure of *The Mystic Masseur* conveys the hollowness of the account. In outlining the essential components of natural narrative, Labov notes that evaluation is a crucial component of narrative syntax. Through this component of evaluation, a narrator reveals involvement in or assessment of the action described,[7] and evaluation in discourse rests on such indicators as desirability, expectability, utility, and so on, but especially on importance or significance.[8] Narrative is one means through which discourse constructs our perceptions of reality, and in which discourse intervenes in the chaos of experience to select, order, reassemble and package experience for manageability. No account has everything (for that would be boring). Narrative discourse pieces together lives and circumstances fractured in fact, perhaps through observation that is discontinuous or unreliable, a remembering on the basis of *criteria*. What the author constructs in *The Mystic Masseur* is *insignificance* in the protagonist and his setting, juxtaposed to that perception of *significance* and expression of admiration that is expressed by the narrator – an inconsistency that evokes ridicule in the reader. The effects are at once comic and tragic, a dissolution of genres. Comic irony rests on an implicated negation of factuality, scope, substance and so forth in Ganesh's achievements so explicitly lauded by the narrator. Tragic irony emerges with the impossibility of wholeness in the protagonist and narrator that fractured history and chronic social fragmentation have produced, and in the resulting emptiness of their discourse.

This sociohistorical shattering materialises in discourse disconnectivity. Emphasis on time-based (sequential or syntagmatic) delivery is explicitly established at once in the opening: 'Later he was to be…' induces a sense of preordination that is reiterated throughout (1978, 46, 50). Yet indeed (since he is not really to be anything) the events merely follow each other meaninglessly. Disconnectivity in discourse takes the form of irrelevance, of causeless action, or of baseless inference. For example, after insistence on existing outside of the weave, John Stewart returns home to join (of all things) the army. Then, despite Stewart's rejection of position and formality he is referred to by Ganesh as Lord Stewart (41, 42). Disconnectivity in discourse also reinforces a theme of ascetic detachment intertwined in the account of Ganesh's condition as misfit. From baseless stipulations (the child's medicine *never* to be taken after meals), through unexplained dependence on signs (1978, 31), to indiscriminate walkouts (213), the protagonist progresses causelessly from one stage to the next. Events are *said* to conspire to prevent him from being a 'mediocre pundit' an 'unsuccessful lawyer,' a 'dangerous doctor' or one of a number of 'penurious mystics' (205–6) – all actually quite accurate descriptors – and to account for his rise from teacher to masseur to mystic and finally to MLC, a continuous dematerialising to empty acronym.

Underlying the teleological order explicitly projected by the narrator is an implied authorial theory of chaos in the unpredictable unravelling of disparate strands that negates the possibility of identity formation. Not only is there no identity to discover from the shattered past but even the construction of identity (on, say, the Stuart Hall model[9]) is denied. Instead the novel deconstructs identity through revelation of fragmentation and fraudulence. The failure of identity construction (ethnic, intellectual and so forth) at an individual level mirrors a failure of national construction.

Logical connections are also negated through consistent misinterpretation of circumstances that are pivotal to the action. At the end, what appears to be a sugar estate strike (which Ganesh is accidentally called on to mediate) turns out to be a lockout in the slack season and explodes in violence. The narrative recasts misinterpretation as revelation, however. Following on his fortunate escape, Ganesh declares himself to have been used as a tool by 'communists,' a label he seizes on in desperation, and he becomes a fervent defender of colonialism, Providence having 'opened his eyes' (1978, 218). Not surprisingly, his full worth comes to be recognised in the award of the MBE.

Narratologists distinguish narrative perspective (who sees) from narrative voice (who speaks), but they are obviously related. The irrelevance, misinterpretation and contradiction that frame the hollow celebration of Ganesh's achievements are conveyed through dialogic discourse. The narrating 'historian's' voice alternates with the mystic's dialogue; Ganesh's discourse debates with the twittering Narayan (The Little Bird); and Ganesh's address alternates with others such as Beharry's public statements about Ganesh. This diversity of voices enables a web of tensions between surface claims and underlying voids. The narrative voice is that of the university man, versus the country pundit, whose uneducated voice is also highlighted through contrasts to characters like Indarsingh with his British accent (Demn good), and the colonial school headmaster (22, 23).

For most of the novel, Ganesh's voice locates him geographically and socially, but the narrator's voice is associated with greater social mobility. Although the narrator represents his own voice as the child who was a fellow occupant of Ganesh's space, he speaks mainly in the voice of an external and objective observer, in the official language. However, the authoritative narrative voice is steadily discredited.

In the first place the authoritative tone is implicitly discredited in that its claims are unsubstantiated. In such statements as, 'Later he was to be famous and honoured' (11), the use of a passive form in which agency is suppressed compels the question: 'honoured by whom?' and directs an interrogation of the I/eye ('none of us foresaw,' 18) and an unmasking of narrative fraudulence. Secondly, the narrator's credulous account is framed in the narrator's own direct experience of Ganesh's fraudulence. Chapter One and the epilogue frame the biography with the biographer's two personal experiences of interaction with Ganesh, in both of which Ganesh operates under a faked identity.

Thirdly, the testimony is circular: the first person narrative undermines all its possibilities as an eyewitness account for authenticating the record, by citing the very records it should authenticate. Moreover, the direct knowledge of Ganesh is undermined by hindsight competence – a 'little-did-I-know' type of awareness that limits our confidence in the experiencing 'I' or eye. In a variety of ways, the history of Ganesh *is* a tale told by an idiot signifying nothing. This first person narrator is set up as a filter (as internal focaliser) through which Ganesh is evaluated, while narrative reliability regarding the evaluation of Ganesh is continuously emphasised as suspect.

Moreover, this slippage between overtly objective narrative on the one hand and, on the other, the personal experience of the narrator as character goes beyond the panfictionality, or blurring of distinction between fiction and fact, noted earlier. The absolute collapse of boundaries between fictional and non-fictional worlds amounts to a transgression of levels or metalepsis that destroys certainty about control over the account. In *The Mystic Masseur* this is a subversive metalepsis because it interrogates, undermines and subverts the distinction between real and fictive in the world Naipaul constructs.[10]

Not only the 'I' persona's collusion with Ganesh propagandists, but his own remoteness from most of the action, destabilise narrative reliability. However, reliability is a function of both commitment to truth-value and accuracy of information. The narrator who propounds, 'the episode is significant' (21), and who hastens to associate his own history with the Ganesh account is morally as well as intellectually implicated in the falsity. This historicising that employs the autobiographical form is geared to connect the present self to past experience so as to produce both continuity (through time) and distance (from events and situations).

I have noted that complementing the narrator's disconnection from actual circumstances are strategies (including those of narrative voice) for distancing events and persons within the text. Ganesh's ascetic remoteness, conveyed as distance in space (12), as intellectual distance (332), and as emotional distance (202), is a distance maintained through deictic elements like adverbs (*away* etc.), and through silence, terseness and indirect responses in dialogue (the discursive disconnectivity noted earlier). Disconnection itself is a crucial issue and at various levels the characters employ discourse to recover the irretrievable, to assemble and revision the past, and to construct an identity. However, identity – like the discourse employed to construct it (the proposed discourse that is Ganesh's book) and like the 'I' narrator's biography of Ganesh – cannot be built because the past is irreversibly ruptured, history irrecoverably fragmented. The discourse is fissive both in form and content; the hollowness of the present corresponds to an evaporation of meaning.

The authorial stance in the face of this collective fraudulence is a curious one. For Naipaul, who claims, 'I am the sum of my books'[11] as he negotiates arrival at a literary discourse through half a century – fiction giving way to non-fictional forms, travelogue, history and autobiography, in an interrogation of roots by routes – arrival at a literary discourse parallels a finding of his own space: 'But home was hardly a place I could return to. Home was something in my head. It was something I had lost.'[12] In *The Mystic Masseur*, the lost homeland, replaced by the imaginary homeland, prompts rituals like the one that sends Ganesh figuratively home to India to study; prompts his reluctance to abandon the journey and his failure to accept it on the figurative level only; and prompts the irritation of his elders when he ascribes meaning to the exercise.

The author shares his narrator's progress from rural East Indian life with its fragments of Indian heritage, through Queen's Royal College (QRC) in Port of Spain, to England, and shares his protagonist's compulsion to autobiography as a re-membering of the Self in the face of obliteration. Helen Hayward remarks that Naipaul's

> multiple re-workings of the materials of his life suggest… the provisionality of constructions of the self. They lead to the inference that the self is open to variable interpretations and that the writing of autobiography is for Naipaul an ongoing project of self-invention.[13]

Naipaul himself elaborates what Hayward terms his ongoing self-invention in pointing to the essence of writing fiction not as a reporting of one's experience but as a distillation: 'The beauty of fiction is that one can do it through other people.'[14]

As a prequel to his later detached and reductive vision, *The Mystic Masseur* deconstructs meaninglessly inflated discourse in consistently metadiscursive commentary (20–1). First, the discourse conveys hypersensitivity to problems of expression. It highlights attention to a withholding of discourse concerning Ganesh 'because his gift of healing was a holy thing' (12). Characters are described as speaking guardedly, communication as often cryptic, and matters relating to ritual as quite properly uninterpretable (30–3). Throughout, meaningless talk is complemented by meaningless written material. From his early years at QRC, Ganesh reads without any apparent connection with or concern for content. Later he reads to Ramlogan who pretends illiteracy so as to maintain communication with the potential son-in-law (34). Ganesh's library comes to be arbitrarily founded on twenty copies of *Science of Thought Review*, on booklets on *The Art of Salesmanship* and, eventually, on Everyman volumes that are valued in relation to their number and measured by the inch. Scribal discourse remains material that is measurable, decorative and esoteric. Ganesh goes through a romantic attachment to paper itself, appreciated for its smell rather than its utility (76), a fascination that culminates in his appreciation for a gimmicky toilet paper roll towards the end of the novel.

In circumstances in which discourse constitutes a bodily function like eating (Suruj Poopa is accosted by his wife for always having his mouth open 'If it ain't eating, is talking' 83), Ganesh's writing begins as little more than marks on a surface, starting with his learning to write on a blackboard. Later, rather like Leela's writing, which is shattered by nonfunctional punctuation, his words often lack intrinsic meaning and carry only a pragmatic function: 'pretty wordings' or 'nice wordings' (49, 202). He writes publishers Smith and Smith (how anonymous can they be?) as to whether they would be interested in his writing books, without reference to his proposed content (76), and it is the hugeness of a printer that spurs him rather than anything he has to say. Unaccountably, the author eventually suppresses *The Years of Guilt,* the autobiography published by Ganesh Publishing Company that supposedly lends credence to the narrator's account. The huge nebulous project of writing is taken up without explanation, and also laid down without explanation. '"Got to write my book," Ganesh said aloud. "Got to"' (82). Yet before the production of this book, he is surrounded by a world of non-signifying signs. Elite Electric Printery tautologically announces on its notice: 'When better printing is printing we will print it' (82). The wedding invitation, his first literary adventure, includes *RSVP* as an entirely meaningless flourish, and types of truncated discourse are everywhere invoked, from the telegram with its inadequate information through reference to letters, articles, a calendar and advertisements, the latter an empty frame of carefully ruled columns.

Rather than an intellectual exercise, writing connotes power, the power associated with magic. Writing is valued for its most primitive function, as a charm (110, 111). Parallel to this it functions as a game like the acrostic (200), undermining its serious role in preparing Ganesh for enhanced power as a healer. In any case, the mystical role of writing changes, as he lays aside the mystic for the politician and moves from Fuente Grove to St Clair (2, 11). Soon, writing gains pragmatic value, as a means of record keeping (59); then writing becomes a money churner, promising credit and requiring a ledger for recording profit (105). The mystical value of writing gives way to mundane utilitarian purposes.

To the end, Ganesh's own inscriptions of spirituality remain obscure and empty of content, culminating in two discourses. One is *What God Told Me,* which reports that he received a direct address from God, although the message itself is not revealed to us. The other, the crowning mark of his career, is *Profitable Evacuation*, inspired by the musical toilet paper rack that plays Yankee Doodle Dandee as it dispenses paper (ibid., 157). While Ganesh the politician is ridiculed in calypso for legislative constipation, the narrator continues to celebrate him as both popular and productive. It is hard to miss the implicature that Ganesh and his undiscriminating narrator commit crap to paper. This implicature (of crap) relates directly to the novel's emphasis on lack of signification, and suggests an underlying theory of value in Naipaul's novel, conveyed through his manipulation of narrative.

A crucial role of narrative discourse is its capacity for re-memberment and thus its potential for healing, for reviewing trauma, engaging with fragmentation and addressing dismemberment. Ganesh's vocation of healing – physically by massage, mystically by psychic intervention and sociopolitically by mediation and reconciliation – are all fictional even as, in the colonial situation that is the novel's setting, such re-memberment is artificial. This derelict existence, comprising entrapment in a claustrophobic situation and entanglement in sterile customs of forgotten meaning, is rendered more desperate by dreams of escape. In *The Mystic Masseur* Naipaul's narrative deconstructs discourse that is unenlightened and reveals discourse that is enslaved to colonial ideology as cheap and hollow. The narrative plays with the superficialities of alternatives to proper names, like Suruj Poopa, that deny individuation. The narrative exposes the meaninglessness of titles adopted without basis in achievement – as in the redefinition of the BA, as in Ganesh's adoption of the word *mystic* as weightier than *pundit*, as in Narayan's inclination to name change (173, 198), and as in Ganesh's ultimate renaming of himself (See 1978, 1221, 173, 198).

Naipaul's metadiscourse interrogates literary discourse itself as an assertion of power, 'I go give them this book, and I go make Trinidad hold it head and bawl' (95), as a poorly conceived educational tool for students to learn by rote, as a showpiece that (like Leela's pictures) is allocated space as long as it demonstrates status. 'It are not going to hang in my drawing room,' Leela stipulates in rejecting nonconformable pieces of art.

In *The Mystic Masseur*, literary discourse by the successful and educated may comprise mindless or irresponsible reporting as in the case of the narrator. Such discourse also reveals self-interest, as in the case of the Colonial Office which describes Ganesh first as an 'irresponsible agitator with no following,' then as the 'most popular man in Trinidad' (213, 215). Ganesh demonstrates individual inadequacy; but intellectual fraudulence in the Colonial Office confirms its agenda for contriving and maintaining a local political void, for bequeathing intellectual failure in those who emanate from the society, who claim to think and write on its behalf but do so uncritically and perpetuate the construction of nothing. Naipaulian discourse in *The Mystic Masseur* represents this nothingness through techniques such as false documentation, inversions of epiphany, interrogations of reality through panfictionality and metalepis, narrative evaluation delivered through explicature but undermined by implicature, disconnectivity in discourse and other strategies that cumulatively project a conceptual void; not a situation in which no one has created anything, so much as one in which nothing (a nothing palpable as crap) has been actively constructed and perpetrated.

The suppressed passion in Ganesh, conveyed with the assumed objectivity of his narrator, parallels the absence of passion in the author's dry, wry construction. If valid autobiography involves self-construction relative to a construction of history and community, *The Mystic Masseur*, this Naipaulian re-membering, assumes the shape of fiction, a fiction about a man who wants to re-member himself through writing, inscribed by an undiscriminating admirer. Both protagonist and narrator are fraudulent writers, one of whom can in fact construct nothing of significance and the other who ascribes significance to meaninglessness. Both writers cumulatively perpetuate the vacuum constructed by colonialism.

Notes

1. V.S. Naipaul, *The Mystic Masseur* (1957; repr., Harmondsworth: Penguin, 1978), 49.
2. Morris Beja, 'Epiphany and Epiphanies,' *A Companion to Joyce Studies*, eds. Zack Bowen and James F. Carens (London: Greenwood, 1984), 719.

3. For more on panfictionality, see Marie-Laure Ryan, 'Postmodernism and the Doctrine of Panfictionality,' *Narrative* 5, no. 2 (1997): 149.
4. As argued by W. Van Peer and Pander Maat, 'Perspectivization and Sympathy: Effects of Narrative Points of View,' *Empirical Approaches to Literature and Aesthetics*, eds. Roger J. Kreuz and M.S. MacNealy (Norward, NJ: Ablex, 1996), 143–54; and Joe Bray, 'The "Dual" Voice of Free Indirect Discourse: A Reading Experiment,' *Language and Literature* 16 (2007): 46.
5. See William Labov, *Language in the Inner City: Studies in the Black English Vernacular Sociolinguistic Patterns* (Philadelphia: University of Pennsylvania Press, 1972), 366–93.
6. Catherine Emmot, *Narrative Comprehension: A Discourse Perspective* (Oxford: Clarendon, 1997), 164.
7. Cf. Carmen Rosa Caldas-Coulthard, 'Cross-Cultural Representation of Otherness in Media Discourse,' in *Critical Discourse Analysis: Theory and Interdisciplinarity*, eds. Gilbert Weiss and Ruth Wodak (New York: Palgrave Macmillan, 2003), 263.
8. Positive or negative significance is propagated in discourse by devices of scope (especially height); precedence; goodness or divinity/sanctity; logical inevitability/necessity; actuality, truth or substance, and so forth. In representing reality, narrative manipulates such devices. On significance/importance projected in discourse, see Phil Graham, 'Critical Discourse Analysis and Evaluative Meaning: Interdisciplinarity as a Critical Turn,' in *Critical Discourse Analysis: Theory and Interdisciplinarity*, eds. Gilbert Weiss and Ruth Wodak (New York: Palgrave Macmillan, 2003), 115.
9. As discussed, for example, in Stuart Hall, 'Cultural Identity and Diaspora,' in *Colonial Discourse and Post Colonial Theory: A Reader*, eds. Patrick Williams and Laura Chruman, (London: Harvester Wheatsheaf,1993), 401–402.
10. See Manfred Jahn, *Narratology: A Guide to the Theory of Narrative* (English Department, University of Cologne, 2005), N2.3.5; David Herman, 'Towards a Formal Description of Narrative Metalepsis,' *Journal of Literary Semantics* 26, no.2 (1997): 132–52; Debra Malina, *Breaking the Frame: Metalepsis and the Construction of the Subject* (Columbus: Ohio State University Press, 2002).
11. Naipaul, 'Two Worlds.' Nobel Lecture. the-south-asian.com, January 2002. Accessed December 9, 2007. www.the-south-asian.com/Jan2002/Naipaul-Nobel-Lecture1.htm.
12. Naipaul, *A Bend in the River* (1979; repr., Harmondsworth: Penguin, 1980), 114.
13. Helen Hayward, *The Enigma of V.S. Naipaul: Sources and Contents* (Oxford: Macmillan, 2002), 72, and see also 56.
14. Cited in Hayward (2002, 65). Naipaul interviewed by Margaret Drabble, *Bookcase*, November 26, 1977. Transcript of BBC broadcast, André Deutsch Archive, 96, IFS folder.

7

KEEPING AN EYE ON NAIPAUL:
Naipaul and the Play of the Visual

Jean Antoine-Dunne

Art in the twentieth and twenty-first centuries has been deeply transformed by the emergence of cinema, the new art of modernity. Theorists, critics and artists have written much about the importance of cinema to human perception and to ways of seeing, but as yet little has been written about the impact of cinema on Caribbean writing. Yet this influence stretches from Naipaul to Walcott and from Brathwaite to Brodber and beyond. My concern here is to show that Naipaul's thinking through of his relationship to the world is projected, in part, through the use of techniques and structures absorbed from cinema.

Writers such as Lynne Macedo and Keith Warner have identified constant references to the cinema and its shaping influence in Naipaul's work. They have linked these instances to Naipaul's conception of the lack of a secure sense among Caribbean peoples and his increasingly dim view of human existence. Caribbean peoples, for example, in such readings construct their ideal selves against the backdrop of movies and movie characters. Naipaul has himself suggested in *Reading and Writing* that he might well have considered an alternative career as a filmmaker were he a young man today.[1] (He has not indicated whether he would be a director, scriptwriter or cinematographer).

Macedo in *Fiction and Film: The Influence of Cinema on Writers from Jamaica and Trinidad,* details some of the thematic parallels between Naipaul and film auteurs such as Hitchcock: their concern with shifting identities; their shared exploration of destructive relationships, including the deep pessimism about such relationships; the threat posed by females within heterosexual relationships and the fragility of men.[2] These cinematic images appear in the early works as ways of filling a lack in the Caribbean psyche. There are some overt examples that come immediately to mind. In *Miguel Street* (1959) the first chapter is named after Humphrey Bogart of 'Casablanca' fame and in *A Flag on the Island* (1967) where Henry and Frank both evolve into characters – a longstanding word in Naipaul for those who adopt poses – the cinema is used as a mechanism for underlining the illusionary nature of the surface ambitions of those like Selma whose desires extend no further than the image taken from the cinema. This is reflected in the early part of the novella when Selma reflects, 'A three-piece suite. One of those deep ones. You sink into them. I'd buy a nice counterpane, satiny and thick and crisscrossed with deep lines. I saw Norma Shearer using one in *Escape*.'[3] These words find an echo years later when Frank returns and sees that, 'On the bed lay a quilted satin eiderdown' (*A Flag* 1967, 22). The final deflation occurs when Frank comments, 'Poor Selma. I pulled the lavatory chain twice' (1967, 230).

The Jamaican film, 'The Harder They Come', (1972) by Perry Henzell encapsulates much of what Naipaul is referring to in Henzell's use of such filmic references and metaphors.[4] In this 1972 Jamaican movie, the hero/anti-hero Ivan sits in a cinema, absorbs the images of cinema and remakes himself as a cult hero according to those images he has viewed on screen. Naipaul's characters also appear to be constantly remaking themselves and filling in the gaps of their existences by cinematic icons and ideas, often, as in *Miguel Street,* with the complicity of their communities.

In a sense, our perception of all of the characters of *Miguel Street* is filtered through the idea of cinema. The characters need illusions to support their impoverished lives. They are, nonetheless, part of a community. Their existences are concrete. In the early novels the filmic illusion is not wholly or necessarily a negative. It can also be viewed as a way of extending the imagination and widening the horizons of those who live in small, narrowly defined and constricting island communities.

Cinematography, as the art of cinema, may from this perspective be seen as a formative influence on Naipaul's characterisation particularly in the ways in which fragmentation gives rise to distorted images that allow for psychological impact: for example the close-up shots of Seth's khaki clothes, big hands, boots, the cigarette holder in his mouth that become constant visual rhymes, and which act as indices to his function as a figure of power within the Tulsi empire. These veer towards the psychological impact of cinema's close shots that, by virtue of their closeness, give rise to an effect of distortion and psychological impact.

The sense of the absurd contained in the grotesqueness of closely scrutinised and mapped humanity finds its most potent evocation in a short story in *Flag on the Island*, 'The Enemy.' The mother is here already an indication of Naipaul's obsession with the maternal figure. This is continued in the late novel *Half a Life* (2001) in the character of Saronjini where one of the often-repeated ideas is Willie's dependence on Ana and on his sister.[5]

In the 1967 short story, hate is expressed as the hatred the mother feels for the father. The psychological problem of this transference of the mother's feelings to her son is made clear via the route of visual description. The father is a driver:

> He wasn't a slave driver, but a driver of free people, but my father used to behave as though the people were slaves. He rode about the estates on a big clumsy brown horse, cracking his whip at the labourers and people said – I really don't believe this – that he used to kick the labourers (*Flag* 1967, 77).

The caricature of the broken-down horse and the ridiculous figure fantasising about power in the twentieth century is punctuated by the words, 'I really don't believe this,' in this way underlining the comic and the fictional. Yet what carries much of the force of the imaging is the gradual decline into paranoia of the father, detailed through the psychologically heightened excess of the horror movie:

> I went to the window. It was a pitch-black night, and the world was a wild and lonely place, with only the wind and the rain on the leaves. I had to fight to pull the window in, and before I could close it, I saw the sky light up with a crack of lightning.
>
> I shut the window and waited for the thunder.
>
> It sounded like a steamroller on the roof.
>
> My father said, 'Boy, don't frighten. Say what I tell you to say.'
>
> I went and sat at the foot of the rocking chair and I began to say, 'Rama! Rama! Sita Rama!'
>
> My father joined in. He was shivering with cold and fright.
>
> Suddenly he shouted, 'Boy, they here. They here. I hear them talking under the house. They could do what they like in all this noise and nobody could hear them.'

> I said. 'Don't fraid, I have this cutlass here, and you have your gun.' (1967, 82)

This sequence may be explained away as literary melodrama or the distortions of a child's memory. Nonetheless, its calling into play of the special effects of the horror genre and its use of intensified images, accesses our recollection of cinema and the sound systems of cinema.

Naipaul's delight in the art of seeing, alongside the rhythm of words in his early novels, creates the elation that makes us see the world of Trinidad or in its more specific incarnations, the world of Elvira, or the interior of Hanuman House or the world of *The Mystic Masseur*. There is a love here that is more than the cynicism that one often associates with Naipaul. This exuberance of sound and image nonetheless also allows for the kind of paradoxical division that we see in a novel like *The Mystic Masseur*, which is in effect a novel in two parts.[6] The first is shaped by Naipaul's self-induced laughter at his own desire to write and his delight in the world of characters and culture specific memories from Trinidad through the channel of sense. The delicious savouring of the paper in the stationer's or the peeping into the printing establishment or the caressing glance at Ramsumair at the wedding feast as his eyes feast on surfaces, on fruit hanging from trees or decorations of homemade lights all engage our senses in a particular way so that we experience the uniqueness of a Trinidadian way of being. The second part traces the decline into absurdity, to the spectacle and emptiness of G. Ramsay Muir.

Naipaul's use of the playful arrangement of visual objects is not unique in that it is linked to the ways in which a modernist writer such as Beckett provides deep artistic truths about the nature of the modern condition.[7] What is interesting in Naipaul is the way that he sets up a relationship with his world that allows for this sensuous and loving apprehension and almost simultaneously enables a savage deconstruction of the very perception and mindset that either emerges from or has emerged from that world of surface things. We see clothes literally 'dancing out of the window' in *A Flag on the Island*, and 'taking on a life of their own' (1967, 180) as a prelude to one of Naipaul's muted references to Carnival (in itself an art of movement). The dance of the visual opens a window on the petty thievery, prostitution, black market economy and a world dominated by a black-white consciousness.

There are other cinematic techniques that approximate this use of visual play throughout the body of Naipaul's work. These include the use of the close-up as a vehicle of meaning (113). The close scrutiny of individual details can allow the reader through his appreciation of the visuality in the experience, to respond to complex emotions generated by the text. The figure of the Zulu's cap in the story 'In a Free State,' for example, plays with the ways in which what we see may not be what is true. This kind of play triggers a response that defines the nature of the two men, two worldviews and two social and political problems: 'Bobby leaned to touch the plaid cap, and for a while they held the cap together, Bobby fingering the material, the Zulu allowing the cap to be fingered.'[8]

This is a gesture that suggests the fondling of flesh, but the visual message inherent in this moves towards more complex ideas: 'On the plaid cap his fingers moved until they were over one of the Zulu's' (*In a Free State* 1971, 115). The silence and the contempt in the eyes of the Zulu and the moist weakness in the face of Bobby set the scene for what occurs next. The interlude has the timing and impact of the filmic caesura: 'Then, without moving his hand or changing his expression, the Zulu spat in his face' (115).

Context is everything. Shots situated within a carefully constructed line that is based on the conflictual play of fragments whereby the addition of one plus one does not lead to two but to a qualitatively different concept allow visuals to transform themselves and their objective realities through conflict. In fact, 'In a Free State' makes constant use of montage. The narrator is often like a camera looking in from the outside and occasionally zooming in on incongruous details that take on the significance of defining images:

> The new photograph of the president, the man of the forest with his hair now in the English style, stood between colored prints of English scenes. There were old magazines: photographs of parties, dances, country houses, furniture; an England, as it were, for export, carefully photographed, with what was offending left out (1971, 140).

These details add up to an idea that is more than each individual object and work in a way that is similar to a collection of shots that take on meaning by their juxtaposition.

There are many such examples where the narrative takes us on a journey, which directs the eye or iris in the same way that a moving camera carries us along a particular terrain. The build up of visual images in a moving line parallels editing principles taken from film. The narrative can speak by interpolating an idea of the human within a moving landscape in the same way that a camera intercuts a scenic fragment with a human figure to provide a psychological or emotional tone. One sees this again in a small example also from 'In a Free State.' The character Bobby is looking at a landscape after his encounter with the fine boned man of the King's tribe. His mind wanders to the man's face and he forces himself to remember the failed homosexual pick up at the bar. The narrative uses an intercutting device:

> Bobby said softly 'God.' Then, leaning again on the steering wheel, he made himself think of the bar of the New Shropshire. 'God. God.' He looked up. 'God.' But now his voice had changed. 'God, how beautiful.' He was speaking of the play of sunlight in the green field (1971, 159).

The words 'God, how beautiful' provide a complex of ideas, here rendered possible through the intercutting of images that we see more frequently in films that use fast cutting techniques of montage. Images of the boy, the Zulu, the bar, are made doubly complex and evocative by the narrator's words: 'He was speaking of the play of sunlight in the green field' (159). There is in all this something of the power of silent cinema with its play of overtonal lines where conflict marks the leap to a new concept.

Cinema as an art of illusion, however, is in itself as an idea brought into play in other works, not simply to demonstrate the mimicry of the insecure self but to denote a state of being. This difference, a difference located in new landscapes and a dissolving idea of home becomes evident after the writing of *The Middle Passage.* The novel, *Mr Stone and the Knights Companion*, sets a new tone, one that suggests in some instances an illusion of a self that is dislocated from its bearings: 'And again Mr Stone has the delicious sensation of flying in his chair. Mr Keenan's reaction was a caricature of astonishment and incredulity. For seconds he held himself in his conspiratorial stoop, held his smile.'[9] Mr Stone is defined in chiaroscuro by the concrete presence of the cat that stalks his movements, and is substantially different from any of the characters of the early novels. It is not simply that the location is different and that nationality is different – Mr Stone is English and in England – the nature of his illusionary world is also different. Unlike the early novels, where surface description aligned to movement gives a sense of the vitality that exists beneath the surface of such descriptions, Mr Stone lives in a world where time passes and time decays and the figure of the young black cat at the end of the novel brings into focus the nature of Stone's hubris, as a destructive element in the face of time and his own insubstantial presence.

What emerges in the later Naipaul is the idea, like a belief system, that illusion has finally replaced reality. It is no longer the matter of basing one's reality on an illusion to shore up one's sense of inadequacy or lack of real identity. Instead illusion becomes lens and fact. Mr Stone's recognition of the finitude of the real world and his fear of death is pitted against a pervasive movement that demonstrates the growing unreality of his situation via an increasing lack of control over events. His wife takes over his home; his aspirations concerning the knight's companion are taken over by someone else. By the end of the novel his space has been so invaded that he has become a figure of real futility simply because he has succumbed to all his illusions.

'Tell Me Who to Kill', of *In a Free State,* also merges fantasy with reality in such a way that we are left finally with a radical uncertainty about events; such is the nature of the nightmare that has replaced the possibility of cinema's regenerative powers, no matter how whimsical this may seem. The word 'regenerative' is used here because Naipaul shares with Walcott and Brathwaite a profound sense of the potency of the moving image or the image aligned to movement, as a formative process that might allow for a truthful representation of the complex web of relations within human persons here and elsewhere, and for portraying the rich interconnections that exist within Caribbean societies. Their attention to the visual makes cinema as the supreme art of seeing, a key strategy in writing about the Caribbean.

There are echoes of its influence in a writer like Kamau Brathwaite where the graphic shapes to be found in visual technologies give language the means to echo the very shape of hurt.[10] The multilayered tapestries of painterly lines and images of Wilson Harris in a work such as *The Tree of the Sun* (1978) suggest the superimpositions of cinematic projection and become a way of interrogating historic and psychological trauma.[11] In Jean Rhys's *Wide Sargasso Sea* (1966), the visual patterning of words and images explodes on the page in the self-immolating fire of Caribbean belief, but beyond this, Rhys foregrounds the differences in ways of seeing between those who come from the Caribbean and those from beyond its borders.[12] Derek Walcott explores the interconnections and interpenetrations that exist in Antillean communities via a route that begins in the reversals of the photographic image and moves towards a benediction of the healing power of cinema's audio-visuality and image-making properties and rests finally on the interchangeability to be found in painting and poetry.[13]

One of my students reminded me the other day that the word re-member is about remembering parts that have been dismembered. That is what film is about, the reconstruction of parts, which is why it is an art that makes use of the structures of memory. Oddly enough this idea of filmic structure as a way of renegotiating the past enables an even closer link with Walcott. Much of what Walcott has written about the negative effect of history has been in some sense shaped by Naipaul. I use the word shape because I am thinking specifically about the way he reinvents and constructs a visual idea and a visual image of Naipaul's 'nothing was created.' This nothing becomes the cavernous O, the opening or the abyss out of which the great novel poem *Omeros* (1990) is shaped.[14] In *Tiepolo's Hound* (2000), Walcott goes in search of a detail of light that defines an epoch.[15] Naipaul's works retain a defining sense of what it was and still is to be a Caribbean person. His works, however, increasingly rest in the shadow of the light of this world. That regenerative light or way of seeing that had within it laughter, satire, grotesqueness and love, becomes converted to another world and increasingly lingers in the shadows of a half-remembered idea that is more fiction than fact and that has become estranged from its origins.

Naipaul's *Half a Life* (2001) is a narrative that brings together a number of fictions. Willie's father lives a fiction. As a writer, Willie looks dispassionately at other people's fictional worlds: the angry young man in his flat whose view of the world is only from his window, and the editor who only wants an audience. Willie himself is a creator of fictions based tenuously on a life he has left behind. In a real sense this novel is like a faint memory of *The Mystic Masseur*. Willie writes scripts for the BBC. He shapes narratives based on dramatic situations taken from movies he has seen (2001, 85). He rewrites his life based on these fictions. He also exhausts them. Exhausted, he becomes a writer in the confessional mode. [16] In this mode the distance between reality and illusion finally collapses.

The narrator of *Half a Life* is distant and objective. He looks at the antics of a world completely outside of himself. This is the tone that Willie's final confession adopts as he tells to his sister, Saronjini, the story of his sojourn in Africa. The narrator gives us a dry account of Willie as he is about to leave for Africa in a state of unreality: 'He wondered whether he would be able to hold on to his own language' (2001, 124). After his fall and during his stay in hospital he asks Ana: 'Do you think it would be possible for someone to look at all my bruises and cuts and work out what has happened to me? Work out what I have done to myself?' (2001, 127). This is pretty much all that he takes with him when he goes to his sister. The rest of the story is a reconstruction of events told after the fact. The novel suggests that Willie's futile existence is nothing more than a series of stories that he has himself constructed out of events he does not really understand. For him there is no true reality. The end has occurred before there could be a beginning. This fact also marks a profound distance between the later fiction and the fiction of the period of *The Mystic Masseur.*

A Bend in the River provides a closing example of this new form of seeing distilled from the cinematic. The evolving fictional layers reveal Ferdinand's multiple roles and shrunken stature and disclose the emptiness and disillusion that lie beneath Indar's sophisticated exterior and language. The constructive possibilities of film also provide a truth about the fragmented nature of the lives of those who write history and who believe in that history as it is written. This construction mimics the ways in which memory shapes images. At the end of the party, Salim, to the evocative music of Joan Baez, says of Yvette:

> I went over the pictures I had of her that evening, ran the film over again, so to speak, reconstructing and reinterpreting what I had seen, re-creating that woman, fixing her in the posture that had bewitched me, her white feet together, one leg drawn up, one leg flat and bent, remaking her face, her smile, touching the whole picture with the mood of the Joan Baez songs and all that they had released in me, and adding to it this extra mood of moonlight, the rapids, and the white hyacinths of this great river of Africa.[17]

His words encapsulate the ways in which the novel edits events and builds a tonal line. A new mood is created out of fragments of the past. Such editing places in a new light the reconstruction of Africa by the President: his fictional self/selves become part of a constant play of illusion fashioned on the structures of cinema. Such shapes and structures allow a reworking of material and become increasingly more about the shape of things and the ways in which the patterning of image and sound can elicit ideas by their very juxtaposition.

Notes

1. V.S. Naipaul, *Reading and Writing: A Personal Account* (New York: New York Review of Books, 2000); Keith Warner, *On Location: Cinema and Film in the Anglophone Caribbean* (London: Macmillian, 2000).
2. Lynne Macedo, *Fiction and Film. The Influence of Cinema on Writers from Jamaica and Trinidad* (Chichester: Dido, 2003).
3. Naipaul, *Miguel Street.* (1959; repr., New York: Vintage Books, 1984); *A Flag on the Island* (London: André Deutsch, 1967), 178.
4. Screenplay by Perry Henzell and Trevor Rhone (International Films, Inc., 1972).
5. Naipaul, *Half a Life* (New York: Alfred Knopf, 2001).
6. Naipaul, *The Mystic Masseur* (1957; repr., London: Penguin, 1964).
7. I am using the word 'play' here in the sense used by Theodor Adorno. *Aesthetic Theory.* Gretel Adorno and Rolf Tiedemann eds. Translated by C. Lenhardt. 1970. Reprint (London: Routledge and Kegan, 1984).
8. Naipaul, *In a Free State* (London: André Deutsch, 1971), 114.
9. Naipaul, *Mr Stone and the Knights Companion* (London: Four Square, 1966), 62–3.
10. See for example the fairly recent Kamau Brathwaite, *Born to Slow Horses* (Middletown, Connecticut: Wesleyan University Press, 2005), where this is further developed.
11. Wilson Harris, *The Tree of the Sun* (London: Faber and Faber, 1978).
12. Jean Rhys, *Wide Sargasso Sea* (1966; repr., London: Penguin, 2000).
13. Derek Walcott, *Omeros* (London: Faber and Faber, 1990).
14. See Jean Antoine-Dunne, 'Time and Space in their Indissoluble Connection: Towards an Audio-Visual Caribbean Aesthetic,' in *The Montage Principle: Einstein in New Cultural and Critical Contents*, eds. Jean Antoine-Dunne with Paula Quigley. (Amsterdam: Rodopi, 2004), 125–52.
15. Derek Walcott, *Tiepolo's Hound* (New York: Farrar, Straus and Giroux, 2000).
16. See Gordon Rohlehr's essay 'The Confessional Element in Naipaul's Fiction,' in this volume.
17. Naipaul, *A Bend in the River* (London: André Deutsch, 1979).

8

A MALA IN OBEISANCE:
Hinduism in Selected Texts by V.S. Naipaul

Vijay Maharaj

Naipaul declares in *An Area of Darkness*, 'that, though growing up in an orthodox family, I remained almost totally ignorant of Hinduism.'[1] This sweeping generalisation is, however, undermined immediately by the self-questioning that follows: 'What, then, survived of Hinduism in me? Perhaps I had received a certain supporting philosophy. I cannot say; my uncle often put it to me that my denial was an admissible type of Hinduism.' That the thought of philosophical support should have come to him at all and that a conversation of this nature should have taken place between uncle and nephew are indications of the writer's embeddedness in Hindu tradition. The sceptic and the seeker-of-clarification are the two categories of interrogators to whom all the *Shastras*, or Hindu scriptural texts, are addressed.[2] As his uncle may have well been capable of explaining, the deliberate installation, constant questioning and referencing of his Hindu background in his writing place him squarely within one or the other of these categories at various times. He may have told him that the pursuit of faith and knowledge are seen in the *Bhagavad-Gita* as two sides of the same coin: the first blossoms in acquiescence and the second in self-doubt, criticism, discussion and questioning. They lead one into the other.

This Hindu influence in Naipaul's work is recognised.[3] However, postcolonial criticism and theory, which is often applied to texts written by people from the fringes of imperial centres, privileges interpretation of the texts as responses to imperial culture. This is a debilitating approach to Caribbean literary texts because it tends to forestall and devalue interpretations that explore the texts' relationships with the often fragmented, dislocated cultures that the authors inherit from their ancestral groups or their relationships with the often equally fragmented and dislocated cultures of the populations among which the groups have settled.[4] Exploring this aspect of postcolonial literary studies is a task in itself. This paper therefore problematises postcolonial criticism and theory by reading Naipaul in relation to a local Hindu tradition, the *katha*. The underlying contention is that Naipaul's work is not just influenced by his Hindu background but is part of a long Hindu tradition of religious and philosophical speculation intrinsic to the Caribbean *katha* tradition.

I argue that Naipaul's oeuvre speculates about a number of key Hindu philosophical concepts and is a form of the Caribbean *katha*. The folk *katha* is a practice of reading or reciting and interpretation of religious texts in relation to social texts of all varieties for the purpose of bringing meaning to events in people's day-to-day lives. In so doing, it provides spaces and techniques for self-examination, self-fashioning and refashioning. Yet, the Caribbean *katha* is not a reproduction of an Indian practice; it is a reinvention specifically tailored to the contingencies of the lives of the indentured and their descendants.[5] Naipaul continues the process of reinvention for the same purpose for a wider audience, to make meaning and suggest ways of self-construction. Indeed, this attribute of his oeuvre can also be seen as an act of self-assertion and self-preservation. The embedded *katha* is obvious if one follows Naipaul's dictum that 'part of the point of a novel [comes] from half rejecting the fiction, or looking through it to reality.'[6] To look through Naipaul's writing is to find traces and sub-texts of Hinduism as the germ plasm around which the narratives grow.[7] This essay explores some of his work to uncover the germ plasm and identify Naipaul's position in the tradition and his synthesis of elements of the tradition with the requirements of literary discourse.

Despite Naipaul's youthful boast in *An Area of Darkness* that 'I was without belief or interest in belief; I was incapable of worship' (1964, 41), as he admits in later texts such as *Finding a Centre* and *Reading and Writing*, his involvement with Hindu tradition is undeniable. This statement in *An Area of Darkness* is in fact immediately preceded by the recognition of the need for belief and worship in times of adversity, and of the more specific need for them to be within the traditions of Hinduism. When his friend, Ramon, dies, he notes:

> We were a tiny, special part of that featureless, unknown country, [India] meaningful to us, if we thought about it, only in that we were its remote descendants. I wished his body to be handled with reverence, and I wished it to be handled according to the old rites. This alone would spare him final nonentity (*1964,* 40–1).

Although separated from the sub-continent by time and distance, the need for its religions and philosophy remains, if only as a bulwark against nonentity. This is compounded by the need to sanctify as Naipaul's observations in *The Enigma of Arrival* demonstrate: 'But at her death there was in her family a wish to give sanctity to the occasion, a wish for old rites, for things that were felt specifically to represent us and our past.'[8] The presence of an Indian heritage and people's need for it are the central pivot on which Naipaul's speculations revolve and it is evident from his first published work, *The Mystic Masseur*, and onwards, even when the signs of religious and philosophical speculations are coded to make them palatable or invisible to the primary international audience.

This encoding leads John Thieme to talk about allusions. He asserts that 'the most significant body of allusions in the novel is to the various aspects of Hinduism,'[9] but he sees these allusions relating to Naipaul's documentation of the acculturation of Indians in Trinidad. It can be argued, however, that *The Mystic Masseur* not only alludes to aspects of Hinduism in order to document acculturation, but it embodies a Hindu concept of the human condition. It achieves this by performing a beautifully coordinated doubled triple movement. The text is an act of social criticism and it establishes an authorial perspective that becomes Naipaul's hallmark. Naipaul constructs his protagonist in such a way that he can as easily be read within the European tradition of the picaroon hero, or the Caribbean tradition of Anansi, as he can be read within Hindu traditions. In the latter regard, the text can be seen as performing an act of religious worship. The coup d'état in joining of these disparate elements is that one does not hear the grinding echoes of different cultures meeting because Naipaul's aesthetics involves a blurring of the boundaries between the three categories. Naipaul's *katha* is, thus, exactly like the folk *katha*, which pulls together diverse discourses in a synthesizing action that is relatively smooth and soundless. This approach becomes progressively stronger as Naipaul continues to write.

In *The Overcrowded Barracoon*, Naipaul refers to this act of blurring when he notes that, '[l]ike the medieval sculptor of the North interpreting the Old

Testament stories in terms of the life he knew, I needed to be able to adapt.'[10] He adapts Hindu philosophy to the demands of the literary text and to the representation of the lives and circumstances of his characters. In *The Mystic Masseur*, he adapts the iconography of *Ganesh*, the God, to construct Ganesh, the protagonist. The God, *Ganesh*, represents the human being in Hinduism. Gan-esh in fact means lord/master/leader (*esh*) of created beings (*gan*). He is depicted as a mighty elephant, the *paramatman*, who sits on a mouse, the *jivatman*. The image is meant to show that the individual is *paramatman*, the Creator, God, but in embodied form the person is severely limited in demonstrating godlike qualities because of corporeal confinement represented in the mouse.[11] Confinement of the spirit is the most immediately obvious element of the iconography that is unveiled in *The Mystic Masseur*. Ganesh, the protagonist, like his father, has a great deal of potential. Within the confines of the colonial condition, however, this potential is severely curtailed. Every area of their lives is filled with difficulties and Ganesh must play the role of *Ganesh*, the God, in many of his aspects, in order to assert himself and carve a place in the social structure of the Caribbean. He does this by displaying that aspect of *Ganesh* called *Lambodar*, he-of-enormous-appetite-for-all-things-of-this-world, symbolised by the great belly of the elephant. Like *Lambodar*, Ganesh consumes everything that comes his way, appropriating them, making them his own, using them to his own purposes. Ganesh is constructed in such a way as to show that he possesses the attribute of *Ekadant*, the single-minded, totally committed, and focused one. Ganesh intends to be successful, at what he does not know, but he expends undivided effort on the idea of success and of victory. The single-mindedness is Ekadantian.

Apart from developing these overt similarities between God and the human being, with a light touch in a celebratory, comic tone, *The Mystic Masseur* also displays a perspective that the author embraces throughout his career. Thieme notes that: 'Nowhere is there any suggestion that Ganesh could be other than he is' (1987, 43). The deeper philosophical ground of this statement lies in Hinduism's refusal to label the things of this world as either good or evil. In Hinduism, unsullied good and evil are confined to the realm of the *devtas* and the *asuras* – for want of a better translation, the gods and the devils. In the realm of the human, there is no unadulterated good or evil. Naipaul is careful to demonstrate this in *The Mystic Masseur* and continues to demonstrate it in his 33 subsequent works. He generally insists that systems, institutions, and other social constructions impact on the individual so that s/he is unable to be other than s/he is. There is no book in which Naipaul can be said to blame the individual for what may be called his/her evil. In this regard, his attitude is Hindu.

Apart from playfully representing God and man as akin, in an optimistic and convivial fashion that steers clear of judgement, the text can also be seen as performing an offhanded gesture of worship. Every child brought up in a Hindu environment learns that, before any enterprise is undertaken, it is important to pray to *Ganesh* in the form of *Vigneshwar*, the remover of obstacles, for the removal of intellectual and other difficulties. Naipaul would have grown up with this idea of *Ganesh* as *Vigneshwar* and as *Vinayak*, the guardian of the doorway and of movement from one area of life to another. To the Hindu in the Caribbean, *The Mystic Masseur* with its point-by-point adaptation of the attributes of the god can be seen as such an act of worship.[12] It does not seem unrealistic or far-fetched to think that in his difficulties with finding his voice, his material, and a publisher for his works, Naipaul would have gestured towards obeisance to the god, *Ganesh*, however obliquely. Whether one sees this as a 'propitiatory technique' common to writers is irrelevant.[13] It is no less 'touching and attractive' than the 'ancient drama' of ritual performances, 'absurdly surviving in a Trinidad yard' (*An Area* 1964, 34).

In the works that follow *The Mystic Masseur*, Naipaul also engages in iconographic adaptations. This is apparent, for example, in *A House for Mr Biswas*.[14] The fictional name, Hanuman House, given to the house called Lion House is a symbol of resistance and courage. Naipaul's objective in this act of renaming is to critique the traditional Hindu social structure that denies individuality and enterprise. *Hanuman*, the Hindu deity, is worshipped for the protection he bestows against illnesses, natural and other calamities, accidents and problems of all types. Similar expectations are set up in the novel for the fictional house and the idea of community it represents. However, the text demonstrates that in its new setting the house cannot last and its protection cannot be extended beyond its shadow. Beyond this is a world where individual enterprise is of utmost importance and the house does not equip its denizens with the tools for survival and prosperity in that environment. The community thus eventually disintegrates under the pressure of changes over which no one has control. In effect Naipaul seems to be making a Nietzschean statement by naming the house Hanuman: God is dead! *Hanuman* is dead! He cannot protect in these new surroundings!

This is not an untoward act in Hinduism since the scriptural texts are replete with ideas about changing systems of worship and new and more efficacious manifestations of the *paramatman*. Within the context of a dead *Hanuman*, Naipaul also appears to be making a Nietzschean declaration about the superman: the person who transcends the need for the herd, who can use the resources of his own spirit to survive.

This idea is dramatised in Mr Biswas's quest in which the idea of confinement of the human spirit re-emerges. Mr Biswas is confined not just by Hanuman House but also by his own body. This is vividly depicted, for example, in one of many descriptions: 'He didn't feel a small man, but clothes which hung so despairingly from the nail on the mud wall were definitely the clothes of a small man' (1961, 157). Mr Biswas must fight to maintain an idea of self, of his own value and of his own bigness despite the evidence of smallness with which he is confronted. His battles finally win him an accommodation in which he can be at peace with the world. The spirit is larger than the body in which it is housed and to identify with the former, even to sense it to the minute extent that Biswas does, is to be able to act to fulfil oneself and to transcend the lure of the herd.

However, the gap between the spirit and body is also a chasm into which the individual can plummet. Naipaul demonstrates that it is the space through which *Maya* or the illusion of omnipotence can enter consciousness. This is the chasm into which Ralph Kripalsingh falls in *The Mimic Men*.[15] Imbued with a sense of destiny and of personal greatness that he has mentally conjured from the discourse of the Indian national movement and from his ill-fitting colonial education, as an escape from the trivialities and confusions of his own life, Ralph becomes entrapped in a world of fantasy. At one moment he is, in his fantasies, an Aryan horseman on the Asiatic plain and at another a knight performing penance on behalf of all. Through Ralph, Naipaul questions a national subjectivity that finds a sense of self-worth and dignity only through romanticised notions and clichéd claims of rich, glorious and ancient heritages that belie the realities of the claimants. Singh, like Hok, Brown and the other young men who seek leadership roles in the national independence movement 'live in a private hemisphere of fantasy' (1967, 11), and are, as a result, psychologically challenged. Naipaul posits the reliance on constructions of heritage as a false consciousness, to use a Marxian turn of phrase, an abdication of responsibility and dissociation from reality.[16] Singh admits: 'I did not feel responsible for what had befallen me; I always felt separate from what I did' (71). What Naipaul demonstrates in this way, in *The Mimic Men* and *A House for Mr Biswas*, is that the balancing act between the elephant and the mouse is a delicate one that can tilt dangerously in one or the other direction; both extremes are unacceptable.

Yet another kind of balancing act is of far greater importance to Naipaul in his later books. In these, his concern, as critics have observed, is the individual's fundamental ensnarement by aspects of Hindu philosophy, particularly the idea of *karma*. However, contrary to the common critical claims that Naipaul rejects *karma*, it can be shown that this is not so. He interrogates the concept as 'the Hindu killer, the Hindu calm, which tells us that we pay in this life for what we have done in past lives,' but he also notes that it is an injunction about 'our duty to ourselves [and] our future lives.'[17] *Karma* is a mandate for acceptance of life's events but it is not fatalism. It is also a call to action since it is only through action taken now that one repays the debts incurred in the past, ensures a quality life in the present and a better life in the future. His books demonstrate that the problem of misunderstanding the concept of *karma* causes people to accept but not act and thus facilitates a lack of personal responsibility. Naipaul's greatest concern is that the *karma* killer results in 'the smugness…the imperviousness to criticism, the refusal to *see*, double-talk and double-think' (*An Area* 1964, 35), and thus to a denial of life, commitment and responsibility. To counter this, his writing engages in intense repeated speculations about *karma* that consider, from many angles, the tension between the idea of predestination and free will on which it rests.

These are the aspects of *karma* that he vehemently critiques in *A House for Mr Biswas*. The vehemence can be seen as the author's inheritance from his father as a direct outgrowth of his rejection of the community's passivity and consequent poverty of mind and spirit. It is lucidly conveyed in the condemnation of the grandfather in the opening pages of *A House for Mr Biswas*. 'Bipti's father, futile with asthma, propped himself up on his string bed and said, as he always did on unhappy occasions, "Fate. There is nothing we can do about it"' (15). Many aspects of this brief scene negate the principle of action in the term *karma* that the grandfather would have used. First of all, he is likely to be suffering with asthma because of working on the plantations but he has never taken a stand on this. Secondly, he is on a string bed that cannot add comfort to his breathing. He has abdicated personal responsibility for his own health and Naipaul suggests by the tone of the narrative that financial poverty is not the only problem. There is a greater problem of poverty of mind and spirit. Finally, his daughter need not have been condemned by *karma* to continue to live with Raghu's miserliness. Her father could have acted on her behalf as could she, but they do not. Biswas's life, set against this background, presents a perfect foil. Against difficulties that are far more complex than those the old man faces, he takes a stand, no matter how haltingly. Naipaul thus posits, in opposition to the fatalism that *karma* has become, a concept of *karma* that demands the full possession of the moment and the place that one is in at any given time, coupled with detachment or distance from the time and space that prevents possessiveness. Possession without possessiveness however demands constant self-reflexivity and an ensuing historical consciousness and it is to these that Naipaul begins to turn his attention from *Finding the Centre* onwards.

In *Finding the Centre*, Naipaul revisits Hanuman House and acknowledges that it had, for all its shortcomings, bestowed on him and its other inhabitants 'a high sense of self.'[18] He also revisits many other pronouncements and assertions that he had previously made in order to undo them. Previous prejudices are turned upside down, former assertions are revised and their substance and assumptions are queried. In this text and in others after there is always this recursivity. The writer is constantly involved in a process of divesting himself of previous judgements and conceptions in order to fully grasp the significance of the moment. The narratives after *Finding the Centre* are thus increasingly acts of reflection. In the process of reflection, the self becomes both subject and object – the subject of reflection and the object of refashioning. This approach achieves literary fruition in *The Enigma of Arrival* and *A Way in the World*.

These two texts have been criticised by some who try to identify them as belonging to a particular genre. The kind of problem that ensues is evident in Walcott's observation, for example, that *The Enigma of Arrival* 'is negligible as a novel and crucial as autobiography or vice versa' (123). The same charge may well also be made of *A Way in the World*.[20] Given the trajectory of development in Naipaul's oeuvre as traced in this essay, however, such observations are of uncertain value. Naipaul has walked a path that rejects categories and in these two narratives a flagrant refusal of the categories of theory, history, fiction and autobiography, as mutually exclusive. Together, *The Enigma of Arrival* and *A Way in the World* comprise an autobiographical duo but the narratives are specifically constructed to continue the epistemological interrogation set up in *Finding the Centre*. However, whereas *Enigma* is an interpretive introspection on the writer's life and is thus self-centred and self-absorbed, *A Way in the World* is concerned with the role of the other in self-formation. The latter begins where the former ends, with the narrator's acceptance that the highest pursuit of the artist's vocation is the conceptualisation of 'life and man as mystery, the true religion of men, the grief and the glory' (*Enigma* 1987, 354). In addition, although *Enigma* is more openly declarative of Naipaul's quarrel with Indian 'smugness' and 'refusal to see' and with shoddy Brahminical practices that are performed without due reflection or care, it is in *A Way in the World* that his own speculation coincides with and reflects the strongest but most carefully concealed element of Hindu philosophy.

Naipaul calls *A Way in the World* 'the magnum opus of my maturity,' an appellation with which one must concur because of the text's richness, depth and complexity.[21] In this work, he re-presents the Vedic concept of *Nirguna Brahman*, the formless conjoined creator and creation before it becomes separated into *purusha* and *prakriti*, creator and created, self and other. The Vedas have no way of describing this because it is prior to and in excess of description. The term that is therefore most frequently used to refer to *Nirguna Brahman* is *Neti Neti* – not this, not that, not any thing, unnameable, indefinable. In the central fictional core of the narrative, Naipaul presents the human confrontation with this essential core of the self through the unheimlich experience of a revolutionary who visits the Guyanese interior. This man goes to Guyana to involve the Native Americans in a revolutionary uprising. On his arrival in their village, he is taken to a pool to bathe, but the pool in its extreme clarity is completely black. When he is submerged in this black water, he finds that although his eyes are open, he can see nothing. Suddenly he does not know where his body begins and where the water ends and all his senses of perception cease to function. He finds that he can formulate no thoughts and loses his grip on reality entirely. His being is suffused with terror. This is not an experience of Thanatos, of Death; it is an experience of sheer unadulterated nothingness. It is an experience that is alluded to in the declaration in the *Taittiriya Upanishad*, 'Non-existent does one become if one knows Brahman as Non-Being.'[22] The revolutionary comes out of the experience of Nirguna Brahman, or Self as Non-Being, a changed person. He suddenly understands that there is no self-in-the-world if there is no other. He begins, therefore to experience the people of the forest as individuals, to know each one singly in a complete reversal of the way he conceived of them en masse within the framework of his revolutionary ideology.

This experience is used to demonstrate that critical element of Hindu philosophy, which stipulates that unless the individual is capable of recognising his fragile positioning between his selfhood as a manifestation of paramatma, and his oneness and differences from other such manifestations then he will live wrongly. It is on this understanding of the self and the value of the individual that Naipaul develops his reconstruction of history which is an unravelling of Kripalsingh's Conradian vision of history that

> ...give[s] expression to the restlessness, the deep disorder, which the great explorations, the overthrow in three continents of established social organization, the unnatural bringing together of peoples who could achieve fulfilment only within the security of their won societies and the landscapes hymned by their ancestors. (*Mimic Men* 1967, 38)

In its place Naipaul delineates a world in which the human condition is a condition of being 'strangers to ourselves' (*A Way* 1994, 11). The genetic inheritance of each 'stranger' stretches far back into an unfathomable past that has always involved self-construction. This self-construction is based on interaction with an other who is in turn a stranger to himself or herself. Self-construction has therefore always occurred through a process of mixing, of creolisation, if you will. The self that Naipaul conceives here is not unlike Édouard Glissant's idea of the opacity of the self;[23] but whereas Glissant suggests that one at least knows one's own self, Naipaul conjectures that even that is opaque. The two however are similarly proposing that the individual is unique, and that a certain tentativeness, a willingness to suspend judgement and a willingness to draw only provisional conclusions about the other are the bases on which interactions of the future must occur. It is the way of countering the colonial subjectivity which Naipaul first defined non-fictionally in *The Middle Passage*: 'In the colonial society every man had to be for himself; every man had to grasp whatever dignity and power he was allowed; he owed no loyalty to the island and scarcely any to his group.'[24] It is a new basis for community that is being suggested here, a more respectful and gentle way of being that counters a long and seemingly never-ending history of violence. The foremost aesthetic feature of *A Way in the World* in this context is its quintessentially Hindu attribute of non-proselytism and non-conversion.

Although it contains a message with the potential to revolutionise culture and bring about the universal civilisation that Naipaul speaks about, 'where it was necessary to be an individual and responsible; where people developed vocations, and were stirred by ambition and achievement, and believed in perfectibility,'[25] there is no attempt to convert.

What emerges from this exploration is the fact that Naipaul's oeuvre is in effect a literary, philosophical and ideological enterprise (in the sense of self-consciously articulating a world vision) that deploys Hindu philosophical concepts to address critical questions about the meaning of the self, ways of self-construction, ways of being-in-the-world, the nature of the relation between self and other and ways of living with the other. It illustrates the locatedness of the writing subject and the fact that self-representation is deeply rooted in spatial and historical legacies. I have argued, in fact, that Naipaul's work is a series of *kathas* on the nature of *paramatman*, *karma* and *nirguna* and *saguna Brahma*, which establishes a complex relationship with the writer's Hindu heritage.

However, if one contrasts the *katha* as it is practised in the Hindu folk tradition in the Caribbean and Naipaul's practice of it, differences are obvious even if these are differences of form and context only, rather than of purpose. Naipaul left Trinidad with the sole aim of becoming a writer. He wanted to carve his name into the Western literary tradition, as it has been conceptualised by T.S. Eliot and others. In this, he was, like many other young Caribbean people, reared for export, for setting out into the world to claim a craft or profession and so to claim the world and be forever removed from the petty concerns of the region that had produced him. He was to find, like so many others, then and now, that knowing home and self was the critical stepping-stone to knowing and claiming the world. The telltale marks of this undertaking make Naipaul's *kathas* clearly distinguishable from the folk *katha*; yet in many fundamental respects, the two overlap and are intent on a similar purpose, meaning-making, and self-construction.

However, Naipaul's work is distinguished from the *katha* in that, like all modern art, it attempts to be conscious of its own being or its art-ness and self-consciously manipulates the media it uses and the discourses it engages. The folk *katha*, on the other hand, is largely unconscious and unconcerned about its use of various media and discourses and crosses boundaries unthinkingly. While the folk *katha* self-confidently proclaims its relation and relevance to reality, Naipaul's art says that it is an act of representation or reflection in a particular genre and in a particular form that the writer has worked hard to discover as most appropriate to his material. Naipaul's *kathas* are thus self-conscious in their use of the media for desired artistic effects. In addition, whereas the folk *katha* is immediately concerned with the moment and with an overt statement on the reality which confronts the community to which it speaks, Naipaul's art is always concerned to maintain a certain distance from 'reality' and its immediate concerns in order to make a statement that has a wider resonance than the immediate needs of any singular community. Unlike the exponent of the traditional *katha* Naipaul's target audience is not a Hindu audience but an international one whose extratextual references may be many but may rarely include Hindu scriptures. The messages that are imbued with the inheritance of his Hindu background are thus covertly embedded and their links to the *katha* tradition may be obscured but they are there nevertheless. In addition, whereas the comments about reality in the *katha* are of paramount importance, in Naipaul's works the 'art' and the comments are of equal significance.

Moreover, in literary discourse the artist is an individual whose responsibility is to produce objects that can be considered art and, better yet, great art. It was to this goal that Naipaul dedicated his efforts. In the religious arena in which the pundit's *katha* is expounded his/her individuality is of minimal importance. His/her responsibility is to help people to better understand the problems that face them in their day-to-day lives. The *katha* is important, not its exponent. The listener is interested in and remembers the *katha*, not its exponent. The reality that is captured in a folk *katha* is more important than the artistry with which it is rendered. The situation in Naipaul's work is reversed. In addition, unlike the pundit whose relationship to the scriptural texts is usually one that accepts the texts' authority, Naipaul adopts a critical position. His discourses are nonetheless a *mala* or garland of obeisance to his Hindu heritage.

The closing concern of this essay, however, is that Naipaul's *kathas* have the potential to be as important to the community as the folk *katha*, but in order for this to be realised the narratives need to be shared by the community as familiar texts to which reference can be made in all situations. To read Naipaul in the way this paper has done is to remove his work from the area of 'litricher and poultry' to which it has been confined, which excludes Elias,[26] and by extension other young Caribbean people, and to bring it into the realm of a discourse with immediate impact on the quotidian Caribbean.

Making this happen should be a priority of Naipaulian scholarship especially that emanating from the Caribbean.

Notes

1. V.S. Naipaul, *An Area of Darkness: An Experience of India* (London: André Deutsch, 1964), 32.
2. Further information on all the elements of Hinduism discussed in this paper can be easily accessed on the web at http://hinduwebsite.com. It is of course also available in many specialist academic texts.
3. See for example Landeg White, *V.S. Naipaul: A Critical Introduction* (London: Macmillan, 1975); John Thieme, *The Web of Tradition: Uses of Allusion in V.S. Naipaul's Fiction* (Hertford: Hansib Publications, 1987); and Selwyn Cudjoe, *V.S. Naipaul: A Materialist Reading* (Amherst: The University of Massachusetts Press, 1988).
4. For a more extensive discussion of this threat that postcolonialism presents to Caribbean literary criticism, see Jennifer Rahim's essay, '"A Quartet of Daffodils" Only: Negotiating the Specific and the Relational in the Context of Multiculturalism and Globalisation,' In *Caribbean Literature in a Global Context,* eds. Funso Aiyejina and Paula Morgan (San Juan, Trinidad: Lexicon Trinidad Ltd, 2006). In the essay, Rahim contends that 'the region's discourses are therefore repositioned on the margins of a postcolonial agenda institutionalized in the West, even as conceptual use is made of them' (43). See also Rowland Smith, ed. *Postcolonizing the Commonwealth: Studies in Literature and Culture* (Ontario: Wilfred Laurier UP, 2000), which contains similar critiques of postcolonial studies.
5. See Aisha Khan, *Callaloo Nation: Metaphors of Race and Religious Identity among South Asians in Trinidad* (Jamaica, Barbados and Trinidad and Tobago: The University Press of the West Indies, 2004), for an extensive description of the performance of the *katha*, which she spells *kuttha*, in Trinidad and Tobago.
6. Naipaul, *Reading and Writing: A Personal Account* (New York: New York Review of Books, 2000), 23.
7. This thesis may seem quite simple and obvious to some readers who have never been in doubt about Naipaul's Hinduism but it involves a number of complicated issues concerning the relationship between the first diaspora Indians and their cultural baggage as well as problems of representing religious and philosophical speculation in modern and postmodern art.
8. Naipaul, The *Enigma of Arrival: A Novel in Five Sections* (London: Penguin Books, 1987), 316.
9. Theime, *The Web of Tradition: Uses and Allusions in V.S. Naipaul's Fiction*, 43; Naipaul, *The Mystic Masseur* (London: André Deutsch, 1957), 43.
10. Naipaul, *The Overcrowded Barracoon and other articles* (London: André Deutsch, 1972), 25.
11. See Paul Courtright, *Ganesha: Lord of Obstacles, Lord of Beginnings.* (New York: Oxford University Press, 1985).

12. In the Lion House in Chaguanas, Trinidad, where Naipaul grew up, there was a statue of *Ganesh* guarding the doorway, a statue that he would have passed on countless occasions, a statue whose significance would have been known to him.
13. See Edward Hoagland, 'Staking His Life on One Grand Vision', *New York Times on the Web,* September 16, 1984. http://www.nytimes.com/books/98/06/07/specials/naipaul-center.html In addition, in an interview with Mel Gussow, Naipaul observes: 'All my titles for the last 12 or 13 years have had slightly triumphant suggestions – not so much triumphant as good luck suggestions.' He also notes that he used 'BBC non-rustle paper and numbered only every fifth page in a similar gesture.' In Mel Gussow, 'V.S. Naipaul: "It Is Out of This Violence I've Always Written,"' *New York Times on the Web,* September 16, 1984. http://www.nytimes.com/books/98/06/07/specials/naipaul-violence.html.
14. Naipaul, *A House for Mr. Biswas* (London: André Deutsch, 1961).
15. Naipaul, *The Mimic Men* (London: André Deutsch, 1967).
16. I agree with the way that Thieme (1987, 135), discusses the absurdity of Ralph's conclusion that he is living the four stages of life outlined in the Hindu texts and will not rehash it here. It should be noted though that Naipaul's representation is directed at calling attention to not just Ralph's absurdity but to nationalism's.
17. Naipaul, *India: A Wounded Civilization* (London: André Deutsch, 1977), 25.
18. Naipaul, *Finding the Centre: Two Narratives* (London: André Deutsch, 1984), 57.
19. Derek Walcott 'The Garden Path,' *The New Republic* (April 18, 1987), 123.
20. Naipaul, *A Way in the World* (New York: Knopf, 1994).
21. Mel Gussow, 'Naipaul in Search of Himself: A Conversation,' *New York Times,* April 24, 1994.
22. *Tąittiriya Upanishad* II.6.1.
23. Édouard Glissant. *Poetics of Relation.* trans. Betsy Wing (Ann Arbor: University of Michigan Press, 1997).
24. Naipaul, *The Middle Passage: The Caribbean Revisited* (London: André Deutsch, 1962), 78.
25. Naipaul, 'Our Universal Civilization,' *New York Times on the Web,* November 5, 1990. http://www.nytimes.com/books/98/06/07/specials/naipaul-universal.html
26. Naipaul, *Miguel Street* (London: André Deutsch, 1959), 41.

9

THE SHADOW OF HANUMAN:
V.S. Naipaul and the 'Unhomely' House of Fiction

Jennifer Rahim

The search for habitable forms to house his fictional and non-fictional material has always preoccupied V.S. Naipaul. This concern with the means of narration is largely rooted in his acute awareness of himself as a writer of Indian descent, originating from the West Indian island of Trinidad and Tobago. Trinidad's multicultural composition with its history of colony and its location in the mouth of the Orinoco river of Venezuela made it, according to Naipaul, 'not strictly of South America, and not strictly of the Caribbean.'[1] He thereby draws attention to a creative sensibility shaped by having been historically positioned, like his native geography, in-between worlds, on the shifting ground of contentious epistemological battles, sociopolitical reconstructions, and cultural negotiations between natal and adopted traditions set in motion by Europe's expansion into the New World. In a reflection on the relationship of a writer with such a background to the literary traditions he inherited as a colonial subject, Naipaul makes the following point about the novel:

> It is something that people in my culture have borrowed from other people and the danger is that we tend...to recreate an alien form, an alien novel, the whole form and concept of life is totally alien to the society. We impose one on the other. My attempt has been, in a way, to dredge down a little deeper to the truth about one's own situation.[2]

The creative dredging of 'situation' for what might be considered an organically derived aesthetic response to experience, with all its implied ideological tensions and power relations, no doubt brought the early recognition of his complex relationship to the act of narration. Naipaul's intercultural inheritance meant that he would have been inescapably inserted into the European literary tradition of his colonial education, the influence of a West Indian folk tradition and, of course, the myths of his Hindu ancestral affiliation. In the case of the latter, Selwyn Cudjoe, for instance, posits a credible argument for the author's 'creative transformation of Hindu classical literature' in his early fiction (1988, 64). He argues that in *A House for Mr Biswas*, 'the author inverts and destroys' the narrative unity of the *Ramayana* epic of Rama and Sita to capture the 'historical reality' of a Biswas and Shama set adrift in the 'disunity of the new world.'[3] Further, he notes that the benevolent ally of Rama, the monkey-God, Hanuman, becomes, in the author's remaking, the 'slightly sinister' deity that oversees more than adorns the Tulsi's family-house (70).

This paper is primarily interested in Naipaul's figurative evocation of the monkey figure in two texts. In his epic novel, *A House for Mr Biswas*, Hanuman plays a significant symbolic role in the text's quest plot. Apart from the statue that crowns the balustrades of Hanuman House, life-size images of the deity adorn its interior pillars and so echo the Chaguanas, Indian style house of Naipaul's maternal grandmother where he grew up ('Two Worlds' 2003, 187). The figure also appears in his personal essay, 'Prologue to an Autobiography,'[4] but more obliquely. There, he describes his posture as he wrote the stories of *Miguel Street* (1959), in the BBC freelancers' room as a 'monkey crouch' ('Prologue' 2003, 60). Both texts invite consideration of the monkey as a metaphor of consciousness and style, grounded, though not solely contained, in the inescapable Hindu sensibility of his upbringing.

New World writers have always searched for aesthetic strategies to represent the complexity of their diverse, diasporic societies given their long histories of anti-imperial struggle as inheritors of multiple, though not always equally valued knowledge systems and cultural traditions. In the process of developing a literature of their own, the creative turn of writers from subject societies to the belief systems, myths, and folk narratives of their various ancestral pasts has been pivotal in asserting cultural agency against oppressive regimes, as well as for articulating the emergence of new identity spaces formed by cross cultural contact. Much like the ever-popular spider, Ananse, one such folk figure that has been a seminal aesthetic force in the articulation of a New World poetics is the trickster-monkey.

Understandably, given the long history of transatlantic slavery, African-derived origins of the monkey-myth have enjoyed some prominence in the New World imagination. Henry Louis Gates, for instance, notes that it has occupied a significant place in the mythologies and rhetorical practices of the African diaspora, inclusive of the Caribbean. He argues that the trickster topos which appears as a monkey, sometimes as a black small man, is the Pan-African relative of the divine trickster/linguist of the Yoruba tradition, Esu-Elegbara, also known as the crossroads God, Legba in the Fon tradition.[5] Monkey myths, however, display diverse origins and cross-cultural links. Josè Piedra's study, 'From Monkey Tales to Cuban Songs: On Signification', draws attention to this fact, arguing that the 'extraordinary Monkey' in New World traditions has appeared 'under many guises, names and cultural origins' that derive from not only African, but also 'Egyptian, Celtic and Indian mythologies.'[6]

This transcultural character of the monkey topos, therefore, consciously or unconsciously marks the collective mythopoetic imagination of the diverse ethnic groups that comprise the Americas. All these worlds and their traditions constitute a psycho-cultural dialectic of imagination that approximates to what Wilson Harris calls the voices of 'a murmuring vibration in the Shadow-organ of space,' where he argues one 'could hear one's voice issuing from the body of a stranger.'[7] In exploring V.S. Naipaul's deployment of the monkey-figure, this paper gives focus to the literary uses of the Hindu deity, Hanuman, its Asian relative. Yet in doing so, it is cognisant of the author's positioning as a diasporic Indian on whose cultural sensibilities several mythological traditions have made impact. Monolithic or ethnocentric readings of the monkey topos will no doubt limit the interpretative possibilities of New World writers whose imperial histories have ideologically and aesthetically unhoused them in more ways than one. Their social milieux therefore require that they simultaneously engage several cultural histories, geographical spaces and narrative traditions in their search for stylistic strategies to accommodate the diversity of their worlds.

The aesthetic outcome of this experience of displacement Homi Bhabha describes as the 'unhomely' in today's 'House of Fiction.'[8] Foremost in his mind is the experience of writers whose fictions 'negotiate the powers of cultural difference in a range of historical conditions and social contradictions' that emerge from agonising ancestral dislocations, fragmentations and inevitable renewals, and so are 'paradigmatic' of the postcolonial experience. Bhabha's interpretation of Naipaul's *A House for Mr Biswas*, for instance, points to the text's 'tragic-comic failure to create a dwelling place' for the protagonist as evidence of 'the *shock* [emphasis mine] of recognition of the world-in-the-home, the home-in-the-world' (1992, 142). He calls the resultant blurring of the borders between private and public space, past and present time, inside and outside positions 'the unhomely moment' which 'creeps up on you stealthily as your own shadow' (141–2). In other words, it is an occasion of existential crisis and collapse when the self recognises its shadow (self) as not quite the same, as altered by the presence of an Other/other.[9] In the turmoil of that recognition 'another world becomes visible' (141), making absolute returns to old identities and cultural spaces impossible. This examination of Naipaul's textual evocations of the monkey totem is therefore read in the context of such destablising processes of change and the struggle to make a place for oneself in an uncertain world.

Nowhere does Naipaul express his intellectual and spiritual terror of the world he inherited more cogently than the parallel he creates between himself and the story of exile enacted in the Ramlila. In *Reading and Writing*, he writes:

> the story of Rama's unjust banishment to the dangerous forest was something I had always known. It lay below the writing I was to get to know later in the city, the Anderson and Aesop I was to read on my own, and the things my father was to read to me. [10]

That theme of exile therefore existed as the subtext of all the literature he was exposed to and, one could assume, would later write. It is manifested most acutely as a fear of abandonment and annihilation echoed, for instance, in Mrs Tulsis's pronouncement after the birth of Biswas's daughter Savi that his children, 'would survive: they couldn't be killed' (*House* 533). It surfaces again in the final chapter of *The Enigma of Arrival*, 'The Ceremony of Farewell,' where Naipaul recalls the puja he attended for his deceased sister, Sati. In the midst of loss and death, an almost unbelievable realisation of survival dawns that discloses a pre-existent cloud of terror and doubt: 'We had made ourselves anew.... There was no ship of antique shape now to take us back. We had come out of the nightmare; and there was nowhere else to go.'[11]

Cudjoe's careful analysis of *A House for Mr Biswas* as a reinvention of the *Ramayana* epic to represent the 'ambiguity of a new social situation' (1988, 65), is therefore corroborated by Naipaul's personal affinity to the Ramlila. This reading gives further credence to the author's method of mythological reconstruction as a means of narrating New World experience. Interestingly, however, while the Rama/Biswas, Sita/Shama reversal is noted, along with the 'scarcely' distinguishable 'whitewashed features' of the Hanuman statue perched on the Tulsi's mansion (1982, 81), Cudjoe does not draw attention to the deity's role as storyteller. According to Philip Lutgendorf, the 'Ramayana tradition' holds that Hanuman is 'the original narrator of the tale of Rama,' but his 'perfect narrative became irretrievably "lost" surviving only in fragments through the lenses of human storytellers: Valmiki, Kampan, Krittibasa, Tulsidas, and so on.'[12]

In the Hindu pantheon, writing is more readily associated with Lord Ganesha, the elephant-God, whom Naipaul evokes in *The Mystic Masseur*, a satirical account of the would-be writer, Ganesh Ramsumair. However, Lutgendorf reminds us that Hanuman traditionally holds the status of divine storyteller whose tale is further authenticated by the fact that he is a key participant. His 'lost' but intentionally 'pure' *Ramayana* text, however, by virtue of its subsequent retellings transfer the tale from a sacrosanct 'truth' narrative to the subjective and re-creative terrain of storytelling and myth. So attention is drawn to the flexibility and open-endedness of all signification practices. Notions of originality and authenticity are therefore brought into question. In this regard, Robert Antoni's *Divina Trace* is of interest since his text notably transgresses these borders in its radical reconstruction of the *Ramayana* as a New World creation story.[13]

Section two of Antoni's novel, 'A Piece of Pommerac,' features Hanuman in three disparate but subtly related discourses. Ultimately all versions escape complete decipherability due to character doublings, multiple narrators, role reversals and, in the case of the middle book, 'Hanuman Speaks of the Monkey Tribes,' a coded 'monkey language' that parodies the 'truth' claims of all signification practices and discourses whether scientific, philosophical or religious. The institutionalised indicators of textual authority and authenticity such as linearity, rationality and originality are thereby displaced. In these versions, Hanuman is not the original narrator of the Rama and Sita tale as tradition holds, but the 'cuss' wielding 'monkeyscribe' of a 'yana' dictated by a deceased 'Uncle Valmiki,' the Caribbean transmutation of the revered creator of the *Ramayana* archetype, Valmiki.

In Antoni's retelling, the very notion of 'creative mimicry' is turned on its head as the epic poet is the deified muse who dictates to a self-doubting less than extraordinary monkey that can 'only scribble verbatim what he me tell' (*Divina Trace* 1991, 214). Yet mimicry as mere copying is undermined because Hanuman reproduces the master's text in 'mirror-form' or 'reverse' of what he hears, as well as invents his own version of incidents. He is therefore not the dependable guide of religious lore, but a partial narrator of Corpus Christi's fragmentary history, where factual discontinuities, faith and cultural diversities are enmeshed in a seemingly unending genealogy of cross-fertilisations that comprise an as yet not fully decipherable Creole nation-story.

Unlike Antoni, Naipaul makes no overt connection between the narrator of *A House for Mr Biswas* and Hanuman; however, the deity hovers in the shadow of the text's omniscient narrator, who in turn is but a shadow of the author. Additionally, the imaginative licence he takes with the *Ramayana* is arguably less transgressive than Antoni's. Yet, *A House for Mr Biswas* writes back to the 'master' texts of the author's ancestral tradition by making its content relevant to his historical and social context. The novel not only invites cognizance of the crisis of signification in the changing social ethos of colonial Trinidad, but (in its indigenisation of the Rama and Sita myth) adds a New World version to Hanuman's mythic long tail/tale.[14] Therefore, Biswas's unaccommodated state which fuels his agonised search for a literal and existential architectural fit is arguably analogous to the author's own search for a house of style, coming from a context where the myriad historical displacements of the postcolonial experience are incompatible, as Bhabha argues, with the aesthetic and ideological assumptions inlaid in a claim such as Iris Murdoch's that the 'novel must be a house for free people to live in.'[15] Calling to mind Harris's early dissatisfactions with the impulse to 'consolidation' in the nineteenth century novel,[16] Bhabha provocatively interrupts Murdoch's statement by asking the following questions: 'Must the novel be a house? What kind of narrative can house unfree people? Is the novel also a house where the unhomely can live?' ('The World' 1992, 142).

Certainly, Hanuman House is the overarching symbol of an acute condition of 'the unhomely' in the circumstances of Biswas's story. The slow disintegration of the Tulsi dynasty and Biswas's sense of existential displacement are, in fact, evidence of the uncomfortable emergence of a new cultural sensibility, national space and world order in which he is simultaneously trying to locate himself. Once inside the Tulsi fortress, it becomes clear that its 'thick' stoic walls and windowless rooms are not impervious to the advance of an encroaching world. This invasion is parodied, for instance, in the household's adoption of the Christian tradition of eating salmon on Good Friday, the influence, the narrator suggests, of the 'orthodox Roman Catholic Hindu Mrs Tulsi' (*House* 1982, 138). Then there is Seth's exasperated exclamation that 'this house is like a republic already' (123) in reaction to Mr Biswas's 'paddle your own canoe' rebelliousness (107). The motto that establishes him as a sign of transience that interrupts the accustomed relational frames of the clan, their myths of containment and politics of stability.

Additionally, overseen as it is by the partially recognisable shadow of a 'slightly sinister' Hanuman, an aura of duplicity and trickery surrounds the Tulsis' dwelling where life proceeds in a chimerical mingling of shadow and light, appearance and reality, past and present. These dualities are evident, for instance, in Shama's prank in providing black stockings for an African customer whom she thinks is unrealistically demanding flesh-coloured ones; Mr Biswas's role as the marginalised house fool and pretender; Mrs. Tulsi's feigned bouts of sickness that mask her authoritarian excesses; and the wooden bridge that almost umbilically connects the modern concrete building and the original termite-eaten house. More significantly, the trauma associated with change is displayed in the uneasy disparity between the internal life of Hanuman House and the reality of the world outside. The narrator articulates Mr Biswas's sense of being ambivalently situated between the old assurances of the now disintegrating feudal law of the Tulsi clan and the attractions of independence offered by the emerging modern nation as follows: 'At Hanuman House everything had appeared simple and reasonable. Outside, he was stunned.... [Yet] in the press of daughters, sons-in-laws and children, he had begun to feel lost, unimportant and even frightened' (1982, 95–6).

In a certain sense, Naipaul's temperamentally ambivalent Hanuman can be read as a symbol of the discomforting effects of change that attend a world in transition where unfamiliar hybridities may disconcert and even 'shock,' but ultimately signal the arrival of the new. This role as cultural bridge intersects somewhat with a brief appearance of the figure in Lakshmi Persaud's *Butterfly in the Wind.* Early in the novel, Kamala, the young narrator, triumphantly shares her reconciliation with the illogic of a nursery rhyme about a cow that jumped over the moon by interfacing it with a tale her grandmother told about Hanuman who once swallowed the moon, having mistaken it for an 'attractive berry.'[17] Incidentally, the better known story tells of Hanuman's swallowing of the sun, not the moon, which results in him being wounded by a thunderbolt.[18] Nevertheless, whether Kamala's recall of the tale is a product of the disorientation caused by the imposed 'contrary' material of her Western-style education; a diasporic transmutation of the original on her grandmother's part; or an 'error' of memory, the deity fuels an accommodative leap of imagination across the apparently disparate and unevenly valued sources of cultural knowledge.

The literal 'dark' and perceptual destabilisation produced as a result of Hanuman's playful swallowing of the sun/moon aptly symbolises the psycho-spiritual disorientation generated by the sudden clash of cultures. However, the often traumatic dynamic of cross-cultural encounter is quickly resolved as Kamala reasons, 'if the moon can be kept in one's mouth, a cow can jump over it' (*Butterfly in the Wind* 1990, 17). The effect is that the familiar and unfamiliar find common ground on the basis of a recognisable point of comparison and so evokes, though only superficially, what Wilson Harris theorises as the creolising trick of an '*involuntary* association' in which difference is accommodated via a perceived similarity of traits.[19] While Harris's theorising of the process suggests a transforming confluence that disturbs the neat borders that demark otherness, Persaud seems satisfied with maintaining an associative parallel that allows for the recognition, and even appreciation of similarity, but preserves the integrity of the separate cultural traditions.[20] This careful policing of the borders of difference is perhaps symptomatic of a fear of cultural erosion or even contamination in the burgeoning multicultural environment.

Naipaul, in contrast, offers no simple resolutions. Hanuman is assigned a multifaceted, contradictory nature: he is simultaneously prankish, sinister and kind – the ambivalent overseer of a house where worlds intersect, albeit uncomfortably, in Trinidad's changing socio-political and cultural space. Of this the text is the aesthetic image. This paradoxical play of traits embodied by the monkey god is actually not uncharacteristic since in the Hindu pantheon he belongs to a 'class of ambivalent deities,' as the eleventh avatar of Rudra/Shiva (the destroyer).[21] Although the deity's benevolence is popularly recognised in orthodox Hinduism, it is his tricky, duplicitous trait that Naipaul chooses to negotiate the text's mytho-religious reworking of the Rama and Sita story of exile and homecoming. For Biswas, there is no triumphant return to stability, no illuminated pathway of return to a lost, original home, symbolised by his disconsolate movement from one imperfect, partially completed house to the next.

Yet the evocation of Hanuman's ambivalent nature provokes a consideration of Biswas's condition as being more than one of divine abandonment in the 'wilderness' of Trinidad. Rather, one is invited to ask if Naipaul is in fact pointing to the need for a reinterpretation and rediscovery of the deity's meanings and functions in the altered realities of a modern, New World order. Is it possible to suggest that Hanuman has undergone some sort of imaginative and diasporic transformation or maybe even a process of creolisation in sociocultural conditions where fresh ways of seeing and daring creative methods are required? Is Naipaul teasing out his own aesthetic/spiritual connection between the New World writer/storyteller/seeker and the figure of the monkey?

A response to these questions seems discernible in his 'Prologue to an Autobiography' where he takes his time to give details about his writing posture in the BBC's freelancers' room, then located in the Langham Hotel:

> My shoulders were thrown back as far as they could go; my spine was arched. My knees were drawn right up; my shoes rested on the topmost struts of the chair, left side and right side. So, with my legs wide apart, I sat at the typewriter with something like a monkey crouch (2003, 60).

Though sleight of hand, he returns to the monkey figure about 20 years after it first appeared in *A House for Mr Biswas*. The pose, he admits to be 'unusual,' but seems, in retrospect, to offer it as a kind of trademark or an odd particularity of style, which he remembers holding as he wrote the infectious tales of *Miguel Street*, stories of his early Trinidadian experience. This is a writer who knows the game of self-construction, as well as his relationship to the tricky art of narration. As a New World mimic man of style, he straddled streams of narrative, religious and philosophical influences on which he is free to draw. Memory is evoked as the conspiratorial agent that traverses barriers of time, space and consciousness to engineer an imaginative return to the 'material' of home from which he had sought to detach himself. That 'moment' in the freelancers' room is therefore staged as a pivotal chapter in his writing journey because it offered him the wisdom that 'to write, it was necessary to go back. It was the beginning of self-knowledge' ('Prologue' 2003, 79).

Further, this strategic positioning of the writer, awkwardly yet productively constrained by a monkey crouch, mirrors his discovery of an economy of style that emerges after much misdirected attempts to write. Naipaul explains that the arrival of the first two sentences, one fact and the other invention, which began the enigmatic story 'Bogart' opened the way for the style he adopted, for they had 'created the world of the street' and 'set up a rhythm, a speed, which dictated all that was to follow' ('Prologue' 2003, 58). Yet the writer, particularly one with a colonial background, is always a kind of mimic man as the image of the monkey self-ironically suggests. So even as one is tempted to claim that he discovers something of an indigenous style in the Langham Hotel, this has to be understood in relation to his as yet unsettled hybridised identity as a colonial caught in an ongoing process of cultural and imaginative 'diaspora-ization,' to borrow what Stuart Hall acknowledges as an 'ugly term.'[22]

In this regard, a direct connection can be made with James Clifford's 'hotel chronotope' and Naipaul's representation of himself as the relocated immigrant, West Indian (monkey) writer.[23] On the one hand, the freelancers' room is paradoxically characterised by a 'hotel atmosphere,' busy with 'chat' 'movement.' On the other, a haughty 'Victorian-Edwardian' gloom hangs over it evoking the economy of servitude, suggested by the author's speculation that it might have been a pantry ('Prologue' 2003, 60). Histories, cultures, traditions and geographies traffic and interchange as island and metropole, past and present, permanence and temporality, scribal and oral, inspiration and craft, memory and invention come to bear on a location that is plagued by its own uncertainties and governed by transience. Moreover, marked as it is by travel and encounter, the room is the quintessential metaphor of the modern, cross-cultural global matrix in which the writer is inserted.

Hybridity and travel characterise in Naipaul's self-portrait as the monkey-scribe that imaginatively governs the hotel/writing room. As mimic, illusive mischief-maker and mocker, the figure functions as an intercultural and transcultural totem of 'creative ambivalence' which, in this instance, expands the meaning of Brathwaite's 'indigenization' as part of the process of 'Caribbean culturation,' to more actively incorporate both the intercultural and transnational features of Caribbean identity.[24] This radical decentering of cultural and imaginative locations perhaps accounts for the fact that, unlikes

A House for Mr Biswas, the trickster-monkey in the 'Prologue' is not overtly identified with the Hindu pantheon, but is left open to the play of ethnic and transcultural links that inform Naipaul's bank of mythology as a New World writer.

One such connection is the crossroads figure of the Afro-Creole Caribbean folk tradition, the spider Ananse. Interestingly, this figure lurks in the shadow of his reference to Earnest Eytle, a fellow freelancer from Guyana.[25] Naipaul recalls that during thinking pauses in his writing, Eylte habitually swept his hand down his forehead 'like a man brushing away cobwebs' ('Prologue' 2003, 60), evoking a connection with death, the man and the writing, thereby allegorising the issue of aesthetic renewal and the (post) colonial writer. The spider 'trace,' so to speak, which is also a sign of the (spider) monkey, is central to the Caribbean's oral tradition and invites associations with the ritual ending of the storyteller's tale: 'crick-crack.' The communal and open-ended qualities signal the need for participatory responses such as the one Merle Hodge offers in her novel *Crick Crack Monkey*, the title of which alludes to the characteristic interface of orality with Caribbean literary practice, as well as the creative trickery of narration.[26] The Hindu association is therefore an insufficient base for reading Naipaul's posture since it appears that the author is subtly weaving himself into a more diverse symbolic and narrative tradition that includes but expands beyond Hanuman.

Arguably, then, in keeping with the text's subtle intercultural mythological play, the monkey image is further elaborated to interface with the 'dancing dwarf,' which surfaces in his semi-autobiographical story 'How I Left Miguel Street,' to which he returns in the 'Prologue,' as he does with the 'Bogart' story. In that story of leave-taking, the protagonist remembers: 'I left them all and walked briskly towards the aeroplane, not looking back, looking only at my shadow before me, a dancing dwarf on the tarmac' (Prologue' 2003, 78). The creature is the shadow of the colonial mimic (monkey) man, a sign of his inescapable and disruptive double-consciousness or more appropriately multiple-consciousness. Of course, several things happen at once. Naipaul as the self-alienated 'colonised man,' is 'tethered' to the complexity of his own shadow that 'splits' and (self) satirises his 'presence,' historically fractures and culturally re-synthesises his 'being,' located as he is on the ground of creative ambivalence between resistance and assimilation.[27]

As he departs from his native island, the many mythological traditions and cultural influences of his formation as an Indian growing up in the multicultural environment of colonial Trinidad leave with him. Like the diminutive, trickster monkey that simultaneously mimics and creatively inspires the young Naipaul at the typewriter, the dwarf, with its half-formed, childish nature represents his awareness that he is a physical and literary 'small man' seeking to infiltrate, by imaginative cunning, the great tradition of Western literature. More importantly, as the dwarf plays mischievously on the airport's tarmac, the site of departures and arrivals, the creature is the trickster mascot that prefigures the life of writing to which he journeys, just as the 'Prologue,' with its intricate plays between fact and fiction, old and new writing acts, foreshadow the fictional 'autobiography' to come – most likely *The Enigma of Arrival*. Every act of writing is therefore a shadow of what has gone before where the distinctions between truth and fiction, as well as the historical past and present are blurred. This accounts for the many returns to previous texts, that narrative design on which the 'Prologue' is structured as he moves intuitively, step by step, towards fresh ground and insight. Hence the logic of his declaration that his 'last book contained all the others' ('Two Worlds' 2003, 183).

As a symbol of all that lies 'outside the orbit of consciousness,'[28] a connection is forged between the dwarf and Naipaul's sense of writing as a mysterious and 'intuitive' journey to 'widening vision and a widening world.'[29] His process is therefore the patient incremental accumulation of knowledge. This approach to writing as a path to illumination is not merely intellectual, but is also deeply spiritual, having its roots in Naipaul's belief that he continues a vocation given to him by his father, Seepersad Naipaul, his literary predecessor who chose writing as a 'version of the pundit's vocation' ('Prologue' 2003, 96). It is highly significant that the prologue of *A House for Mr Biswas* ends with an image of the idle, yellow typewriter, since its colour is an erratic act of rebellion against the black border that the colonial newspaper, the *Sentinel*, had carried in an elaborate show of mourning for the Pope's death (*House* 1982, 13). The typewriter would be the vehicle of illumination against ignorance and the fragmentary knowledge and ideological biases of his colonial formation. Writing in this context seems to intersect with the triumphant dance of Shiva, of whom Hanuman is a manifestation, on the prostrate body of a dwarf.[30] The son, however, would transcend his father's limitations through the telling of many more tales.

Conclusion

In writing about Kamau Brathwaite's use of the 'twin-natured' Ananse and Legba in *The Arrivants* as symbols of the 'ambiguity of the New World experience,' Gordon Rohlehr draws a useful parallel with Wilson Harris's conviction that the artist must move beyond historical ruin to renewal. He argues that in accordance with this vision, Brathwaite begins with 'the image of diminished man – (Ananse, Legba)' and 'moves slowly and circuitously towards a vision of creative possibility,' knowing that

> ...it will require a long journey through spiritual time and space, before either the artist or the society is in a position to invoke Ananse in his capacity as 'creator' or Legba in his restored capacity as the god of beginning and rebirth.[31]

While Naipaul is largely read as being preoccupied with the ruin of history, having as he claims, 'come into a world past its peak' (*Enigma* 1987, 26), it is possible to discern connections to a similar mythopoetic process of loss and renewal in his deployment of the monkey totem.

Apart from bearing the mark of an ambivalent, dual nature, Hanuman, almost like Legba who is 'keeper of the door of the material world and *Les Invisibles*,' is literally the wounded, cosmic middleman, half-human and divine, who travels between worlds and builds causeways across oceans.[32] He is an agent of contact who initiates and oversees the disruptive uncertainties that visit re-creative change, a function that is embedded in his connection with Shiva, the deity of change and time or variously 'the eater of worlds' who mirrors Hanuman's own ravenous appetite (Lutgendorf 2007, 188). In Naipaul's usage, the deity's ambivalent shadow seems to interplay with its many diasporic manifestations as it oversees the necessary movement towards adaptation and survival. The young Naipaul discovers the creative possibilities of such negotiations in the Langham Hotel to which he returns much later with deeper understanding at the memorial puja for Sati, which he remembers as staged on the terrazzo floor of her suburban house and officiated by a comfortably 'ecumenical' pundit. In that context, the realisation arrives that 'we remade the world for ourselves' (*Enigma* 313, 318).

At the conclusion of *The Enigma of Arrival*, Naipaul seems less troubled by the inevitability of cultural confluence and sheds the anxious and guilt-ridden condition of consorting with difference in the Tulsi household in

A House for Mr Biswas. This early text shares, but with less defensiveness, Persaud's anxiety about change in *Butterfly in the Wind*, where one can discern the operation of a cautious hybridity that is circumspect about the meeting with cultural difference. For Persaud, Hanuman is a temporary bridge across differences and also preserver of a distinctively Hindu identity placed on the defensive in the Westernised colonial environment of the school. Naipaul is likewise disturbed. He seems more accepting, however, though ironically so, of the ambivalence of being positioned between worlds. He does not display Antoni's recklessly playful deconstruction of cultural borders, although in the 'Prologue' his monkey-scribe seems to revel in the creative possibilities of the transnational, 'unhomely' imagination, and in *The Enigma of Arrival* the writer appears to acknowledge the miracle of survival in throes of change.

For Naipaul, inherent in what it means to be a writer from the West Indies is the slow and circuitous coming to terms with the fact that structural frameworks and ideological certainties of an old order have been disrupted, leaving in their wake a world without easy closures; no happy returns to ancestral homes; no reassuring retreats to a culturally pure space or group; as yet no ready made architecture of style to contain its new realities. Yet, as a sign of pregnant liminality, clever shape-shifter and restorer of cosmic order empowered to leap through time and space, the figure of Hanuman teases the imagination into a consideration of its function as an appropriate totem for the New World's diasporic ethos of cross cultural confluence and travel, as well as the aesthetic and philosophical embodiment of what is necessary to narrate its stories.

Notes

1. Naipaul, V.S. 'Two Worlds.' In *Literary Occasions: Essays* (London: Picador, 2003), 183.
2. Quoted in Selwyn Cudjoe, *V.S. Naipaul: A Materialist Reading* (Amherst: The University of Massachusetts Press, 1988), 28.
3. Cudjoe 1988, 64–5; *A House for Mr Biswas* (1961; repr., London: Penguin Books, 1982). Apart from *A House for Mr Biswas*, Cudjoe mentions *The Mystic Masseur* (1967) in this regard. See Cudjoe 1988, 42–5, 64.
4. In *Literary Occasions: Essays* (2003), 60.
5. See Henry Louis Gates, Jr, *The Signifying Monkey: A Theory of African American Literary Criticism* (New York and Oxford: Oxford University Press, 1988), chapters 1, 5 and 17.

6. José Piedra, 'From Monkey Tales to Cuban Songs: On Signification,' *MLN* 1000, no.2, Hispanic Issue (March 1985): 362. He notes its appearance in Cuban discourse the Latin American literature.
7. Wilson Harris, *The Four Banks of the River Space* (London: Faber and Faber, 1990), 153. Harris quotes this passage from *The Four Banks* at length in the essay 'The Unfinished Genesis of the Imagination,' in order to make the intricate point about the interconnectivity of inner and outer time, space, consciousness, cultures and bodies that together enact a paradoxical drama of destruction and renewal, guilt and redemption. For Harris the 'therapeutic edge' to the histories of violence that wound the collective human psyche is dependent on the bridging and healing of the fissures caused by the failure to visualise 'the stranger in ourselves' (Bundy 1999, 248–60).
8. Homi Bhabha, 'The World and the Home,' *Social Text*, No. 31/32, Third World and Post-Colonial Issues (1992): 141.
9. Bhabha, *The Location of Culture* (London: Routledge, 1994), 85–6. He uses the phrase 'almost the same, *but not quite*,' to refer to the '*ambivalence* of mimicry' where the gap between 'imitation' and 'mockery' destabilises the colonising demand for sameness.
10. Naipaul, *Reading and Writing: A Personal Account* (New York: The New York Review of Books, 2000), 12–13.
11. Naipaul, *The Enigma of Arrival* (London: Penguin Books, 1987), 317.
12. See Phillip Lutgendorf, *Hanuman's Tale: The Messages of a Divine Monkey* (Oxford: Oxford University Press, 2007), where he traces the various versions and representations of Hanuman in Hinduism, which includes the story of the magical growth of the deity's tail (35–88).
13. Robert Antoni, *Divina Trace* (London: Robin Clark, 1991).
14. See Lutgendorf (2007), 132. In one of the versions, Hanuman is struck by Indra with a thunderbolt for his deed. The blow leaves him with a permanently disfigured left chin that results in his name that means 'one having a distinctive chin.'
15. Quoted in Bhabha, 'The World and the Home,' (1992), 142.
16. 'Tradition and the West Indian Novel,' in *Tradition, the Writer and Society: Critical Essays* (London: New Beacon Publications, 1967), 28.
17. Lakshmi Persaud, *Butterfly in the Wind* (London: Peepal Tree Press, 1990), 17.
18. See note 14.
19. Harris, 'Creoleness: The Crossroads of A Civilization?' *Selected Essays: The Unfinished Genesis of the Imagination.* ed. Andrew Bundy (London: Routledge, 1999), 239.
20. Interestingly, the same logic of association is repeated later in the text when she is deeply traumatised by her exposure to Catholicism, which she describes as an entry to 'a place unknown to her' (1990, 141), where 'a certain kind of reasoning was beginning to gnaw at the roots of all the things [she] held dear' (1990, 144). Any inner turbulence caused is easily resolved by the intervention of her father's swift wisdom. He simply reasons, 'one group is using hell to keep us in line and the other is using reincarnation' (1990, 146).

21. Lutgendorf (2007, 44). He also notes the deity's ambivalent positioning between 'the dark side of the Vedic cosmos' according to ancient worship and Valmiki's placement of him in the 'luminous realm of the celestial Vishnu' in his epic (87–8).
22. Stuart Hall, 'New Ethnicities,' In *Stuart Hall: Critical Dialogues in Cultural Studies*, eds. David Morley and Kuan-Hsing Chen. (London: Routledge, 1996), 447. Hall uses the term to refer to the 'unsettling' process of 'hybritization' that characterises the 'black experience,' which in his reading of 'black' includes the Asian diaspora.
23. See James Clifford, *Routes: Travel and Translation in the Late Twentieth Century* (Cambridge: Harvard University Press, 1997), chapter 1. He identifies the 'hotel chronotope' as representative of the modern metaphor of travel and exchange; one that is plagued by its own 'levels of ambivalence' since it is 'negatively viewed as transience, superficiality, tourism, exile, and rootlessness,' and 'positively conceived as exploration, research, escape and transforming encounter…' (1997, 31).
24. The term is employed here in Edward 'Kamau' Brathwaite's sense to mean the 'ambivalent acceptance-rejection syndrome' that marks 'Caribbean culturation' in which 'imitation (acculturation)' is the basis for 'native creation (indigenization).' *Contradictory Omens: Cultural diversity and integration in the Caribbean* (Kingston: Savacou Publications, 1974), 15–6.
25. Earnest Eytle is best known for his book on Sir Frank Worrell. See *Frank Worrell* (London: Hodder & Stoughton, 1963) with a foreword by Sir Learie Constantine and chapter commentaries by Frank Worrell.
26. See Merle Hodge's *Crick Crack* Monkey (1970; repr., London: Heinemann, 1981), 13.
27. Bhabha argues that 'the image of post-Enlightenment man tethered to, *not* confronted by, his dark reflection, the shadow of colonized man, that splits his presence, distorts his outline, breaches his boundaries, repeats his action at a distance, disturbs and divides the very time of his being' in 'Remembering Fanon: Self, Psyche and the Colonial Condition,' in *Colonial Discourse and Post-colonial Theory: A Reader,* eds. Patrick Williams and Laura Chrisman (New York: Prentice Hall/ Harvester Wheatsheaf, 1994),27. The link lends support to the cross-cultural nuances of monkey/dwarf image.
28. J. E. Cirlot, *A Dictionary of Symbols* (Mineola, New York: Dover Publications, 2002), 91.
29. Naipaul, 'Foreword to *A House for Mr Biswas,*' In *Literary Occasions: Essays*, 132.
30. The dance is indicative of the triumph of wisdom over ignorance. See Cirlot (2002), 91.
31. Edward Brathwaite, *The Arrivants: A New World Trilogy* (Oxford: Oxford University Press, 1973); Gordon Rohlehr, *Pathfinder: Black Awakening in the Arrivants of Edward Kamau Brathwaite* (Port of Spain, Trinidad: 1981), 195–6.
32. Rohlehr (1981), 194. Also, Legba is the Fon version of Esu, and as Gates demonstrates is called the 'father of the Monkey' in Fon myth. See Gates (1988), 17.

Section Three

Rethinking Naipaul on the Thresholds of History and New Horizons

10

V.S. NAIPAUL AND THE INTERIOR EXPEDITIONS: *'It is Impossible to Make a Step Without the Indians'*

Sandra Pouchet Paquet

'It is impossible to make a step without the Indians' is a phrase that William Hilhouse, surveyor and plantation owner in the Demerara region of colonial Guyana, used in his 'Account of British Guiana.'[1] In his essay '"It's Impossible to Make a Step without the Indians": Nineteenth-Century Geographical Exploration and the Amerindians of British Guiana,' D. Graham Burnett describes Hillhouse's 'Account' as a colonial handbook that never found a publisher (2002, 13). Burnett calls attention to the way that published accounts of expeditions of surveyors and explorers like Hilhouse and Richard Schomburgk

> ...did a certain kind of colonial work, narrowly shaping the histories and characters of indigenous people to conform to the needs of the colony. Still closer examination of that writing provided dramatic evidence that this work involved minimizing Amerindian knowledge and power in an effort to reflect the superiority of the European and to validate the virtue of the colonial project (2002, 33–4).

This essay explores some of the ways in which V.S. Naipaul shapes the histories and characters of indigenous peoples in Trinidad and Guyana in *The Middle Passage: Impressions of Five Societies – British, French and Dutch in the West Indies and South America* (1962), in *The Loss of El Dorado: A*

History (1969), *A Way in the World* (1994) (subtitled a 'novel' in the 1995 Vintage edition), *Reading and Writing: a Personal Account* (2000), and the Nobel Lecture 'Two Worlds' (2001), with a view to assessing unresolved incongruities in his various representations.[2] I argue that in respect to the way he shapes the history and character of indigenous peoples over a span of some 39 years, Naipaul moves away from the traditional imperial models of cross-cultural exploration he identifies in the travel narratives of Aldous Huxley, D.H. Lawrence, and Evelyn Waugh, through a more rigorous imaginative inquiry into history, to something approaching what Wilson Harris might describe as 'an art of compassion' that unravels the blocked formations of a colonial relationship.[3]

In a reversal of the historical chronology that this analytical approach might imply, I would like to begin by noting the elegiac tone with which Naipaul situates the original inhabitants of his native Chaguanas in his 2001 Nobel Lecture:

> Chaguanas was a strange name, in spelling and pronunciation, and many of the Indian people – they were in the majority in the area – preferred to call it by the Indian caste name of Chauhan. I was 34 when I found out about the name of my birthplace. I was living in London, had been living in England for 16 years. I was writing my ninth book. This was a history of Trinidad, a human history, trying to re-create people and their stories. I used to go to the British Museum to read the Spanish documents about the region (n.p.).

Naipaul recounts his shock on discovering a letter from King Philip IV of Spain dated October 12, 1625 to the Governor of Trinidad, perhaps Don Luís de Monsalves (1624–31), instructing him to punish the Chaguanes for their intractability to Spanish rule and for conspiring with the English:

> What the governor did I don't know. I could find no further reference to the Chaguanes in the documents in the Museum.... What is true is that the little tribe of over a thousand – who would have been living on both sides of the Gulf of Paria – disappeared so completely that no one in the town of Chaguanas or Chauhan knew anything about them. And the thought came to me in the Museum that I was the first person since 1625 to whom that letter of the king of Spain had a real meaning. And that letter had been

> dug out of the archives only in 1896 or 1897. A disappearance, and then the silence of centuries (Nobel Lecture n.p.). [4]

Naipaul pauses to lament the erasure of the Chaguanes from the annals of Trinidad's history and the consciousness of those who succeeded them in that landscape over time.[5] The absence of the Chaguanes from popular consciousness in Trinidad, and the compulsion to reiterate the fact of their erasure marks this discovery as an epiphany of sorts in the unravelling of the maze of deception within historical revelation and self-revelation.

In the previous year, Naipaul had published *Reading and Writing* with the New York Review of Books. In the title essay, Naipaul expresses similar sentiments in a brief mention of the same sequence of events: time spent in the British Museum studying old documents, among them, a selection from the Spanish archives (32–3).

Naipaul writes on this occasion that his quest for local history in the British Museum, that is, a history of the former island colony, uncovered a framework for revisiting earlier judgments about indigenous peoples whom he nonetheless condemns to inescapable ruin in our time. Yet, he writes that he remains haunted, by 'the thought of the vanished aborigines, on whose land and among whose spirits we all lived' (35), which suggests a recognition of mutuality or shared experience in lieu of the seemingly absolute Otherness that characterises *The Middle Passage*:

> This was more than a fact about aborigines. It to some extent altered my own past. I could no longer think of the *Ramlila* I had seen as a child as occurring at the very beginning of things. I had imaginatively to make room for people of another kind on the *Ramlila* ground. Fiction by itself would not have taken me to this larger comprehension (*Reading and Writing 2000,* 35–6).

Naipaul's assessment of the experience so many years after the actual event is interesting, in that, he makes a clear argument for the subversive value of historical/colonial records despite the partial truths and poverty of conception that characterises them; they enable a revisualisation of time and space and a consciousness of the relativity of the self's relationship to cultural environment, and myths of racial and ethnic origin. Altered concepts of place, space, and landscape reveal a hidden dimension in history that is self-revelatory and potentially transforming. The critique of his efforts in *The*

Middle Passage (1962), long after the fact in *Reading and Writing*, suggests that his altered vision occasions a Wilson Harris-like 'unraveling of self-deception within self-revelation.'[6] In Naipaul's words, one result was 'to have a new vision of what one had been born into and to have an intimation of a sequence of historical events going far back' (*Reading and Writing*, 30). The experience Naipaul describes, though written with a clarity and purposefulness that differs sharply from Wilson Harris's characteristic style, constitutively resembles Harris's concept of 'creative erosion,' which links the discovery of 'alternative realities,' previously obscured in the void of colonial history, 'to a new scale or illumination of the meaning of "community."'[7]

While an elegiac sense of loss pervades Naipaul's more recent references to the erasure of an aboriginal people in Trinidad, my purpose here is to connect the dots, so to speak, to question the interior journey over time that the written record implies; a journey that for my purposes begins with the publication of Naipaul's *The Middle Passage* some 50 years ago. If historical research and writing are an essential part of that journey, as Naipaul explains in *Reading and Writing*, travel and travel writing with its distinct expeditionary values are also an essential component of this pilgrim's progress:

> For all its faults, the book [*The Middle Passage*], like the fiction books that had gone before, was for me an extension of knowledge and feeling. It wouldn't have been possible for me to unlearn what I had learned. Fiction, the exploration of one's immediate circumstances, had taken me a lot of the way. Travel had taken me further (1979, 30–1).

Naipaul's observation confirms a dynamic relationship among the different genres he employs in individual texts and over time as enabling different elements of learning and thus of personal growth. It is as though each has limitations from which he has to liberate himself. In respect to *The Middle Passage*, he writes much later in *Reading and Writing* of his difficulty in travelling 'for a book' (2000, 30).

This trouble with the 'I' of the travel writer is observable in the hierarchical judgments the narrator makes in *The Middle Passage* in respect to the Amerindians he encounters in Guyana. His first impulse is to distance and differentiate in the time-honoured reductive colonial fashion: 'This was my first sight of these people, known fearfully to Trinidadians as "wild Indians" and contemptuously referred to as "Bucks" by coastland Guianese' (*Middle*

Passage 1979, 104). The alien space the Amerindians occupy within the state that is their native land is at first unsympathetically underscored in relation to Afro-Guyanese:

> The exotics were not the Amerindians whom I was seeing in quantity for the first time, but the two Negro policemen in smart black uniforms and bush hats. And this, too, was a singular reversal of the roles, this policing of Amerindians by Negroes: in the days of slavery the Amerindians were employed to hunt down runaway slaves. And now these policemen spoke to me of the Amerindians as of some primitive, unpredictable people, who needed to be watched (*Middle Passage* 1979, 105).

Though the narrator in turn distances himself from the policemen suggesting the superior status of the traveller as observer-recorder and evaluator of cultural mores, the policemen's judgment is reinforced when, on the next page, the narrator comments on savannah fires: 'The fires are started by ranchers who wish to burn away the grass-choking sedge; and more indiscriminately, in defiance of the law, by Amerindians, who like to see the savannah burn;' and for good measure, he adds, 'at times, I was told, whole mountains are on fire. After such a fire the savannah becomes truly lunar; a landscape in with curling copper leaves hang on gnarled, artificial-looking trees rising out of the black ground' (*Middle Passage* 1979, 106–7).

In *The Loss of El Dorado*, published seven years later, Naipaul offers a correction to this assessment of the Amerindians as mindless arsonists, when he recounts that they in fact once used fire in the savannahs very successfully as a weapon of attack: 'Sudden fire on the brown grasslands encircled and consumed all the hundred and seventy men. Two years later the local Indians, exaggerating, told Raleigh they had killed three hundred' (*The Loss of El Dorado* 1973, 39). This explanation is later repeated by an elder of the Amerindian community in Chapter Three of *A Way in the World*. Yet in the earlier travel narrative *The Middle Passage*, the sense of latent Amerindian menace lingers in the narrative with unexamined observations such as, 'Everyone knows that Amerindians hunted down runaway slaves; it was something I heard again and again, from white and black; and on the Rumpununi, and wherever one sees Amerindians, it is a chilling memory' (1979, 107). In the absence of any recognition that this hunting of runaway slaves was an arrangement managed by European settlers and administrators with specific tribal groups, the myth of the compulsive hunter of men and the bloodthirsty savage is uncritically reified, perhaps for the reader's edification and certainly to assuage the narrator's guilt at finding them repulsive. Though Naipaul cites Michael Swan's *The Marches of El Dorado* (1958), and Swan's book was published with a range of references to his predecessors in expeditionary writing, including the works of Walter Roth so admired by Wilson Harris, this does not result in further investigation into the history and character of the Amerindians in Guyana at the time. He is distracted by the immediate reality of Amerindian/African hostilities, which in turn blinds him to the gap in his historical understanding. Similarly, he cites Richard Schomburgk not for the wealth of knowledge the latter had acquired about indigenous peoples, but rather to make a point about the Victoria lily, which Schomburgk got credit for 'discovering' which made him famous.

In *The Middle Passage*, cross-cultural exploration is stymied by a lack of communication between the observer-narrator and the Amerindians whom he observes, a hypersensitivity to observed cultural differences, and the predictable sense of vulnerability, perhaps fear, that the narrator expresses: 'I had tried hard to feel an interest in the Amerindians as a whole, but had failed. I couldn't read their faces; I couldn't understand their language, and could never gauge at what level communication was possible' (1979, 111). Recognising the nature of the problem in part, the narrative deteriorates into a projection of a felt personal failure onto the Amerindians themselves in the deepening mask of their Otherness. He continues:

> Among more complex peoples there are certain individuals who have the power to transmit to you their sense of defeat and purposelessness: emotional parasites who flourish by draining you of the vitality you preserve with difficulty. The Amerindians had this effect on me (1979, 111).

I quote from *The Middle Passage* extensively as a way of measuring the quality of change in Naipaul's recent empathetic engagement with the erasure of the Chaguanes from Trinidad and Tobago's history. From conventional representations of a childlike and doomed people, doomed because of their inability, not their refusal but their inability to change, Naipaul enshrines a moving, even sentimental account in the Nobel Lecture of a rite involving a seasonal visitation of mainland aborigenes to the island:

> The rite must have been of enormous importance to survive the upheavals of 400 years, and the extinction of the aborigines in Trinidad…And now the memory is all lost; and that sacred site, if it existed, has become common ground (Nobel Lecture n.p.).

In this instance, the horizon of culture-contact is problematised in personal terms and in the context of colonial history. However, Naipaul had already initiated this mantra in his Foreword to the 1973 Penguin edition of *The Loss of El Dorado: A History*. Situating himself as he has done so often, by naming his birthplace, his race, and his colonial upbringing in Trinidad, Naipaul writes of his childhood in Chaguanas:

> All this seemed so settled and complete it was hard to think of Chaguanas being otherwise. It was hard to feel any wonder at the fact that, more than four hundred years after Columbus, there were Indians in a part of the world he had called the Indies; and that the people he had called Indians had vanished. They had left no monuments; they were not missed. Chaguanas was a place-name, no more; many Indians turned it into 'Chauhan,' a Hindu caste-name. Wonder came later, with my own sense of being cut off from a past; and wonder grew during the writing of this book. One day in the British Museum… (*El Dorado,* 13).

This statement appended to the Penguin edition four years after the book was first published betrays lingering incongruities in Naipaul's narrative of the history and character of the Amerindians in *The Loss of El Dorado*.

At the end of the first of the two narratives that comprise this history, a narrative that begins more or less in 1595 with Sir Walter Raleigh's raid on Trinidad and ends more or less with Raleigh's return to the Tower of London in 1617, Naipaul observes by way of conclusion that

> The Indians had changed. They had been dulled by defeat and disappointments, and there is no trace in their stupefied descendents today of that intelligence and quickness which attracted Raleigh and made them such feared enemies, masters of the waters (*El Dorado* 1973, 107).

Yet, this perfunctory and unexplained statement comes at the end of a narrative shot through with admiration for the Amerindian people who struggled with mixed results to maintain some degree of independence in the face of a mushrooming European onslaught on their persons and their territory. Drawing largely on English and Spanish archives, in *The Loss of El Dorado* Naipaul culls from these narratives a compelling portrait of Amerindian resistance and accommodation in their attempts to manage their collective fate. The Amerindians are anything but capricious and indolent and passive in character. In fact they are masters of the seas and rivers, with a geographical knowledge of their territory on which the Europeans were totally dependent (1973, 56). Alliances with Amerindian tribes meant the difference between survival and death, victory and defeat for the Europeans, who relied on them as guides and pilots and interpreters, and also for provisions without which they soon starved: 'The Spaniards, even in extremity, never planted; they depended on the Indians for food. When the Indians withdrew, when no crops were planted, the Spaniards starved' (*The Loss of El Dorado* 1973, 74).

In fact, Naipaul describes the strategic withdrawal of the Indians from Spanish settlements as 'the worst sort of Indian war, famine' (77); and there was also their growing proficiency with guns (85), not to mention the poisonings, which the Amerindians understood (when selectively administered) could disrupt the hierarchical structure of a Spanish settlement and leave it in disarray (78). As Burnett argues – though in respect to a later period – there was a direct link between the loyalty of Amerindians and territorial possession (2002, 25). As Naipaul describes them, they are highly mobile and self-sufficient people in a fertile landscape that they know intimately; they are skilled hunters, fishermen, and warriors and provided bread, fish, game, and determined the direction of expeditions across difficult terrain. Bartering with Amerindians for seeming trifles produced by the Europeans is a small part of the terms of cultural-contact, which left the Europeans dependent on the Amerindians and the latter sensitive to their need to understand the culture and disposition of the invaders, their languages and religion, and their warring with each other.

Perhaps, the most regressive uncreative element of *The Loss of El Dorado* is the way Naipaul sets the Caribs apart as a special order of savage largely because of a perceived disposition to cannibalism. Naipaul recounts with vigour stories of Carib raids and cannibalism on terrified Amerindians and Europeans alike. In fairness to Naipaul, so-called 'cannibalism' as a practice among groups of people designated as uncivilised and savage had not yet received the kind of critical and corrective examination subsequent to the publication of *The Loss of El Dorado*. Indeed, Wilson Harris would be among the first to revise and correct earlier determinations that the Caribs lusted for human blood. Still, there is really no excuse, even for a Naipaul seemingly interred alive among documents in the British Museum, to write with such uncritical relish and indifference to the incongruities evident in this account of one of Antonio de Berrio's expeditions:

> They [Berrio and his men] ate the horses. They hollowed out four canoes from tree-trunks and dropped down the river until they came to Carib country. The Caribs ate men. Twice a year Carib fleets of up to thirty canoes went up the river, hunting; for three hundred and fifty leagues the river banks had been depopulated, eaten out. But the hunting party Berrio met was friendly. They offered food. They also offered to guide Berrio part of the way to El Dorado (*The Loss of El Dorado* 1973, 27).

Naipaul is aware that to be designated Carib/cannibal is to be outside the protection of the Spanish crown, to be a ready target for enslavement or extermination. He also writes about Carib alliances with the Dutch in the tobacco trade and trade in cloth, though when these alliances are with the Spanish they are identified as Indians. He writes of an Indian warning system to protect traders and their illegal trade. Yet still, he appears to relish the Europeans' strategic depiction of the Caribs as eaters of human flesh, as the 'bad' Indians as opposed to the 'good' Indians, whatever that distinction might mean in written reports detailing progress and failure to Spain, or England.

I want to turn to one chapter in *A Way in the World* in particular, as a way of demonstrating how Naipaul problematises the horizon of culture-contact in this remarkable multi-genre work that grapples directly with the problem of form Harris had addressed in 'Tradition, the Writer and Society.' In *A Way in the World: A Novel*, Naipaul employs elements of fiction, history, and autobiography in ironic counterpoint in part to demonstrate the dialectical relationship between his fiction and non-fiction that engenders what he has described as 'a new vision of what one had been born into' (*Reading and Writing* 2000, 30). This structural arrangement also facilitates self-parody and self-scrutiny as key elements of a creative rereading and critical rewriting of the earlier work analysed here. In Chapter three, 'New Clothes: An Unwritten Story,' Naipaul plays with the idea of reversible fictions. He begins by revisiting his account of travelling into the interior of Guyana in *The Middle Passage* with something of an apology that acknowledges his inexperience as a writer and awe of his environment at the time. Then he carefully refashions the earlier account into a specific setting for his resensitised perspective. With profound irony Naipaul retells his earlier narrative experience as a fiction in which the narrator's journey up river into Amerindian territory in order to foment a rebellion of the indigenous people of the interior against the coastal inheritors of colonial power and authority (African and Indian and Portuguese), is also a psychic journey through self doubt and cynicism about the futility of his undertaking, the clutter of his metropolitan sense of superiority, to an overt empathy and identification with the Amerindian community, though admittedly after a casual homoerotic experience with one of his two young Amerindian guides. Anticipating the pain he will bring the community that hosts him, he admits his 'love for these people, which contains the wish that no harm should come to them' (*A Way* 1995, 66):

> It is pain rather than love which now suffuses the narrator's vision, and corrupts everything he sees. It is all like something he has already lost: the late afternoon light, the friendly women and children, the very blue smoke. And all the half-formulated doubts, mere impulses, of the last few days harden into a determination to turn his back on these people, to put them out of his mind (66).

Whatever the narrator does finally, and the ending is left open, a new understanding of the Amerindian community he seeks to lead into rebellion is in place. His prior perception of their innocence and naiveté and vulnerability is altered. He observes:

> And they, people without writing and books, depend completely on sight and memory; they have greater gifts that way. They will commit an infinity of details about him to memory: his voice, gait, gestures. He will exist in the minds of these people as he will exist nowhere else. And after he has gone away they will remember him as the man who stayed long and wasn't straight with them, who promised many things and then went away (66–7).

The narrator is in fact at the threshold of a new understanding of what Harris has called the paradoxical 'mutuality of cultures.'[8] He will have evidence very shortly that the Amerindians do not live in a timeless void as he assumes. Indeed, they have a long memory of historical events and betrayals that date back at least to Walter Raleigh, one of his forerunners. Once he opens himself to them as an engaged listener, he sees them for the active, self-reflective, historically aware, and dynamic people that they are, who have a keen sense of the past and thus a context for evaluating his presence among them independently of the role he assumes – that they let him assume in their community.

This is but one example of several that I could draw from *A Way in the World* of an elaborate process of critical rereading and creative rewriting evident in this work. By stressing the chronology of its composition and the dialectical relationship over time between Naipaul's fiction and non-fiction, I have tried to detail what is, in fact, an organising theme of *A Way in the World*, and that is the evolution of this writer's consciousness from the thrall of colonial models of thought. It is about different ways of looking and seeing, about representations of reality and turning reality into fiction. The narrative strategy involves a discontinuity in discourse that is at once self-reflective and reconstructive. Think of this, if you will, as an outline of a particular trajectory of intellectual thought and history that informs Naipaul's work. I chose to focus on the changing shape of the history and character of indigenous people in his work because this trope is so exquisitely wrought in colonialist discourses of travel and expedition, and for this reason pivotal in unravelling the formations of colonial thought in our culture and society. Naipaul is making an important point about our cultural disposition when he writes in *The Loss of El Dorado*, with particular reference to Trinidad and coastal Guyana, 'It is the absence of the Indians that distorts the time-scale in these parts of the Indies' (1973, 56).

Notes

1. Hilhouse is cited in D. Graham Burnett, '"It's Impossible to Make a Step without the Indians": Nineteenth-Century Geographical Exploration and the Amerindians of British Guiana,' *Ethnohistory* 49 no. 1 (Winter 2002): 36, endnote 34. In 1834, the Royal Geographic Society of London published Hilhouse's 'Journal of a Voyage up the Massaroony in 1831,' *Journal of the Royal Geographical Society of London*, vol. 4, 1834, 25–40, and 'Memoir on the Warow Land of British Guiana' *Journal of the Royal Geographical Society of London*, vol. 4, 1834, 321–33. In 1837, *RPGS* also published Hilhouse's 'Journal of an Expedition up the River Cuyuny, in British Guayana, in March, 1837,' *Journal of the Royal Geographical Society of London*, vol. 7, 1837, 446–54. William Hilhouse, *Indian Notices, or Sketches of the Habits, Characters, Languages, Superstitions, and Climate of the Several Nations, with Remarks on their Capacity for Colonization, Present Government, and Suggestions for Future Improvement*

and Civilization, Etc. Also the Ichthyology of the Fresh Waters of the Interior. 1st edn (Georgetown: Printed for the Author for Private Circulation, 1825), 8; edited by M.N. Menezes, (Georgetown: National Commission for Research Materials on Guyana, 1978), xiii, facs ed.

2. The first two of these publications later appear as *The Middle Passage: The Caribbean Revisited* (Harmondsworth: Penguin, 1979), and *The Loss of El Dorado* (Harmondsworth: Penguin, 1973); *A Way in the World: A Novel* (New York: Vintage, 1995); *Reading and Writing: A Personal Account* (New York: New York Review of Books, 2000); Nobel Lecture. *Caribbean Voice.* n.p. Accessed March 14, 2007. www.caribvoice.org/CaribbeanDocuments/naipaul.html.
3. 'Interior of the Novel,' 140, cited in Russell Mcdougall, 'Walter Roth, Wilson Harris and a Caribbean/Postcolonial Theory of Modernism,' *University of Toronto Quarterly* 67.2 (Spring 1998): n.p. accessed February 8, 2007. http:/www.utpjournals.com/product/utq/672/672_mcdougall.html
4. The challenge that the enormity of these archives represents is in part the subject of Antonio Benítez-Rojo's brilliant novel *The Sea of Lentils* (*El mar de las lentejas*) first published in Spanish in 1985.
5. Naipaul continues: 'They were a small tribe, and they were aboriginal. Such people – on the mainland, in what was called B.G., British Guiana – were known to us, and were a kind of joke. People who were loud and ill-behaved, were known, to all groups in Trinidad, I think, as warrahoons. I used to think it was a made-up word, made up to suggest wildness. It was only when I began to travel in Venezuela, in my 40s, that I understood that a word like that was the name of a rather large aboriginal tribe there' (Nobel Lecture n.p.).
6. Wilson Harris, 'The Native Phenomenon.' *Common Wealth.* ed. Anna Rutherford, (Aarhus: Akademisk Boghandel, 1971), 148.
7. Harris, 'The Phenomenal Legacy.' *Explorations: A Selection of Talks and Articles, 1966–1981.* ed. Hena Maes-Jelinek (Mundelstrup: Dangaroo, 1981), 45–6.
8. Harris, 'The Quest for Form,' *Kunapipi* 1 (1983): 23.

11

THE NOVELIST AND HISTORY – PLEASURES AND PROBLEMS:

V.S. Naipaul's The Loss of El Dorado – A History, The Enigma of Arrival – A Novel, *and* A Way in the World – A Sequence

Lawrence Scott

Asked to speak as a writer after producing four books of my own, at this time of Vidia Naipaul's writing life, is in part, for a relatively new and younger writer, an opportunity to pay homage, and to describe and analyse critically how my homage came to be paid along the way in the development of my own writing. One of the histories in this discussion, 'the novelist and history,' is the history of my reading of V.S. Naipaul's work.

Naipaul was never an easy writer to carry with one as a *friend*. I use the word metaphorically. I found it important to be obsessed by certain writers for a time. Yet almost from the start one had to steer a way between the myth of the man and the writing itself. The public rhetoric did not always encourage one to keep an eye on the books, and if one was not careful, the distractions of the rhetoric which helped to burnish the myth of the writer, as Eddie Baugh has said elsewhere in this volume, could break the obsession.

The reflections I want to share with you I am putting under the heading of the novelist and the writing of history: the pleasures and problems in that for the writer. They are my pleasures and problems and Naipaul's, as I see them. This business of history seemed to be something I was involved in right from the start in my own writing. It is *my* interest as a writer then, those matters which involve me in my own books, that will inform my reflections on Naipaul's books and that I have chosen to talk about.

In 1980, I sat down on a small verandah up in the Cascade Hills above Port of Spain to begin writing with the intent to publish. I remember well a particular morning during that time when I set myself this regime, deciding that I would have to write like Vidia Naipaul if I were to be a writer. Ambitious, eh?

Now that I think back on that, it was curious in one sense that I was doing this, and of course, in another sense, not curious at all. Naipaul was a kind of monumental figure, starting so young, producing so much; and the quality of the writing winning him so much recognition, so many claims made by others – and, he was from *my* island. It was a thing at the time for me: Naipaul, Walcott, Anthony and Lovelace had used up everything on the island. There would be nothing more for me to write about. I could merely imitate, be influenced.

I satirised Naipaul at the end of my first novel, *Witchbroom.* My narrator Lavren, coming to the end of his tale and wondering what kind of fate awaits his story in the publishing world, says:

> But he knows when a country bookie comes to town, some little colonial boy, so they will inevitably think of him, they will want to link him to the Indian novelist, their sole point of reference: so they speak of before the Indian novelist there was nothing and since the Indian novelist there has been nothing.[1]

When I was given The Tom-Gallon Award by the Society of Authors in England, for my short story 'The House of Funerals,' the citation read something to the effect that I echoed V.S. Naipaul's style. It must have been Mr Samaroo, my undertaker, in that story, a kind of humour and voice: unconscious influences working their way through from early obsessions.

Let me leave the autobiographical journey for a moment and talk a little more plainly – not as an academic, nor as a historian (I was not trained as either of these) but, rather, as a writer of fictions, looking at fictions, looking at fiction and history. What I find enduring in Naipaul's work is the craft. I am going to examine elements of that craft in relation to the writing of history in three books: *The Loss of El Dorado – A History, The Enigma of Arrival – A Novel* and *A Way in the World – A Sequence.*[2]

For my purposes, I am defining history in three particular ways. Firstly, there is implied history, history as background. Secondly, there is the narrating of history as story, with a sense of people and their lives derived from documents, which we get in a very particular sense in *The Loss of El Dorado – A History.* Thirdly, there is that sense of history created through the use of autobiography, biography and memoir. Examples of this are the alternations of narrative and authorial points of view in *The Enigma of Arrival* and *A Way in the World.* It is the craft of this narration, the use of these 'I's that I want to reflect on, as it is this, in the end, that gives authority to a text and a sense of truth and authenticity to the voice and tone of the text. I was interested too in juxtaposing different kinds of narration in my fictions, in my fictive histories. So, deep sympathies and empathies were established – at least, here. Also, the epigraph of my first novel, *Witchbroom*, taken from Derek Walcott's essay, 'The Muse of History,' points to the connection I wanted to make from the start between fiction and history: '...history is fiction subject to a fitful muse, memory....In time every event becomes an exertion of memory and is thus subject to invention....'[3]

The Loss of El Dorado had been published in 1969, a long time before I started writing for publication. In fact, it struck me, while thinking about this discussion, that Vidia Naipaul was in London in 1967–69, walking along the same streets as myself to the British Library in the summer of love. That was the year I exchanged the habit of a monk for other habits – not quite dressed in beads, and flowers in my hair, off down the King's Road in swinging London, but soon having another habit, the 'habit' of writing. Naipaul, in the summer of love, was submerging himself in the documents which were to send him into a trance that would result in *The Loss of El Dorado*, and (several years later when I returned to Trinidad in 1977) send me into a trance. 'We cannot understand all the traits we have inherited. Sometimes we can be strangers to ourselves,' Naipaul concludes one of his pieces in *A Way in the World* to which I will return later on (1995, 11). How different the experiences, our ways in the world, which have formed us and which would inform the writing.

The first sense of history – that which is implied, the background to a story, properly part of its setting, but not necessarily history that comes forcefully to the fore – is not going to play a principal part of my reflections. For this first sense of history the examples are well known in Naipaul and include most of the early novels, what I call Naipaul's Trinidad novels. These are the ones we came to love for their comic irony, satire and pathos in their depiction of

Trinidad character and life in the 1930s, 1940s and 1950s: East Indian life in particular and the mixed community of *Miguel Street.* I remember re-reading aloud *The Mystic Masseur* and finding it impossible to stop laughing. In these novels the age is implied, or particular events are referred to as indicators. For example, we get a sense of the Second World War and of pre-Independence politics. The pleasure for the reader and the writer in reading and writing this kind of history is that we know where we are, though we may not always agree with the interpretation of the age. We also get a strong sense that this author knows where he is with the world he creates and the point of view he adopts. There is the voice of deep recall which governs all, and this for me was instructive and enriching. Not least, there is also the confidence this writer had gained from the voice of a writing father with his own stories that had launched a son onto a writer's life. You realise that I am paying absolutely no attention to the public rhetoric, recent or otherwise on this issue.

I am thinking of course of the *The Mystic Masseur* itself, *The Suffrage of Elvira, Miguel Street* and of course the great novel of the twentieth century, *A House for Mr Biswas,* the full blooming of this period of Naipaul's. For these alone, together with *The Loss of El Dorado,* I would give Naipaul all the prizes he has been awarded, and he was given prizes for almost each one of them. We are comfortable with this sense of history and made so through the conventions of point of view in the novel, whether we are dealing with an omniscient narrator or an 'I' narrator. It might be too as Kenneth Ramchand says in his 'Partial Truths: A Critical Account of V.S. Naipaul's Later Fiction':

> There are few signs of authorial pressure in the early works… because Naipaul has not yet hardened his opinions and…many of the issues that are to preoccupy him later are as yet only latent or in suspension in the material.[4]

In the later work, did 'I' narrators become the mouth-piece of the author? Was the view too insistent? Was the author too influenced by powers that wanted him to say certain things that they themselves would not dare to speak? That which the craft was in service of became more and more problematic for me. Not that there were no pleasures at all in the writing of the later period – there were. There were always pleasures in the sentences, in the progress of those paragraphs, in the methods of characterisation and in a particular kind of writing in English that constituted the best of its time: the writing of the dialect so well heard. Yet for this reader and writer the pleasures came more from that craft than from the emerging vision, either of contemporary Man (and I use that generic for humanity advisedly), in the midst of the world, or of the societies in the postcolonial world. I am thinking of *In a Free State* and *A Bend in the River.* I am not dealing with the travel writing at all, although of course we can see the effect of the travel writing and the 'journalistic style' on this later fiction.

In *Finding the Centre* Naipaul says about visiting places and travelling writing: 'When my curiosity has been satisfied, when there are no more surprises, the intellectual adventure is over and I become anxious to leave.'[5] That, for me, is not a sufficient basis for the judgements that are made in many of these travel books. It is in *Finding the Centre* that we find the beginning of the juxtaposition of 'I' narratives, where some of the problems of writing history begin and which I will discuss later. Naipaul often talks about the writer's duty to look and to see, but, as the English artist Constable suggests, you can only see if you understand what you are looking at.[6] Intuition may not be enough and the eye has to be formed. Where was Naipaul's eye formed? At a colonial Queen's Royal College, at an Oxford which he now decries, in a house in St James, through (eventually) ceaseless travel, in a pastoral England and in a literary London. There must have been biases formed. What else has formed the eye?

At this time in my reading I also came under other influences and developed other obsessions, other kinds of style and craft. I began to separate from Naipaul, the one novelist of my island. Yet he was not, was he, and never had been. That was the myth. I felt confirmed in my view formed of the later work when I heard Naipaul say in his Nobel Lecture, 'Two Worlds,' 'I have no system, literary or political. I have no guiding political idea.'[7] I am always suspicious of a position like this which claims such a degree of objectivity, such a lack of bias, a distance, which is not entirely possible. So, I question, as a socialist myself, this distancing from ideology for it often coincides with a support, an ideology itself, for a reactionary 'establishment.' This is not entirely the position I hold on all of Naipaul, but I do wonder, like Edward Said, why it seems that a view in some of the books is 'to indict guerrillas for their pretensions rather than indict the imperialism that drove them to insurrection.'[8] *The Loss of El Dorado* is a major exception here. I sense more of a *view* in these later works, narrators and authors converging to an end – what Ramchand calls 'authorial pressure'(1986, 239). Were there other pressures on the author?

Let me go in more detail now into the first of the texts I have chosen, the text that enchanted me, *The Loss of El Dorado – A History,* to make my first points about the pleasures in the writing of history. This text may present problems for conventional historians in its method of narration. I can imagine some of them. However, for me it is a tour de force of a novelist at the height of his narrating powers. I see that in the recent reprint they subtitle it, *A Colonial History*. I prefer the original, *A History*. It would be perverse to argue otherwise, but I do wish to be a little perverse and argue just that: yes, it is a history, but it reads like a novel. It is a kind of fiction in which narration by omniscient point of view, organising other points of view and tones (bread and butter techniques of the writer's craft) come into play to organise the prolific material discovered in the British Library for this story, told as episodes from the sixteenth, seventeenth, eighteenth and nineteenth centuries in Trinidad.

As a beginning writer, writing my own history of Trinidad, *Witchbroom*, 'quirky' as one critic called it, I found this text invaluable. This text was seminal to me, but as I said, I had been two-timing Naipaul. At the same time I found that other great Caribbean history, *The Black Jacobins* by C.L.R. James – which also benefits from the novelist's sense of narration, drama and character – to be inspiring and instructive in the craft of telling a story with a strong sense of history. Coupled with *The Loss of El Dorado* and *The Black Jacobins* was the great novel of South America, *One Hundred Years of Solitude*, which reads like a history. Alejo Carpentier's original sense of *lo real maravilloso,* properly translated as the 'Marvels of the Real,' rather than the popular and misleading translation, 'magic realism.' Certainly this writing has nothing to do with the disparaging 'surrealism' recently mentioned by Naipaul as characterising Latin American literature (though I was influenced by the surrealism, properly understood, of Cesaire and St John Perse). Still let us avoid those petulant outbursts. Shut my ears to the public rhetoric. The late John La Rose, the founder of New Beacon in London (the inheritor of the Beacon in Trinidad) always emphasised this reading Carpentier himself preferred, 'the marvels of the real.' Naipaul gave me a sense of the Tulsies in *A House for Mr Biswas,* like the Buendia in *The Loss of El Dorado.*

If Naipaul did not find a tradition in the Caribbean, in his area of darkness, I certainly did, a rich one, which also included novels by Jean Rhys, Wilson Harris, Earl Lovelace, Sam Selvon, together with the poetry of Martin Carter, Kamau Brathwaite and Derek Walcott, to name a few – without intending any sense of exclusion in not mentioning all. What would I do without poets? This was a vital tradition going back into the 1930s, to writers like C.L.R. James himself, Ralph de Boissiere to whom my most recent novel, *Night Calypso,* pays homage and owes some measure of influence: no father writer for me, but many fellow writers, comrades on this craft.

When Naipaul embarks upon his non-fiction book which becomes *The Loss of El Dorado,* he begins, he says, with a kind of 'innocence,'[9] something not entirely believable, more an example of Naipaul's fictionalising of the writer-self, something that has very much occupied the later Naipaul in essay after essay, almost compulsively, and in two of the texts I am to treat later.

In the records in the British Museum he was looking for 'people and their stories,' as he tells us in *Reading and Writing* 'the best way of organising the material' (2004, 18). He picked his way through documents, letters, records to organise the narrative for one paragraph. This was two years' work involving his own translations. Truly, this book could be said to have been created not in the West Indies but in the British Library. I imagine him, Borgesian style, with his own kind of *lo real maravilloso.* It was not just the material, the story that he finds in these documents, 'the technique...of looking through a multiplicity of impressions to a central human narrative' (2004, 20). It is also the subliminal story which surfaces from time to time in the finding of the story: a story within a story. It is the story of time, fourteen months for a letter to get to the king of Spain, ten years between one account of an event and the surfacing of its continuation; the story of how lives appear and disappear up the Orinoco as he tracks his way through the documents as through a forest or a delta, as if himself an explorer writing his own account. He talks about what this process brought to his travel writing, but it is also very apparent what as a novelist he brings to this writing of a history.

He gives us an account of writing this book in *Reading and Writing* and also in 'Prologue to an Autobiography' and returns to it again in his Nobel Lecture, 'Two Worlds.' He conveys a sense of wonder at finding mention of the Chaguanes Indians in a letter from the King of Spain, October 12, 1625, to the then Governor of Trinidad – linking that reference to his birth place in Chaguanas – a sense of history in records touching Trinidad, because it is discovered in a document. There is an experience he says of feeling 'that I was the first person since 1625 to whom that letter of the King of Spain had a real meaning.'[10] This early experience of excitement and wonder infuses the entire text. It was with this excitement that I was infected when I was writing my own first novel, *Witchbroom*, and came to the sources through Naipaul's history to produce my *Carnival Tales of Lavren Monagas de los Macajuelos*, the last child of a Spanish/French Creole family, my androgynous narrator, Lavren.

The Loss of El Dorado contains 'two forgotten stories' (2001, 3), the first at the end of the search for El Dorado, an Edenic search, the materialist search for gold. There is the foundering expedition of Walter Raleigh and before him the dispossessed conquistador Antonio de Berrio. In recounting this first story the novelist has an eye for the small human details. As John Berger the Swiss writer tells us: 'The true stories of our time have to be able to reconcile a pile of clothes in a drawer with world historical upheavals.'[11] These stories of the sixteenth, seventeenth, eighteenth and nineteenth centuries read not only as a history of a time but as a history which enlightens us about our own time. This is brought about by the urgency of the narrative, the sense of the dramatic which he discovers and creates, the discovery of the characters that he builds and of emotions and events. There is a sense for him that all this activity in the search for El Dorado becomes an abstraction until imagination and intellect shape the narrative. That is its contribution to history writing.

Antonio de Berrio's accounts are lost in the accumulating imperial records at Simancas in Spain. Before they are read, the only story we have is Walter Raleigh's mythic account in *The Discovery of the Large, Rich, and Beautiful Empire of Guiana, with a Relation of the Great and Golden City of Manoa (which the Spaniards Call El Dorado) and the Provinces of Emerica, Aromaia, Amapaia, and Other Countries, with their Rivers Adjoining.*[12] Naipaul adds ironically 'how real it sounds! And he had hardly been on the main Orinoco.' Having not found anything, Raleigh had to write a book saying that he had. It is as if for Naipaul also these events would not exist except for his own organising imagination and intellect. An element of this exists in my narrator, Lavren Monagas, with his clairvoyance – having been hit on the head by a golf ball as a baby, thereby allowing him to read the past and create the future.

It is the sense of absurdity which Naipaul responds to over and over, for example, when he finds Domingo de Vera's account (which hardly goes to four pages) yet discovers that it is that text that fires Raleigh's expedition. As well as timing, it is also the business of paper, ink, pens and printeries that fascinate Naipaul (the writer of books, busy putting together his documents) and that keep coming up in his text. How important pens, paper and printing were, if you were to let others know what you had done – even if you had not, but had to make your way in the world: 'the legend of El Dorado narrative within narrative, witness within witness had become like the finest fiction indistinguishable from the truth' (2001, 24).

In Robert Dudley's adventure in south Trinidad, luckily written down by a Captain Wyatt, who is never to appear again in the records, Naipaul responds to the romance, the adventure, the suspense of arrival and departure from the island in search of gold, and comments:

> They got back to the ship about two or three in the morning. A blank place, that Gulf shore; but they had made it yield the drama of late hours and a midnight wade in full armour. They had had two adventures of fireflies and the tide and they had got a lot of sand (2001, 34).

After Trinidad ceases to be a base for expeditions to El Dorado, it becomes a ghost province, 'in which they needed almost everything' (2001, 102). The Indians became restive and gave the Christians their first martyrs. There is the killing of monks, the suicide of Indians. A year later the exhumed bodies of the monks in St Joseph oozed with fresh blood. Someone wrote a poem, '*Romance muy doloroso,* A Very Sad Story' (2001, 105) – 'the only piece of literature the Spaniards produced in Trinidad' (2001, 101).

In explaining the theme of resistance from 1776–1800 Naipaul gives us a sense of the impact of what he calls the four revolutions: the American, the French, the Negro (Haitian) and what is to be the South American Revolution. The latter is being prepared by Francisco de Miranda, a story he returns to again and again, particularly in *A Way in the World.*

In contrast to this first 'forgotten' story of expedition there is a second – of oppression. Having (in 2007) commemorated the anniversary of 200 years of the abolition of the slave trade, we can enter the second story in *The Loss of El Dorado* with added interest. It contains the episodes of Picton's time as Governor of Trinidad: the numbing story of Louisa Calderon's torture, the details of floggings, the cutting off ears and the burning of 'negroes,' as an extraordinary evocation of the detail, the horror and cruelty of eighteenth and nineteenth century Trinidad where individuals make their way in the world through the intricacies of Spanish and English law. Here the drama comprises the clash between endeavours to have a colony of freed people and to run a slave colony. I am reminded of how Earl Lovelace puts it in his novel,

Salt: 'But now they had another problem: it was not how to keep people in captivity. It was how to set people at liberty.'[13]

Before I move on, I found that my own research of the texts for this discussion uncovered the wonderful story of the rise to power of William Hardin Burnley, the *despositario* who makes himself more and more wealthy, becoming the richest man in Trinidad as owner of the Orange Grove Estate with his 200 slaves. Naipaul offers us one of his many conclusions: 'At the end of the story Trinidad is visibly corrupt.' It goes on to show that 'the English immigrants had gone as colonial as the French and had reduced the complex drives of their culture to the simplicities of money and race.' Is there, in this statement, a truth for us today about our political culture? Of course, for my novel *Witchbroom,* I found confirmation of something which had its origins in one of my own short stories, in the following absurdity: 'The cacao trees were blighted and the revenue of the province dropped to 231 dollars'(2001, 106).

These conclusions are enlivened by the drama and characterisation, and the organising of the large themes of colonial repression founded on bizarre contradictions between the ideals of liberty on the one hand, and the system of slavery on the other. Such contradictions held while the free coloureds were suspected for their republican views and even as they feared that (under the English) they would be flogged in the same way as those who were enslaved. Some historians might consider these partial truths but the persuasive stylist convinces, if not at times overwhelms us, with the authoritative marshalling of the 'facts' which are his 'fictions,' as Ramchand points out. He goes on to comment that Naipaul

> ...is able to unite his selected moments because by this time he has arrived at a philosophy of history in which disillusion, futility and the ultimate meaninglessness of human endeavour in a world that has its own will are structural elements (1986, 233).

I hold that this is still Naipaul, the intuitive writer with a sense of awe and wonder in which the story comes in the writing and takes him by surprise. Futility and disillusion follow later and is the disappointing vision, if we can call it a vision at all, that the craft begins to serve.

After *A Bend in the River*, there were no Naipaul novels as we had come to understand them until the most recent works *Half a Life* and *Magic Seeds.*

At this point there is a kind of crisis for the writer. In *Reading and Writing* he tells us,

> Fiction had taken me as far as it could go. There were certain things it couldn't deal with. It couldn't deal with my years in England; there was no social depth to the experience; it seemed more a matter for autobiography...I didn't know how to move; I was quite lost (2004, 15–6).

Naipaul feels rescued from this disorientation by the narrating 'I' of the travel writer. However, the two novels in which he reflects and makes fictions of this experience are *The Enigma of Arrival – A Novel* and *A Way in the World – A Sequence.* We have to be told that they are fictional, for they are not recognisably so. These writings of history raise more problems than pleasures, though there are some pleasures in the writing of history as memoir, biography, autobiography and fictional autobiography.

When I came to *The Enigma of Arrival* as a writer, I was then writing my own novel, *Aelred's Sin,* a novel with three narrations, set in England with a memory of Les Deux Isles. I was sympathetic to this coming home to England with its eruptions of Trinidad throughout, the journey between one place and the other, the repeated journeys which comprise the novel and the attempt in part by the 'I' narrator at autobiography – but very selectively so that the work remains a 'fiction.' We are on shifting ground. Writing about England, a pastoral England, appealed to my sense of my own experience. I became sympathetic to the self-examination of this complex writer in this sequence of autobiographical pieces, though I could not entirely believe the 'I' as autobiographical, especially in relation to his degree of isolation. It is difficult to fully believe this narrator in 'Jack's Garden.' This is, rather, one of these fictions of the writer. This is not the real self nor a truly fictional self; this is the writer-self, a fiction of the writer-self, 'subject to a fitful muse' to use a Walcott phrase. I feel this is the only way to salvage any truth or authenticity here.

I share sentiments with Derek Walcott when he says of sections of this book, 'I cherished them as the tenderest writing Naipaul had ever done. Tempered and delicate, the mood of these pieces has the subdued subtleties of the weather their pliant sentences celebrated' (1998, 132). Still I also have to agree with Walcott when he says that the 'beautiful prose…is scarred by scrofula, by passages from which one would like to avert one's eye; and these reveal remorselessly, Naipaul's repulsion towards Negroes.'[14] It is so difficult for me, the writer who admires the craft, to read: 'In Trinidad on my return now that the rawness of nerves among black people had become a communal festering' (*Enigma* 2002, 174). Naipaul's mere use of the word 'negro' and 'negroid' jars again and again, festering as his descriptions become negative even as he maintains the tone and language of the documents he had researched.

It can seem that part of the problem for Naipaul, comes from the fact that as he himself says in *The Enigma of Arrival*, the island had become 'his romance, his possession'(2002, 174) as he wrote *The Loss of El Dorado*. As I have said, his recall of Trinidad, a loved place I think, erupts throughout *The Enigma of Arrival*, but the loved places does not include the present reality of people he did not know or experience. He knew by recall the people of *Miguel Street* back in 1959, but not a Port of Spain in 1970, where he returns after writing *The Loss of El Dorado,* where something like 'Haitian anarchy' seemed to threaten 'my island' (*Enigma* 2002, 179, 174). This sums up a sense that even in *The Loss of El Dorado* the revolt of the slaves is not what he is concerned with; remorselessly, the word *negro* litters that book. Yes, the word of the historical documents, but you can be persuaded to feel retrospectively that some other trauma feeds a distaste. It is the collapse of the colonial regimes that he is involved with, and the story is a powerful one of colonial repression. Similarly, in 1970, it is not Black Power that he sees as significant but the despair that it is not his 'romance:' 'I saw all of this under the spell of the book I had written' – *The Loss of El Dorado* – 'the past I had discovered far away in England from the documents and felt that I had almost created, as much as my novels had been created' (2002, 177). He does not draw the conclusions you think he might from his own revolutionary story in *The Loss of El Dorado.*

The craft is one thing, but this is a writer who has bought into an idea of his writer-self, an entirely isolated figure. The beauty of the narration in *The Enigma of Arrival* – the way that 'Jack's Garden' penetrates and is linked with 'The Journey,' 'Ivy,' 'Rooks' and then (in conclusion) 'The Ceremony of Farewell,' a memorial for a dead sister – is architectural craft at its best. Prose as poetry. The way that memory, almost Proustian, fashions both the act of memory itself and its expression is extraordinary, but the vision that it serves cumulatively for us on this little island creeps towards the depressing and dangerous.

I found that in my own research for the history of my most recent novel, *Night Calypso,* it was partly Naipaul's history that still fired my own revolutionary conclusions. Also, contrary to him, the past of 1937, the labour riots were equally revolutionary, but marginalised by Naipaul in *A Way in the World*, as a kind of madness in the characterisation of Butler. The watershed of 1937 suggests alliances against the then colonial power which might now get us out of our present Naipaulian 'area of darkness.' Do we always need an enemy without to galvanise our best potential?

The lonely isolated figure of *The Enigma of Arrival* makes for a sad book, a book 'without love' as Salman Rushdie says, and sad too 'that the warmth and energy of the early work had not intensified with the mastery of his later writing.'[15] That would have been 'something rather special,' rather than 'precise prose' but 'bloodless prose,' as Rushdie assesses it (1991, 148, 150). Not all bloodless, I would say, but conveying little love, except possibly in 'The Ceremony of Farewell' at the end, unless of course you include self-love or at least self-obsession in the fictionalising of the writer-self. This figure leads inevitably to the autobiographical 'I' and the fictional 'I' narrators of *A Way in the World – A Sequence* – another sequence, another fragmented search for self through examination of the past, another go at the history. Yet again, the magic of the craft creates difficulties, this time not for race only, but also for sexuality.

In my own novels and stories I had been struggling with explorations of sexuality, unearthing hidden histories, which would take in the whole range of sexualities, deal with loves that could not previously speak their name. Naipaul offered me Jimmy Ahmed, in *Guerrillas*, with his stunted boys, his disgust and violence, as well as characterisation and exploration used to discredit black revolt. He also offered me Bobby in *In a Free State* – sympathetic at one level but essentially a weak character used to portray white liberalism and its ineffectiveness. Bobby is a victim of attack, self-internalising the disgust he experiences from others about his homosexuality so that any humanity in his own view of 'Africans' consequently diminishes the Africans. The reader can hardly help wondering whether this is Bobby's view only or, at least in part, Naipaul's – one of the examples of slippage or 'leakage.'

In the middle novels, have we sensed already a kind of creeping misogyny and negative characterisation of women, as in *Guerrillas* (that 'nasty book' as C.L.R. James once described it to me) and also *In a Free State* and in *A*

Bend in the River? Are there any strong, fulfilled Naipaulian women, I often wonder? Is that a question for him at all?

In the opening piece of *A Way in the World*, 'Prelude: An Inheritance,' Naipaul offers me the story of Leonard Side whom the narrator who opens and closes the piece characterises as one who would not know that his name was really the Muslim name, Sayed. This comment and the historical allusions at the conclusion of this story seek to give the story some historical stature, but they fail to mask deeper intentions.

Leonard Side is set up for us by a woman-schoolteacher-narrator to whom Naipaul allocates five pages of direct speech which is difficult to distinguish from the voice of the author, so Naipaulian is she in tone and observation. The author hears the story of Leonard Side from the teacher while in a state of 'fever' (1995, 4). That is important. The word 'fever' alerts us to the recurring theme in the portrayal of Leonard Side, and a second reading reveals the reader is manipulated insidiously into a disturbing view of this man and his sexuality.

Leonard Side, 'a decorator of cakes and an arranger of flowers,' gives courses at the Women's Auxiliary Association. When the schoolteacher first meets him to invite him to be a judge of cakes and flower arrangements she finds him in an undertaker's parlour 'doing things with his fingers to a dead body.' He is 'quite good looking,' with 'hairy fingers.' He had made 'a posy of pink rose buds.' Then, when he is making cakes he is 'doing things with dough using those hairy fingers.' When she sees him again he is 'sick and trembling,' 'He had laid himself out' (like a corpse? we ask). Just outside his room is 'the smell of cess pits of St James,' 'runnels of filth from latrines… green and slimy.' The schoolteacher feels frightened for him. She is scared of him because of his 'beauty,' a beauty of 'many Indian men you see in St James,' 'narrow waisted in open necked shirts,' 'a special idea of beauty,' 'people mocking him scorning him.' The piece ends with this comment still with the woman schoolteacher's voice:

> He frightened me because I felt that his feeling for beauty was like an illness; as though some unfamiliar deforming virus had passed through his simple mother to him and was even then – he was in his mid-thirties – something neither of them had begun to understand.[16]

'This was what I heard,' says Naipaul, or the 'I' narrator, who has taken back the narration and openly states that his inheritance is from the 'lewd men' of Lucknow who 'painted their faces and tried to live like women.' The 'persuasive stylist' who began with a historical reference in the first reading also ends with the enigmatic and ambiguous: 'We cannot understand all the traits we have inherited. Sometimes we can be strangers to ourselves' (1995, 10–1). This is Naipaul's voice.

This is clearly the portrait of a gay man who is ill. The language and the pathetic fallacy of the 'cesspit' and the 'slimy' drains point to him and his world as dirty, even as the narrator conveys fear of his beauty. Why does Naipaul try to give the story of Leonard Side to his schoolteacher narrator? What is gained? Is this a mask of sorts? We know what he thought of E.M. Forster and Maynard Keynes from one of those recent outbursts some saw as a ploy to garner cheap publicity for a new book, put forward as his response to their attitude to India, but attacking them as homosexuals.[17] The 'persuasive stylist' tries to takes us in, but the craft is serving some other purpose. Is this the homophobia not of some fictional female schoolteacher, but the author himself, V.S. Naipaul?

Another way to put all of this is to say that Naipaul is old-fashioned, old-fashioned about race, about women, about sexuality; an isolated figure, unaware of how the world around him is changing, with regard to these issues, or, if aware, untouched, unmoved, isolated in a kind of 'conservatism' pursuing now the fictional writer-self in these later days.

We find a suggestive homoerotic episode in 'New Clothes: An Unwritten Story' couched as an historical journey/reflection in the Guianas, where again searching for a narrator we find an unresolved story which becomes associated with feminine repulsion and so sours. While 'appetite grows on the narrator' for the boy, 'the narrator's thought is of the grossness of the big blond woman at the station' (*A Way* 1995, 59). Why we wonder? This is perhaps a version of Gordon Rohlehr's attraction and repulsion theme so well analysed in his own paper in this collection. The question of sexuality seems deeply problematic in Naipaul's work. Representation of women and of 'gay' characters is a significant issue in our time and provokes radical approaches, calling not for the straitjacket of political correctness but for searching moral questions, questions of responsibility.

As the author of *Aelred's Sin*, trying to deal sensitively with homoerotic love and embedded prejudice in religions and states, I note that Naipaul does not follow his own advice to writers regarding 'undermining.' His characterisations rather consolidate the prejudice and bigotry too often peddled by crazed preachers of religions and by thinkers still in thraldom to colonial law and institutions irrelevant to their current societies. We know that the fundamentalist pastors of Trinidad and Tobago and elsewhere do not need this kind of literary support. On the other hand, we know V.S. Naipaul is no friend of religious fundamentalists.

Questions of race and of sexuality, but also of political discrediting become masked by these narrators who are also personae. The portrait of Lebrun in the chapter, 'On the Run,' heavily suggests C.L.R. James. He may also be an amalgam of James and George Padmore and the earlier Constantine. (Is that where the name Lebrun comes from?) In that piece we are again moving between fiction and fact where a character like Butler (the 1930s political leader) gets his real name, and is dismissed as mad. The fictional writer 'Foster Morris,' may satirise English writing on the colonies at the time, or, ironically, adopt the name Foster from the Forster Commission in the 1930s. He is used as a kind of an alter ego with a book entitled 'The Shadowed Livery'– actually the title of an unpublished novel of Naipaul's, as we learn in his letters. His positive views about Butler are later discounted. These seem clever ways for Naipaul to attempt to mask his politics. Why? Characteristics are assembled to discredit the Lebrun/C.L.R. James figure and consequently, for example, the Pan-African Movement. For this is not the author of the *The Black Jacobins* or *Beyond the Boundary* but a discredited figure of socialist politics coming from a Naipaul that tells us he has no political ideology. Often with Naipaul the discrediting, the repulsions he experiences, come with descriptions of smells, of poverty, 'rubbishy food,' 'ground provisions' Grenedians boil on pitch oil tins (*A Way* 1995, 80). Yet there is a sense too that he identifies in passing with these West Indians abroad. Is there no political view? Perhaps there is not, but rather, a mechanism for serving a reactionary establishment. Still, for what audience? I am reminded of Walcott's rhetorical question and use it more generally: 'What is this but style without truth?'('The Garden Path' 1998, 130)

Where does all of this leave me now? Firstly, congratulating a writer of almost 30 books from our region and our island but also wrestling with the craft of a very significant writer of our time. We cannot ignore Naipaul. I found myself recently, while writing a story for the BBC, reminded of Naipaul's beginnings, when he had a sense of Caribbean literary community with Lamming, Selvon and Salkey, when *Miguel Street* (which we all love) was written. That writer had a hand in my recent character Harri Harricharan, I am sure, in a story called *From the Cane*. Indeed, *Miguel Street* is a seminal collection for any writer of the short story and I went to it as I did to Jean Rhys, Michael Anthony, Gabriel Marquez, Sam Selvon, John Stewart and Earl Lovelace for my own collection *Ballad for the New World.* So, while I may not want to dwell with the isolated figure in 'Jack's Garden' too long, I embrace pleasures of re-reading *The Loss of El Dorado*, *Miguel Street* and *A House for Mr Biswas.* I look forward to Naipaul's next publication, which sounds like a book about writing and I am sure it will shed more light on this writer's craft in the writing of fiction and history.

Yet I continue to wonder about the language, and the craft required to shape that language, which we still have to continue to create in order to engage the world from these islands. The challenge is to fashion a literary language which has to wrestle with both the sentences of education and the syntax of the full language that we speak, and through which we relate to each other. I do wonder also about how such a language has to be inseparable from the kind of visions we will continue to have and to make of ourselves, as we create ourselves, with our histories and fictions in this Creole Caribbean, imaginatively entering into each others' experiences across race, religion, sexuality and class, engage the world from here.

Notes

1. Lawrence Scott, *Witchbroom* (London: Heinemann, 1993), 235.
2. V.S. Naipaul, *The Loss of El Dorado – A History* (New York: Alfred P. Knopf, 1970; London: Picador, 2001); *The Enigma of Arrival – A Novel* (Harmondsworth: Viking, 1987); *A Way in the World – A Sequence* (London: Heinemann, 1994; New York: Vintage Books, 1995).
3. Derek Walcott, 'The Muse of History,' *What the Twilight Says* (London: Faber & Faber, 1998), 37.
4. Kenneth Ramchand 'Partial Truths: A Critical Account of V.S. Naipaul's Later Fiction,' in *Essays on Contemporary Post-Colonial Fiction*, eds. Hedwig Bock and Albert Wertheim (Munchen: Max Hueber Verlag, 1986), 226.
5. Naipaul, *Finding the Centre* (Harmondsworth: Penguin Books, 1985), 87.
6. John Constable, 'The History of Landscape Painting,' Third Lecture at the Royal Institution, 1836.
7. Naipaul, 'Postscript: Two Worlds, the Nobel Lecture,' in *Literary Occasions* (London: Picador, 2003), 194.
8. Edward Said, 'Interview' (Newsweek, August 18, 1980).

9. Naipaul, 'Reading and Writing,' in *Literary Occasions* (London: Picador, 2003), 17.
10. Naipaul, 'Two Worlds' (London: Picador, 2003), 185.
11. John Berger, 'Afterword,' in *Nineteen Nineteen*, eds. Hugh Brody, Michael Ignatieff and John Berger (London: Faber & Faber, 1985).
12. Naipaul, 'Two Worlds,' (London: Picador, 2003), 184.
13. Earl Lovelace, *Salt* (New York: Persea Books, 1997), 7.
14. Walcott, 'The Garden Path,' in *What the Twilight Says* (London: Faber & Faber, 1998), 131–32.
15. Salman Rushdie, *Imaginary Homelands* (New York: Penguin Book, 1991), 137.
16. This description of Leonard Side is developed in *A Way in the World*, 9–10.
17. Paul Kelso, 'Naipaul Derides Forster "A Nasty Homosexual,"' *The Guardian* (UK) August 2, 2001.

12

V.S. NAIPAUL AS CRITICAL THINKER

Bhoendradatt Tewarie

V.S. Naipaul has been written and spoken about as a novelist and writer from many perspectives: as a Trinidadian and West Indian writer; as a writer of the Indian/Asian diaspora; as a British writer; as a writer in the context of the postcolonial tradition; as a Third World writer and, generally, as a writer of some substance writing in the English language. This is largely because of the complexity of his background as a writer, the period during which he began to write, the subjects and places that he has chosen to write about, his preferred place of residency for most of his writing career and the ideological cross-currents which have been heatedly debated by admirers and detractors over the course of the evolution of his writing career.

Naipaul has always been a controversial writer principally because of his ideas, but also because of his detached, unsympathetic, sometimes brutal assessments of political realities in the developing world as well as his revulsion toward the tendency to ideological excess and dogmatism wherever it emerges. The truth of the matter is that Naipaul has perpetually found himself swimming against the current as a writer. Why is this so?

Dilemma of Small Societies

I take the liberty of suggesting in this presentation that it is because V.S. Naipaul is a critical thinker. I will get to the definition of this term that, as an enlightened reader, I am sure you are anticipating. However, let us for a moment examine the issues that would have been swirling around V.S. Naipaul as he was struggling to find subject matter at the beginning of his writing career. I will begin at the beginning with a focus on his first four books, all set in Trinidad.

Naipaul arrived in Oxford in 1950 and studied there until 1954. In 1954 he began to write his first book. In 1961 his fourth book was published. He would have been acutely aware of post-Second World War realities as well as the anti-colonial wave that was rising to a crest across the postcolonial world. In the household in which Naipaul grew up, he would have been very aware of Mahatma Gandhi and the anti-imperialist struggle in India leading to Independence in 1947, three years before Naipaul actually left Trinidad. At Oxford, between 1950 and 1954 he would have been exposed to the build up of anti-colonial resentment that would have been the subject of heated debate and discussion at institutions such as Oxford and in cities such as London. He would have been aware of what was happening in Ghana and across the African continent. Federation across the West Indies, its subsequent collapse, and the rise of nationalism in individual territories leading to independence for both Trinidad and Tobago and Jamaica in 1962 could not have escaped him.

Yet none of his first four books take any of these matters, their context, the possible implications of these events into account even though Naipaul acknowledges, in several places, his deep understanding of the swirling postcolonial world around him with all its implications. This is how he writes about it in *The Enigma of Arrival*:

> Because in 1950 in London I was at the beginning of that great movement of peoples that was to take place in the second half of the twentieth century – a movement and a cultural mixing greater than the peopling of the United States, which was essentially a movement of Europeans to the new world. This was a movement between all the continents…cities like London were to change. They were to cease being more or less national cities; they were to become cities of the world, modern-day Romes, establishing the pattern of what great cities should be, in the eyes of islanders like myself and people even more remote in language and culture. They were to be cities visited for learning and elegant goods and manners and freedom by all the barbarian peoples of the globe, people of forests and desert, Arabs, Africans, Malays.[1]

So Naipaul understood very well the time and context in which he lived and against which background he was writing.

Yet *Miguel Street* focuses on the claustrophobic nature of life in a small colonial island of limited options and basically concludes that for the ambitious and/or the talented, escape from such a society in search of greater options is the only reasonable thing for an enterprising person to do. *The Mystic Masseur* presents politics as one option in a small society as a means of escape from the drudgery of a mundane existence. Ganesh Ramsumair is bereft of any communal or national sense and basically seizes the option of personal advancement first inside and, later, in the wider world made possible by the political platform that he has grasped the opportunity to build. Naipaul has on many occasions described *The Suffrage of Elvira* as a farce and he uses that book to focus on the futility of politics in a multi-ethnic, multi-religious colonial society where neither politicians nor people have developed any larger view of themselves or nobler view of possibilities. *A House for Mr Biswas* focuses on one man's story of his life of 41 years and the interweaving narratives and people which connect to that life in various ways as he struggles to meet his multiple obligations and yet find space to pursue his dreams.[2]

Amidst the global upheavals taking place at the time of writing of his early books and the swirling currents being unleashed in his own region, Naipaul's entire focus was on something else – something he considered more important than the political changes. Perhaps, it is too far-fetched to suggest that, in his view, all of this would pass soon enough even if the consequences might pose challenges later; but the prospect does raise its head.

I suggest that at the age of 22 when Naipaul began work on his first book length work, he had already grasped the fundamental dilemma of small societies of a particular kind. Those societies, from his point of view, had no continuous history as a community and therefore no strong sense of themselves or of the possibilities for a common future. Naipaul had already sensed that such communities, consisting as they did of transplanted peoples, would find it very difficult to create a society together and to cohere and would have great difficulty building the capacity required to make genuine development and lasting achievement possible.

Naipaul's early books are very revealing in this regard and his later books and writings make it clear that this issue of the special challenge of small countries, created as a consequence of colonial encounter, has remained one of his obsessions. This obsession manifests itself in Naipaul's early writing.

Miguel Street spans the spectrum of ethnic and racial types in Trinidad, all tragic-comic failures for whom escape from their condition of material and cultural impoverishment is a virtual impossibility. To Bogart, freedom means the absence of commitment or responsibility. Hat is the man who embraces life but lives only for today. The dreams of the poet 'Wordsworth' stifle and die inside of him. Titus Hoyte tries in vain to win notoriety and recognition. Herrera drinks himself into oblivion despite the love of a beautiful woman. In the case of the narrator the entire tone of *Miguel Street* suggests that unless he can escape from Trinidad he will be doomed to a mindless, unambitious, boring career perhaps coupled with excess and debauchery. What makes the narrator leave without even looking back at the end of *Miguel Street* is his recognition that in spite of uncertainties and fears which the outside world may hold, the one certainty that awaits him in *Miguel Street* is failure, stagnation and extinction. So he leaves his society behind in search of life and fortune elsewhere.

When Ganesh Ramsumair, the protagonist of *The Mystic Masseur*, retreats into the countryside following his father's death, he believes that somehow his destiny is bound up with that of his community. Politics, however, gives Ganesh the opportunity to escape from his community and its provincial limitations. Ganesh is able to enter the upper class, he wins status and fame in the outside world, and his emerging interests prompt him to reach outward rather than inward. Culturally he becomes less and less Hindu (just as Hat divests himself of his Indianness). He is transformed into a complete colonial politician, with commitment neither to community nor society. All of his aspirations are now for the self. He comes to perceive that his personal destiny is tied, not to his ethnic community or to the dispossessed in his society but to the colonial office. Thus, in the end he sells out to become a colonial mimic man and stooge. He chooses cultural assimilation as the road to individual freedom. However, individual freedom, won on terms dictated from the outside, will inevitably result in the cultural isolation, disorientation and displacement that so many of Naipaul's later protagonists feel deeply.

In *The Suffrage of Elvira*, the election becomes a symbol of the encroachment of the modern world in a society ill-prepared to deal with the challenges of modern existence. As western ways encroach more and more, as ambitions and aspirations are released, the old world finds it increasingly difficult to survive so that cultural and spiritual dislocation begins to set in. In this novel the election can be won simply by manipulating ethnic blocks because the politicians do not have a concept of society or country and the people are ill-equipped to think creatively on the best options for themselves as a collective. Ethnic chauvinism is thus portrayed as a national intellectual failure. Neither politicians nor citizens see themselves as part of a larger nation; there is no common purpose around which people are able to rally. And so, lacking a sense of common purpose, lacking a sense of wholeness as a community, the citizens of Elvira fall back on tribal loyalties and when the politician Baksh wins, he, in turn, turns his back on his community to pursue wealth-gaining opportunities.

The tremendous vitality of the novel, *A House for Mr Biswas,* ultimately derives from Biswas's insatiable hunger for individual liberty, which drives him to despair, to insanity and ultimately to the audacious act of buying a house without the foggiest notion of where the money was likely to come from. This house becomes a symbol of independence in his lifetime, offering the promise and possibility of individual freedom and personal fulfilment to the children. Implied in those famous lines at the end of this great novel is the notion that Biswas's life has ultimately been worthwhile since he actually succeeds in securing a place for himself in a world that is clearly at odds with his inner needs and deepest aspirations. Yet greater than his own triumph, not from our perspective but from Biswas's, is the world of possibilities that had opened up for his children, Savi and Anand:

> How terrible it would have been, at this time, to be without it: to have died among the Tulsis, amid the squalor of that large, disintegrating and indifferent family; to have left Shama and the children among them in one room; worse to have lived without even attempting to lay claim to one's portion of the earth; to have lived and died as one had been born, unnecessary and unaccommodated (1969, 13–4).

It is my view that Naipaul, in the writing of *Miguel Street,* began to discern clearly the human resource and capacity issues which would inevitably challenge the development of a small country such as Trinidad and Tobago. How would people without the capacity for self-examination, self-scrutiny and self-criticism ever be able to develop themselves and create a vision for development of a country? Was it not also inevitable that anyone with talent and/or ambition would seek to escape? Naipaul saw no future for himself in Trinidad as a boy and would have reflected on the possibilities and options for the country of his birth at Oxford and after. Perhaps, at the time, he saw no future for Trinidad and Tobago either. In *The Mystic Masseur* Naipaul ponders the future of a small, relatively backward colonial country, if the leadership which emerges is not equal to the challenge at hand and is incapable of thinking through a possible way forward. In *The Suffrage of Elvira* the author considers the political limitations of a place that has been artificially created and finds it inherently difficult to cohere. How is a society to be forged, if disparate interests can find no common ground, and if there is no leadership capable of rising to the challenge of lighting the way?

In *A House for Mr Biswas*, what Naipaul recognises is that education of one kind or another (in the case of Biswas it is all self education) is essential to stimulate citizens to assert their individual will and to demand freedom and independence for themselves. Free and independent individuals capable of making choices make democracy possible because institutions for freedom and democracy can only be created by men and women who are free and independent. Also, such a society, with such institutions is only possible where the individual is valued and protected. Few other novels are as explicit as *A House for Mr Biswas* on how little the value of an individual is to the community and society which surrounds him.

While Naipaul may have been sensitive to the upheavals and cross currents that surrounded him after the Second World War, and while from 1954 he was wrestling for a hold on material within his memory to create books of fiction, one of his central concerns may have been how his society would survive in a world of turmoil, change and transition. This dilemma – of small, limited societies and migrating talent – he addressed by critically appraising his society, hoping to find a readership in the process. Naipaul has explored these ideas in various pieces. His story of Anguilla published in *The Overcrowded Barracoon* and titled 'The Shipwrecked Six Thousand' comes to mind immediately. These concerns about smallness of size and an attendant narrowness of perspective persist. In fact, the six short pieces which make up the final section of *The Overcrowded Barracoon*, including the title story which is about Mauritius, all explore this theme in one way or another.[3] And in *A Writer's People: Ways of Looking and Feeling*, V.S. Naipaul writes:

> ...small places with simple economies bred small people with simple destinies. And these islands were very small, infinitely

> smaller than Ibsen's Norway. Their literary possibilities, like their economic possibilities, were as narrow as their human possibilities.[4]

On a visit to Trinidad in 2007 to meet commitments to the University of the West Indies, Naipaul conveyed a more positive view of Trinidad and its possibilities – he felt that the quality of people had improved generally through education and exposure but he still expressed worry about its capacity and potential for development in spite of the oil wealth and about the unlikelihood of truly significant talent choosing to stay. I challenged him on that point of view insisting that many had stayed or chose to come back and that much progress had been made, but he retorted by saying that while a writer might be able to live in today's Trinidad and with travel be able to produce, a scientist of world stature would still need more than Trinidad and Tobago or the West Indies has to offer, even now, in order to attain best-in-the-world stature in his field.

In a recent interview, Naipaul distinguished small ex-colonial societies such as those in the West Indies which he claims were 'left on their own… without any guiding idea' from countries such as Finland, Norway or Switzerland, which though small have had a long and continuous autonomous history and strong sense of community.[5]

Anticipating Globalisation

I want to shift gears a bit to another kind of book that Naipaul has written. *In a Free State* is a remarkable work of fiction consisting of a Prologue, an Epilogue and three seemingly unconnected narrative pieces, which are, in fact, mutually reinforcing.[6] Each of the three main stories, 'One Out of Many,' 'Tell Me Who to Kill' and the title story, 'In a Free State' is about displaced persons, a consequence of the great imperial upheavals, and about how these displaced individuals cope with their various realities. The first story is about a Bombay Indian in Washington; the second, about two Trinidad Indian brothers in London; and the third, about English expatriates in an unnamed African country. The Prologue is about a tramp who has been travelling from country to country for a considerable length of time. The Epilogue ends the book with hundreds of Chinese tourists in the centre of Cairo against the background of traditions and habits which have continued uninterrupted in Egypt for a thousand years.

While the novel is exploring postcolonial realities as they unfold, it is also foreshadowing the emergence of the phenomenon of failing states in postcolonial Africa; the challenge of migration to the metropolitan centres; the aftermath of postcolonial disorder, the psychic realities of displacement, homelessness and exile, both for coloniser and colonised. The book takes into account the changing role of India in the international system, a new Indian migration to the USA and the emerging phenomenon of China in the contemporary world while drawing to our attention the fact that, as the phenomenon of change unleashes itself on the planet, there will continue to be countries that persist in their seemingly timeless ways, relatively impervious to modern Western civilisation. Ideas such as these have, from time to time, steered Naipaul in the direction of controversy.

Naipaul does not anticipate failing states in Africa simply because of errors or incompetence of national governments or even the limitations of national leaders. He is absolutely clear on the complicating factors. This is how, almost in fairytale-like style, he explains the situation in *In a Free State*:

> The King and the President intrigued with the local representatives of white governments. The white men who were appealed to liked the king personally. But the President was stronger; the new army was wholly his, of his tribe; and so the white men decided that the President was to be supported. So that, at last, this weekend, the President was able to send his army against the King's people (1973, 103).

Naipaul is careful not to ignore the complicity of colonial agents in his early Trinidad novels either. When, for instance, Ganesh Ramsumair stands up on behalf of disgruntled workers he is described in colonial reports as 'an irresponsible agitator with no following' (*Mystic Masseur* 1957, 214) but when he turns his back on the working class movement and brands it as communist he is embraced by the colonial office as 'an important political leader' (1957, 216). In *The Suffrage of Elvira*, a documentary film is made about political progress in the colonies, 'the script of which was to be written, poetically, in London by a minor British poet' (1969, 180). The irony is that while the Colonial office views the high election poll as significant, it fails to appreciate that all the basic infrastructure required for genuine democracy is missing.

In a fundamental way, Naipaul, almost two decades before the Berlin Wall fell, anticipates the phenomenon of globalisation and the intensification of the internationalisation process. He also foreshadows the discourse that has emerged about identity, home, citizenship and human security in our time. In 'Prologue, from a Journal: The Tramp at Piraeus' published, in 1971, the seemingly, homeless tramp remarks,

> I've been to Egypt six to seven times, gone around the world about a dozen times. Australia, Canada, all those countries....I've been traveling for thirty-eight years....Youth-hostelling, that's how I do it. Not a thing to be despised. New Zealand, have you been there? I went there in 1934. Between you and me, they're a cut above the Australians. But what's nationality these days? I myself, I think of myself as a citizen of the world (*In a Free State* 1971, 3).

Today, curriculum reform theorists argue that we should be preparing our graduates for global citizenship. In 1971 what were we wrestling with here in our part of the world – the first traumatic signs of our post Independence crisis? How much more postmodernist can one get? Everywhere is home; no place to call home; home is wherever you end up. Perhaps with hindsight now, when one considers small ex-colonial societies with limited opportunities and migrating talent, developing countries alongside the prospect of failing states, continual big-country interference in the developing world in pursuit of self-interested gains, and the spirit of ambition and adventure which always drives humans to explore – all elements of simultaneous, often contending strands of thought in Naipaul's head – it is possible to discern that Naipaul foresaw the inevitability of globalisation. The fall of the Berlin Wall might have intensified globalisation by bringing the other empire to an end, but the end of European empire had already unleashed globalisation and set it in motion. Indeed, European imperialism from the fifteenth century onwards had established its foundations.

In his own mind Naipaul might have seen it more as modernisation and the rise of global cities and of a 'universal civilization' which he would identify later in his talk to the Manhattan Institute in October 1990.[7] However, Naipaul, in the early 1970s had already glimpsed the fact that not everywhere would benefit from this modernisation process – some countries such as the one described in *In a Free State* might regress, an issue intensely explored in *A Bend in the River*,[8] while others surrendering to fundamentalist impulses might retreat from the process altogether. If my reading of these matters is correct, and I am open to persuasion otherwise, then this anticipation of the contradictory currents which now criss-cross our contemporary world represents a remarkable feat for V.S. Naipaul as a writer.

So Naipaul's capacity for critical thought and assessment told him that the foundations had not been properly laid for Independence in the ex-colonies, that failing states might well be the result because of a range of complex circumstances and that a new process of human interrelations would emerge on a global scale, facilitated by what he would describe as 'Our Universal Civilization' which would nevertheless cause a stressful degree of displacement and existential angst, but which could also lead to a degree of liberation available to the individual hitherto unknown in human history and civilisation.

Naipaul has told us that writing did not come easily to him. 'To become a writer, that noble thing,' he has written, 'I had thought it necessary to leave. Actually, to write, it was necessary to go back. It was the beginning of self knowledge. So step by step, book by book...I eased myself into knowledge. To write was to learn.'[9] Naipaul also had to learn after completing his first book that there were many other ways in which to look at the material for writing and that once chosen, the way of looking was certain to influence the writing response and the written product. About the period after writing *Miguel Street* he writes in his recent book, *A Writer's People*,

> I knew even then that there were other ways of looking; that if so to speak I took a step or two or three back and saw more of the setting, it would require another kind of writing. And if, in a greater complication, I wished to explore who I was and who the people in the street were...that would require yet another kind of writing. It was to that complication that my writing took me (2007, 2).

Later, in this same recent book, Naipaul also tells us:

> There is a specificity to writing. Certain settings, certain cultures, have to be written about in a certain way. These ways are not interchangeable, you cannot write about Nigerian tribal life as you would write about the English Midlands. (23)

Naipaul had to scrutinise himself as a writer. He was soon to discover that 'to be an Indian or East Indian from the West Indies is to be a perpetual surprise to people outside the region' (*Overcrowded Barracoon* 1976, 33) and that reality created complications both for him as a writer and for the reception to the material that formed the substance of his writing. The sheer incongruity of being an Indian from Trinidad in Naipaul's early career became a formidable challenge for Naipaul:

> To be an Indian from Trinidad is unlikely...When in 1492 Columbus landed on Guanahani he thought he had got to Cathay. He ought, therefore, to have called the people Chinese...He called them Indians, and Indians they remained, walking Indian file through the Indian corn....
>
> So long as the real Indians remained on the other side of the world there was little confusion. But when in 1845 these Indians began coming over to some of the islands Columbus called the Indies, confusion became total (*Overcrowded Barracoon* 1976, 33, 34).

Naipaul made other discoveries and learnt other things. For instance, he discovered the life of the period from 1906 to the time of his birth (1932) through his father's stories. Naipaul discovered Trinidad's history by poring over original documents and maps which revealed stories of 'discovery, the New World, the dispeopling of the discovered islands; slavery, the creation of the plantation colony; the coming of the idea of revolution; the chaos after revolutions in societies so created' (*Enigma* 1987, 94). Naipaul discovered the options available to a writer through travel, beginning with *The Middle Passage* and through travel, again, Africa, India, the non-Arab Islamic world, Latin America, the United States of America and England where he settled after leaving Trinidad.[10] Naipaul has described all of this as 'areas of darkness around me as a child' that is to say places and things about which he knew very little.[11] It is these areas of darkness that became the subject matter of both his fictional and non-fictional work (Naipaul makes little distinction between these two types of writing) and because they were areas of darkness, he had to discover them in his own original way.

He had to look at things in a particular way and critically assess everything that would come into his experience with a freshness of perspective, '...To write was to learn,' he writes in 'Prologue to an Autobiography' (2003, 67). 'Self assessment...is where learning begins' he says in his Nobel Lecture (2001 n.p.), and it is this freshness of perspective, the suspension of assumptions, the taking of nothing for granted which provides the critical thinking, which ultimately leads to this writer's keen and original insights. The writing process itself became not just a creative act of the imagination but a process of discovery and critical inquiry.

Critical Thinker

Critical self-inquiry, self-discovery and self-knowledge led to critical thought about what it means to be a writer, aware of various ways of looking. The 'confusion' of being an Indian from the West Indies (the equivalent of an area of darkness for the global literary public) was resolved, for instance, on the completion of Naipaul's first five books. These covered the journey of East Indians from India to the New World, addressed disintegration in this new world and took Ralph Singh on another journey to London, the metropolitan centre. Thus the colonial experience of the indentured Indian was extensively explored by the time *The Mimic Men* was written. However, that book also explored the neuroses of Indian and African politicians in the West Indies – something not easily explored in a few paragraphs. The introduction of travel allowed Naipaul to discover new worlds and, with these new worlds, new material that would make up for the exhaustion of material based on limited experience and memory in Trinidad.

Trinidad, however, and his knowledge and experience of Trinidad, always remained Naipaul's point of reference. This becomes clear when one reads a book such as *The Enigma of Arrival* in which his focus is on the English Midlands but his point of reference always tropical, island Trinidad. And this Trinidad reference point has remained a constant in Naipaul's way of seeing because it is fundamental to his critical thinking process. This is what he says in *Enigma*:

> But the island – with the curiosity it had awakened in me for the larger world, the idea of civilization, and the idea of antiquity; and all the anxieties it had quickened in me – the island had given me the world as a writer; had given me the themes that in the second half of the twentieth century had become important; had made me metropolitan (1987, 140).

So Trinidad had given him the world but it is through research that he discovered Trinidad. 'I had to do the books I did because there were no books about those subjects to give me what I wanted. I had to clear up my world, to elucidate it for myself,' he says in his Nobel Lecture, 'Two Words,'

> ...I had to go to the documents in the British Museum and elsewhere, to get the true feel of the history of the colony. I had to travel to India because there was no one to tell me what the India my grandparents had come from was like....And when that Indian need was satisfied, others became apparent: Africa, South America, the Muslim world. The aim has always been to fill out my world picture, and the purpose comes from my childhood: to make me more at ease with myself.

So out of this personal need as an individual to learn, to understand, to locate himself in the world, Naipaul begins a process of critical inquiry into self, society and the world around him through the act of writing. By this act of writing and the creation of books, he illumines his own life and world as he illumines ours, forcing us to think and rethink about our human condition. Naipaul had to think critically about himself to find his way as a writer, about his background and society in order to summon material, and to grope in the darkness of other worlds, in order to arrive at a point of view consistently based on critical inquiry and thought. Let me highlight a few examples that are familiar to you.

Who else but a critical thinker would spend four years at Oxford and brand that world-famous institution a provincial University?[12] Who else but a critical thinker would describe himself as 'a man of a certain race, from a certain place, looking at the world in a certain way and coming to certain conclusions,'[13] or make the statement, 'When I speak of being an exile or a refugee, I'm not just using a metaphor'?[14] and who but a critical thinker would boldly write in 1962, the year Trinidad and Tobago secured its Independence:

> Nationalism was impossible in Trinidad. In the Colonial Society every man had to be for himself; every man had to grasp whatever dignity and power he was allowed; he owed no loyalty to the island and scarcely any to his group (*The Middle Passage* 2001, 72).

He puts it even more controversially and provocatively later in *The Middle Passage*:

> The history of the islands can never be satisfactorily told. Brutality is not the only difficulty. History is built around achievement and creation; and nothing was created in the West Indies (2001, 20).

In 1983, I responded to those critics who had taken Naipaul's statement out of context and to others who have been misrepresenting Naipaul's thinking on this matter by pointing out their error:

> The lack of a sense of community that is demonstrated in *The Suffrage of Elvira* has its roots in the colonial plantation legacy for which the British were responsible. Naipaul's *The Loss of El Dorado* makes it clear that the causes of the contemporary dislocation with which he deals are rooted in colonial history. The charge of non-creation is made against the colonists not the colonized. It is no accident that Naipaul's *Loss of El Dorado* ends in 1813, two decades before slavery was abolished. It is clear that Naipaul's point of view is that the pattern of human relations and the accompanying depravity of human endeavour were already established at that time.[15]

At the time, I also made reference to another critic, Margaret Nightingale, with whose views I concur:

> Naipaul's history of Trinidad concentrates on the period during which patterns of colonial behaviour were established, tracing it to the origins of modern sterility, lack of creativity, racial stratification, roguery and self-denigration he has recorded in The Middle Passage.[16]

Obviously when V.S. Naipaul wrote *The Middle Passage* he was dealing with matters of historical fact that warranted our attention as matters of concern. But by misunderstanding him some critics responded to a legitimate matter of concern without any regard whatsoever for matters of fact.

In my interview of Naipaul (April 11, 2007) he makes it clear that his quarrel is with history and the colonial legacy and definitely not a judgement on the people who in contemporary time must wrestle with their challenges and dilemmas. This is not to seek to soften for a minute the brutality of Naipaul but it is honest brutality or, if you prefer, brutal honesty – a brutal honesty which, on occasion, generates fierce hostility. Similarly, he writes about Argentina during a period of crisis when the country was passionately divided: 'Where jargon turns living issues into abstractions, and where jargon ends by competing with jargon, people don't have causes. They only have enemies.'[17] Again, Naipaul writes as follows about the approach to conversion in the Far East by the Arabs: '…no colonization had been so thorough as the colonization that had come with the Arab faith….No colonization could have been greater than this colonization by faith.' Naipaul continues '…the faith was the complete way, filled everything, left no spare corner of the mind or will or soul.'[18] Thus he describes the process of establishing the foundation for fundamentalism which, borrowing a word from Joseph Conrad, he describes as 'philosophical hysteria' ('Our Universal Civilization' 2002, 513). This is vintage Naipaul responding to ideological excess and dogmatism.

There is more. In *The Middle Passage*, V.S. Naipaul uses the phrase 'half made societies,' but it is a phrase that he has used many times since then. In *Enigma of Arrival*, Naipaul makes reference to his 'half-Indian world' (1988, 103). In his 2001 novel entitled *Half a Life*, Willie Chandran speaks of the 'half and half world'[19] and in *A Writer's People* he describes Vinoba Bhave (a follower of Gandhi, who unsuccessfully tried to emulate him), not only as a foolish man but as 'a kind of half-man' who had lived for a long time as a 'parasite' (2007, 172).

While Naipaul in *Mimic Men* diagnoses colonial neurosis in the West Indies where men can only mimic the idea of manhood; while he makes an assessment that India's dilemma of 'fitting one civilization to another' will lead to crisis, in *A Writer's People*, and while he is repulsed by the idea of converts who wish 'to make their minds and souls a blank, an emptiness, so that they could be nothing but their faith' ('Our Universal Civilization' 2002, 512) his concept of the 'half' – half a life, half-Indian world, half-made societies, half-man, is a bothersome repetitive motif in Naipaul's work. What exactly does it mean? Could it be something as simple as 'half-baked' in the way we normally use it to mean, not quite ready, not quite up to it in the sense of half-baked effort and thus half-baked society? What does half a life mean? What does the 'half and half world' mean? What does 'half-made societies' really mean since, according to Naipaul, some of them are doomed to remain half-made?

In the case of the individual, it is my view that it has to do with two things – identity on the one hand, and achievement of potential on the other. In *Half a Life*, Willie's father who becomes the model for a character in a Somerset Maugham novel finds it hard to 'step out of that role' (2002, 3).

In this sense he is like Ralph Singh playing the role that others expect him to play. Eventually Willie's father finds it impossible to break out of the mould in which he has been cast and so he surrenders to fate: 'I recognized that breaking out had become impossible, and I settled down to live the strange life that fate had bestowed on me' (2002, 4). The life of the father, unfulfilling for him as it is, is nevertheless understandable because of the rules and restrictions and sanctions that govern life in rural India. However, Willie Chandran seizes the opportunity to turn his back on it all and ill-equipped, ill-prepared as he is, ends up in London in the bohemian 1950s to find himself 'unanchored, with no idea of what lay ahead' (2002, 58). Yet if Willie is lost he also begins to understand that he is free of the old shackles and can reinvent himself:

> Willie began to understand that he was free to present himself as he wished. He could, as it were, write his own revolution. The possibilities were dizzying. He could, within reason, remake himself and his past and his ancestry....So, playing with words, he began to re-make himself. It excited him, and began to give him a feeling of power (2002, 60–1).

However, Willie achieves little during the course of his lifetime. In London, in spite of the publication of one book, his life is a disaster. He ends up in parasitic relationship with Ana who takes him with her to her home in Mozambique just at that moment when time and opportunity have run out on Willie in London. At that point, Ana literally saves him from an uncertain fate.

In Portuguese Mozambique, in the midst of an anti-colonial revolutionary struggle, he becomes an idler and womaniser cut off by language from the world that he knows and without an identity that is meaningful to him or anyone else: 'So people couldn't place me and they let me be. I was Ana's London man...' (2002, 145). At the age of 41 he realises that he has been living Ana's life and that the best part of his life is gone and that he has achieved nothing although 'there was another self inside him, in a silent space where all his external life was muffled' (2002, 133).

Critical and Creative

The concept of 'half a life' has been connected (above) with the issues of identity and achievement. After travelling through the Far East, Naipaul discerned what Samuel Huntington would later describe as the 'clash of civilizations.'[20] Naipaul was horrified that an entire people with a history, culture and civilisation would be willing to wipe out all of this in order to become religiously devout and pure. He saw this as an attempt not only to close out the world but to deny reality. This fundamentalist world he saw as doctrinaire, closed, mind-numbing and ritualistic. The world diametrically opposed to this was one that was open, embracing, celebrative of individual freedom and demanding of individual responsibility, a world that had given him an opportunity to strive and to thrive as a writer. This world Naipaul labels 'Our Universal Civilization' and it is a world which Naipaul fully embraces. Not that this world is perfect, but from his point of view, it is the best that humankind has created in all of its history:

> The universal civilization has been a long time in making. It wasn't always universal; it wasn't always as attractive as it is today. The expansion of Europe gave it, for at least three centuries, a racial taint which still causes pain (2002, 516).

Notwithstanding this, however, Naipaul celebrates this civilisation not only because of 'the extraordinary attempt of this civilization to accommodate the rest of the world and all the currents of the world's thought' (516) but also because in that civilisation it is 'necessary to be an individual and responsible,' and also one in which people 'developed vocations and were stirred by ambition and achievement and believed in perfectability' (514–15). Naipaul sees fundamentalism of any kind as diametrically opposed to this universal civilisation. One might attempt to retreat to the fundamentalist world and turn one's back entirely on the universal civilisation but the scientific and technological supports of the universal civilisation would still be required for survival and for sustainability.

However, beyond fundamentalist retreat, civilisations and cultures connect and meet everyday. People from other cultures move to the metropolitan centres. The universal culture spreads outward globally impacting on people, societies and culture. East meets West. Africa interfaces with Europe. What, therefore, is the challenge? We get an insight from *A Writer's People*. In an open democracy such as India, secular in its outlook, Naipaul makes a judgement that India is wrestling with the challenge of 'fitting one civilization to another' (2007, 191) and he anticipates that this will lead to crisis since, from his perspective, 'India has no autonomous intellectual life.' Naipaul makes the following comment about the Bengali intellectual, Nirad Chaudhuri:

> It is astonishing that Chaudhuri could without strain, have contained so many worlds within himself. But then the strain came, with the politics of the nationalist movement, with the new eyes that the movement gave, and everything that was so nicely balanced came tumbling down (82).

Half-made societies, therefore, from Naipaul's perspective are societies that cannot pull together the most meaningful elements of a multi-civilisational, multicultural world to make a psychologically coherent whole; that cannot successfully integrate what is authentically theirs with what is available from other societies and cultures. Half a life, half a man, describes the individual who cannot summon the will to achieve because, moving through multiple cultures and societies or impacted by them, he is unable to effectively contain the many worlds that he carries within him and yet achieve clarity of perspective and a sense of purpose. At the extreme ends are colonial schizophrenia and fundamentalist retreat, but in the middle are the half and half lives proceeding in their mental half and half worlds.

What contributes to the creation of a 'half and half' status in individuals and societies? Naipaul might answer 'intellectual failure.' I might interpret that to mean the absence of critical thinking, that is to say, the failure to assess one's situation realistically and, through a deep understanding, think one's way through well enough to summon the will and courage required to meet the challenge no matter how formidable. 'The world is as it is,' Salim tells us in the first sentence of *A Bend in the River*, 'those who are nothing, who allow themselves to be nothing, have no place in it' (Naipaul 1979, 3). So it is for individuals, so it is for societies. Happiness is there for all to pursue; opportunities are there that all may pursue; development and achievement are there for all to strive for, but only some will truly triumph.

I promised earlier to define what I mean by 'critical thinking.' I begin from a book called *I Know What it Says...What Does it Mean?* by Daniel Kurkland: 'Broadly speaking, critical thinking is concerned with reason, intellectual honesty and open mindedness.'[21] Against this, Kurkland juxtaposes 'emotionalism, intellectual laziness and closed mindedness' and elaborates further: 'critical thinking involves following evidence where it leads…considering all possibilities…being concerned more with finding the truth than with being right.'

Critical thinking is not a matter of accumulating information and critical thinking should not be confused with being argumentative or being critical of other people or things. Those who espouse the value of critical thinking emphasise its value as both the foundation of science as well as the foundation of a liberal democratic society. That is because science requires the critical use of reason for experimentation as well as for the confirmation of theory. For a liberal democracy to function effectively it requires citizens who can think critically about social issues to inform their judgements about good governance and also in order to overcome biases and prejudices. Joanne Kurfiss describes critical thinking as,

> …a process to figure out what to believe or not about a situation, phenomenon, problem or controversy for which no single definitive answer or solution exists. The term implies a diligent open-minded search for understanding, rather than for a discovery of a necessary solution.[22]

There must be sceptics in the audience who may be thinking that Naipaul is a creative writer and what is at work here is really creative thinking or the creative artist or the creative mind at work. While it is true that both critical thinking and creative thinking are high order cognitive skills and that both of these skills may be classified as high achievement of thought, we need to be clear that critical thinking leads the thinker to ask questions and to interrogate the reasons behind something. The creative thinker may well ask why not – that is to say, such a person may well posit an alternative view or way or a solution.

Throughout his writing V.S. Naipaul asks the questions why and how. Why is this so? How did this get to be so? He is seeking to understand; it is a process of discovery. In a fundamental way, when he is wrestling with ideas he is thinking inside the box – evaluating material or a particular context to understand it much more deeply. The creative thinker, however, is also at work because he is a writer who is producing a new, tangible product – a book, essay, article, story as the case might be. One also needs to conceptualise critical and creative thinking as elements that are intertwined strands of a double helix in which, in the case of a writer such as V.S. Naipaul, the two types of thinking – critical thinking and creative thinking – are constantly reinforcing each other.

That is why we find his work thought-provoking, sometimes jolting; that is why some are disappointed at the paucity of solutions to the dark-visioned challenges he poses. Yet that is also why, by looking outside the box as a creative imagination, he is able to conjure up new worlds, book after formidable book, to engage our imagination, provoke a response, entice our souls by illuminating his life and world as well as ours. At the end of the day, the reader is able to engage both his critical insight as well as his creative genius.

We may not like what Naipaul says or how he says it; we may not agree with his point of view at all; after all, the fact that he is a critical thinker does not necessarily make him right on everything. However, we need, at the very least, to understand and appreciate what he is thinking and the meaning of his writing and vision before we ourselves can either accept his perspective, challenge it, dismiss it altogether or present an alternative point of view.

Naipaul's work has been a prompting for other critical thinkers. Lloyd Best's theory of tribes and its implications for national politics in Trinidad and Tobago derives from *The Suffrage of Elvira* and, not only does Samuel Huntington's *Clash of Civilizations* owe a debt to Naipaul but Huntington's work has provoked Amartya Senn to respond in a book entitled *Identity and Violence*.[23] So Naipaul is not simply a critical thinker himself; he is, and has been, a profound influence on other critical thinkers as well.

Notes

1. V.S. Naipaul, *The Enigma of Arrival* (England: Penguin Books, 1987), 130.
2. Naipaul, *A House for Mr Biswas* (England: Penguin Books, 1969), 13–4. *Miguel Street*, (London: Heinemann, 1974); *The Mystic Masseur*, (London: Penguin Books, 1957), *The Suffrage of Elvira* (1958; repr., Harmondsworth: Penguin, 1969).
3. Naipaul, *The Overcrowded Barracoon* (1972; repr., Harmondsworth: Penguin, 1976).
4. Naipaul, *A Writer's People: Ways of Looking and Feeling* (London: Picador, 2007), 16.
5. V.S. Naipaul, interview by Bhoendradatt Tewarie, April 11, 2007. Video presentation at the University of the West Indies, St Augustine, Trinidad and Tobago, as part of the Campus celebration of V.S. Naipaul.
6. Naipaul, *In a Free State* (1971; repr., Harmondsworth: Penguin Books, 1973).
7. Naipaul, 'Our Universal Civilization,' in *The Writer and the World*, ed. Pankaj Mishra (1990; repr., London: Picador, 2003).
8. Naipaul, *A Bend in the River*, (London: André Deutsch, 1979), 3.

9. Naipaul, 'Prologue to an Autobiography' in *Literary Occasions: Essays* (London: Picador, 2003), 67.
10. Naipaul, *The Middle Passage: Impressions of Five Societies, British, French and Dutch, in the West Indies and South America* (1962; repr., London: Picador, 2001), 69.
11. Naipaul, 'Two Worlds,' The Nobel Lecture, Börssalen, Swedish Academy, Stockholm, 7 December 2001. http://nobelprize.org/nobel_prizes/literature/laureates/2001/naipaul-lecture-e.html
12. See Feroza Jussawalla, ed. *Conversations with V.S. Naipaul,* (Jackson: University Press of Mississippi, 1997), 99.
13. R. Z. Sheppard, 'Notes from the Fourth World,' *Time*, May 21, 1979.
14. Paul Theroux, *Sunrise With Seamonsters Travels and Discoveries, 1964–84* (Rolling Meadows, MA: Houghton Mifflin Books, 1985), 95.
15. Bhoendradatt Tewari, 'A Comparative Study of Ethnicity in the Novels of Saul Bellow and V.S. Naipaul' (PhD dissertation, Pennsylvania State University, 1993), 316; V.S. Naipaul, *The Loss of El Dorado,* (Great Britain: André Deutsch, 1969).
16. Margaret Nightingale, 'V.S. Naipaul as Historian: Combating Chaos,' *Southern Review: Literary and Interdisciplinary Essays* 13, no. 3 (1980): 240.
17. Naipaul, *The Return of Eva Perón* (1974; repr., Harmondsworth: Penguin, 1980).
18. Naipaul, 'Our Universal Civilisation,' *The Writer and the World* (New York: Alfred A. Knopf, 2002), 508, 513–4.
19. Naipaul, *Half a Life* (2001; repr., London: Picador, 2002), 150.
20. Samuel P. Huntington. *The Clash of Civilizations and the Remaking of World Order* (1997; repr., London: Simon and Schuster, 2002).
21. Daniel J. Kurkland. *I Know What it Says... What Does it Mean?* (Kentucky: Wadsworth Publishing, 1995), 164.
22. Joanne Kurfiss, 'Helping Faculty Foster Students' Critical Thinking in the Disciplines,' *New Directions for Teaching and Learning*, no. 37 (1989): 42.
23. Amartya Kumar Sen, *Identity and Violence: The Illusion of Destiny* (New York: W.W. Norton and Co., 2006).

13

NAIPAUL'S SENSE OF HISTORY

Bridget Brereton

No passage in V.S. Naipaul's vast corpus of published work has been more frequently quoted and reviled than the following:

> How can the history of this West Indian futility be written? What tone shall the historian adopt?...Shall he, like the West Indian historians, who can only now [1962] begin to face their history, be icily detached and tell the story of the slave trade as if it were just another aspect of mercantilism? The history of the islands can never be satisfactorily told. Brutality is not the only difficulty. History is build around achievement and creation; and nothing was created in the West Indies.[1]

This is the passage that has been justly criticised both for its sheer rhetorical excess and for the disdain and dismissal it seems to reflect: a dismissal not only of the possibility of West Indian creativity, but also of the value of the historian's project, at least when applied to the Caribbean.

Yet the need to understand the past, the imperative to confront one's personal, national, and regional histories unflinchingly, seems to me to be absolutely central in Naipaul's work and worldview. On the basis of a highly selective reading of some of his fiction and non-fiction, I argue that, for Naipaul, the erasure of the past, the failure or refusal to develop well researched and reasonably objective historical narratives, are key indices of underdevelopment and intellectual impoverishment for any people, nation or region of the world. A society which cannot, or will not, examine its past with scholarly rigour is, in his view, a society doomed to be static and uncreative. It is a society which substitutes tradition, barely understood ritual, fundamentalisms of various kinds, for a critical examination of its history. Naipaul admits that this examination is difficult and painful, involving, as it must, the loss of a sense of enclosed security that the traditions, the rituals and the fundamentalisms engender. However, it also opens up the possibility of creativity and development. So far from dismissing the historian's project as futile or a mission impossible, he effectively validates the need for sound historical scholarship and for the critical self-awareness which that scholarship can and should help to develop.

Over and over again, Naipaul has written of the Indo-Hindu Trinidadian community into which he was born, and among which he spent his first 18 years, as one that was abysmally ignorant of its history, and utterly incurious about it. He told a University of the West Indies, St Augustine conference audience in 1975 that 'we [Indo-Caribbeans] came from a culture that has not been much given to self-examination or to historical enquiry...[we] have become people who live as though the past can be denied...[we] have become people without a past.'[2] They inhabited a world in which 'all the questions had already been answered and all the rituals perfected.' Naipaul went on to insist that 'self-examination' and 'self-awareness' through historical research were not only necessary for this community to move out of its self-absorbed and static world, but positively 'revolutionary' in their implications (1982, 5). A quarter of a century later, in his 2001 Nobel Lecture, he makes the same point:

> What was past was past. I suppose that was the general attitude. And we Indians, immigrants from India, had that attitude to the island. We lived for the most part ritualised lives, and were not yet capable of self-assessment, which is where learning begins.[3]

To live within such a worldview was 'to know a kind of security; it was to inhabit a fixed world';[4] but the loss of that security and fixedness, through learning about the past, was essential for creativity and development – whether for the writer himself, or for a society.

'I grew up with two ideas of history, almost two ideas of time,' Naipaul wrote in *Finding the Centre* 1984; 'there was history with dates...[which] affected peoples and places abroad.'[5] This was the history he learned at

Queen's Royal College, of Rome, England, Europe. 'But Chaguanas, where I was born…had no dates;' beyond personal memories was

> …undated time, historical darkness. Out of that darkness (extending to place as well as time) we had all come…I lived easily with that darkness, that lack of knowledge. I never thought to inquire further….To discover the wonder of our situation as children of the New World we had to look into ourselves; and to someone from my kind of Hindu background that wasn't easy (*Finding the Centre* 1984, 58).

'I had no idea of history,' he writes again, this time in his autobiographical novel *The Enigma of Arrival*; 'it was hard to attach something as grand as history to our island.'[6] In 1950, when he first came to England, he was 'like the earliest Spanish travellers to the New World, medieval men with high faith,' lacking curiosity about what they found, without any impulse to enquiry. 'True curiosity comes at a later stage of development' – for the writer as for a society (*Finding* 1984, 143).

Naipaul has stated unequivocally that historical research – scholarly, based on the evidence, as objective as this mode of enquiry can be – is in his view essential for the self-knowledge that all individuals and societies must have if they are to create and develop. He said in 1975:

> I think that it is through scholarship and a wish to understand through scholarship, and not through sentiment, that we can arrive at some understanding of all the strands in our upbringing….I think that through scholarship and intelligent inquiry we will understand more about the past and more about the culture of our grandfathers than they themselves did.[7]

In his own journey to self-knowledge, he has often acknowledged that the years he spent researching and writing *The Loss of El Dorado* (1969), his only full-length work of formal 'history,' were enormously important in helping him to locate his place in the world. He has returned again and again to material he studied in the British Museum and the Public Records Office in London for that book. In his Nobel Lecture, Naipaul describes almost as a personal epiphany his discovery, sitting in the British Museum in 1967 reading old Spanish documents, that his birthplace Chaguanas was named after a small Amerindian ethnic group, the Chaguanes, mentioned in a letter from the King of Spain to the governor of Trinidad in 1625: 'And the thought came to me in the Museum that I was the first person since 1625 to whom that letter...had a real meaning....We lived on the Chaguanes' land' (Naipaul *Nobel* 2001, 3; *Finding* 1984, 50).

His arduous work in the archives, researching the history of Trinidad from the sixteenth to the nineteenth centuries, endowed him with a sense of 'historical wonder' which never left him, and which he clearly believes is essential for intellectual and social development. 'True knowledge of geography, and with it a sense of historical wonder, began to come sixteen years after I had left Trinidad, when for two years I worked on a history of the region,' he wrote in 1984. He was 'trying only to understand how [his] corner of the New World...had become the place it was' (*Finding* 1984, 49). In *The Enigma of Arrival*, Naipaul describes his two years in the archives as 'a great packed education;'

> for the two years that I lived among the documents I sought to reconstruct the human story as best I could...discovery, the New World, the dispeopling of the discovered islands [like the disappearance or obliteration of the Chaguanes]; slavery, the creation of the plantation colony; the coming of the idea of revolution; the chaos after revolutions in societies so created (1987, 101).

Coming from a community and an island with little interest in its past, where 'history' happened only in other places, Naipaul was energised by a new understanding of his place – and therefore his way – in the world:

> I was amazed, reading the documents of my island in London, by the antiquity of the place to which I belonged. Such simple things! Seeing the island as part of the globe, seeing it sharing in the antiquity of the earth! Yet these simple things came to me as revelations (157).

He says much the same in *A Way in the World*, the Naipaul book that resonates most strongly with his earlier archival researches. So much in this 'sequence' (between novel and non-fiction) reflects his profound feel for the early history of Trinidad, his deep understanding of its tragedy, the degradation of slavery and racial oppression; especially, in my view, the section entitled 'In the Gulf of Desolation.'[8]

To achieve the self-awareness on which creativity and critical thought rest, Naipaul believes writers and societies must face up to their past through serious historical examination. Caribbean people, including his own Indo-Trinidadian community, will need to go through this process, even if the price is a loss of ancestral tradition and atavistic security. The terrible ravages wrought by imperialism on the former colonies must be rigorously researched and explicated – for the damage done by the colonial powers is a central theme in nearly all Naipaul's work; he is no 'imperialist stooge' as some of his cruder critics have argued.[9] Yet the crimes and follies of postcolonial elites and others must, equally, be unflinchingly exposed. Societies that fail or refuse to go through this rigorous self-examination may be doomed to remain uncreative and dependent. Perhaps it is no coincidence that Ralph Singh, the flawed protagonist of *The Mimic Men*, wanted to write a history of 'the empires of our time…[which] have altered the world for ever,' but does not, in the end, try very hard to do so.[10]

One nation of the New World which Naipaul finds has failed to confront its past – and has paid a heavy price for that failure – is Argentina, which he visited and wrote about on many occasions:

> A million square miles, an enormous country, twenty-three million people, everything in the world, so rich, and now [1975] in its death throes. Its failure is not a failure of wealth or education. It's an intellectual failure, a failure of people who have been unwilling to face their history. That was a history of genocide, occurring quite recently, followed by the seizing of Indian lands and the establishing of enormous estates…The labour was imported from Europe to service these big estates. These people were fed on special myths. The most debilitating was that they were not South Americans, that they were really Europeans, that their culture distinguished them from the rest of the continent. But they were in fact living in a borrowed culture; they had created nothing; and when the British Empire that protected them withdrew, the whole thing just fell apart (*Introduction* 1982, 8–9).

This basic point is reiterated in his essays about Argentina written between 1972 and 1991. 'There is no history in Argentina,' Naipaul wrote in 1972, 'there are no archives; there are only graffiti and polemics and school lessons.'[11] The War of Independence and its heroes are celebrated but the event 'stands in isolation; it is not related, in the text books or in the popular mind, to what immediately followed: the loss of law, the seeking out of the enemy, endless civil wars, gangster rule' (*The Writers and the World* 2002, 360). Even the nation's great writer, Borges, substitutes 'ancestor worship' for 'the contemplation of his country's history' – and 'Borges is Argentina's greatest man' (360). It was, in Naipaul's acerbic yet not entirely unsympathetic view, 'a collective refusal to see, to come to terms with the land: an artificial, fragmented colonial society, made deficient and bogus by its myths' (361). It was a refusal to 'see' the Indians, destroyed in a fairly recent (1870s–80s) genocide, which is 'dismissed in a line or two in the annals…the Argentine terror is that people in other countries might think of Argentina as an Indian country' (385). The Indians 'disappeared' from the history and the memory; so did the Africans, descendants of slaves from Spanish times. Until the nation confronted its past, and put aside the myths and the disappearances in favour of critical self-examination, Naipaul implies, it would continue to be static and uncreative, failing to live up to its potential (394–426).

He makes much the same kind of point about India, Pakistan and Africa. As Nana Wilson-Tagoe points out, Naipaul believed that Hindu India, as he first encountered it in 1963, was enmeshed in a 'medieval' worldview, in which history was not researched and few were interested in understanding the past.[12] In the first of his books on India, he wrote that myth and binding tradition substituted for critical self-awareness through historical research, much as in the Indo-Trinidadian community he had known in the 1930s and 1940s. These were enclosed societies with an undeveloped sense of history, which – both in India and in Trinidad – impeded the possibility of creativity, imaginative vision and progressive change.[13] The same was broadly true of Islamic Pakistan. Here, Naipaul writes, 'the faith abolished the past. And when the past was abolished like this, more than an idea of history suffered. Human behavior, and ideals of good behavior, could suffer' ('Our Universal' 2002, 509). He illustrates his argument by referring to the 1979 commemoration of the Arab conquest of Sind, the conquest of a Hindu-Buddhist kingdom, occupying much of today's southern Pakistan, by Arab Muslims in the eighth century. A newspaper article about an Arab general tried to be fair to the armies of both sides. It drew an official rebuke from the chairman of Pakistan's National Commission of Historical and Cultural Research (no less) for appearing to 'sympathise' with the Hindu defenders of Sind and for employing the wrong 'phraseology' when describing the Arab 'hero.' 'After 1,200 years,' Naipaul comments,

> …the holy war is still being fought. The hero is the Arab invader, bringer of the faith. The rival whose defeat is to be applauded – and I was reading this in Sind – is the man of Sind. To possess the faith was to possess the only truth; and possession of this truth set many things on its head….The faith altered values, ideas of good behaviour, human judgements ('Our Universal Civilisation' 2002, 511).

Such a society was shutting itself off from 'the ideas of inquiry and the tools of scholarship' and 'whole accumulations' of knowledge (2002, 512). As to Africa, Nana-Tagoe points out that the protagonist of *A Bend in the River,* Salim, sees the capacity to separate the past from the present, to recognise the past as distinct territory from the present, to be historically aware, as crucially linked to the ability to change and grow. To have it, in Salim's view, is to be able 'to assess the consequences of the past with an eye on future action and thinking' (Wilson-Tagoe 1998, 71). Salim believes that 'Africans' lacked this capacity, for the 'tribal world' (like Naipaul's Indo-Trinidadian community of his childhood) did not need historical awareness. Such an enclosed world, lacking all sense of the past, was secure only until it was exposed; then it was defenceless, leading directly to the 'disorder' Salim saw in the Africa of his present (Wilson-Tagoe 1998, 71).

Famously (or infamously), Naipaul often seems to see 'order' only in Europe, the 'metropole,' and disorder or half-made societies everywhere else. To the extent that this is true, it is clearly linked to his notion that these 'older' societies have come to be on easy terms with their history, have invested in scholarship about their past as well as, inevitably, creating their own national myths. This sense of antiquity is movingly expressed in Naipaul's meditations about the Wiltshire countryside in *The Enigma of Arrival*, the most 'personal' of his novels:

> my feeling for the age of the earth and the oldness of man's possession of it, was always with me…That sense of antiquity gave another scale to the activities around one. But at the same time – from this height and with that wide view – there was a feeling of continuity. So the idea of antiquity, at once diminishing and ennobling the current activities of men, as well as the ideas of literature, enveloped this world which…came to me as a lucky find (1987, 20).

The sense of human possession of the land in this 'historical' corner of England, stretching back thousands of years, moved Naipaul. The older ideals of '[h]istory, glory, religion as a wish to do the right thing by oneself – these ideas were still with some people in the valleys round about...[who] still had the idea of being successors and inheritors' (*Enigma* 1987, 50–1). Yet of course, even in his pastoral Wiltshire countryside, there can be no 'pure' sense of historical continuity and progress. Change, decay, renovation are all around. Naipaul is also sharply aware that the 'order' and 'security' he finds in his corner of England rested on wealth, empire and the exploitation of people like his ancestors; that in the 'glory days' of the landed estate, from which he was renting a cottage, there would have been no place for 'people like me' (Wilson-Tagoe 1998, 75–76).

Like most historians working today, Naipaul does not subscribe to any overarching Grand Theory which purports to explain all of the vast, chaotic human past: 'I have no unifying theory of things,' he told a New York audience in 1992. He continues:

> To me situations and people are always specific, always of themselves. That is why one travels and writes: to find out. To work in the other way would be to know the answers before one knew the problems. That is a recognized way of working, I know, especially if one is a political or religious or racial missionary. But I would have found it hard ('Our Universal Civilisation' 2002, 503).

He said much the same thing in his Nobel Lecture: 'I have always moved by intuition alone. I have no system, literary or political. I have no guiding political idea' (2001, 7).

However, one 'guiding idea' that seems to underlie much, if not all of his work is the belief that critical self-awareness, born out of the hard and painful work of examining the past, is vital for individuals, peoples and nations. A historical sense allows for creativity, the full exercise of the imagination, and the capacity for change and growth. 'Men need history,' Naipaul writes at the end of *The Enigma of Arrival*; 'it helps them to have an idea of who they are. But history, like sanctity, can reside in the heart; it is enough that there is something there' (1987, 353). We must be able to make the connections if we are to find our way in the world. Contemplating the city of his youth, Port of Spain, as it appeared after the fires and looting that followed an attempted coup in 1990, he wrote:

> You could see down to what might have been thought buried forever: the thick-walled eighteenth-century Spanish foundations of some buildings. You could see the low gable marks of early, small buildings against higher walls. You could look down, in fact, at more than Spanish foundation: you could look down at red Amerindian soil (*A Way* 1995, 43).

Earlier in the narrative, he wrote in a similar vein: 'we go back and back, forever; we go back all of us to the very beginning; in our blood and bone and brain we carry the memories of thousands of beings' (11).

History is vital; critically examining, and unflinchingly facing up to the past is a necessary process for all individuals – but especially writers – and for all nations, perhaps especially those of the postcolonial world. This seems to me to be one of the key Naipaulian ideas. I believe it provides a good reason for historians (and others, of course) to respect and read and reread Naipaul, whatever their individual judgements on his worldview. Is it time to forgive him for the rhetorical excess of that famous statement with which I began this essay, written all of 45 years ago when he was just 30?

Notes

1. V.S. Naipaul, *The Middle Passage* (1962; repr., London: Picador, 2001), 20.
2. 'Introduction.' *East Indians in the Caribbean*. eds. B. Brereton and W. Dookeran (Millwood, NY: Kraus Thomson, 1982), 4.
3. Naipaul, 'The Nobel Lecture' (2001). http://nobelprize.org/nobel_prizes/literature/laureates /2001/naipaul-lecture-e.html
4. Naipaul, *The Return of Eva Peron with the Killings in Trinidad* (New York: Knopf, 1980), 216.
5. Naipaul, *Finding the Centre* (London: André Deutsch, 1984), 58.
6. Naipaul, *The Enigma of Arrival* (New York: Alfred A. Knopf, 1987), 143.
7. 'Introduction.' *East Indians in the Caribbean*. eds. B. Brereton and W. Dookeran (Millwood, NY: Kraus Thomson, 1982), 6.
8. Naipaul, *A Way in the World* (New York: Vintage, 1995).
9. See Stefano Harney's *Nationalism and Identity: Culture and the Imagination in a Caribbean Diaspora* (London: Zed Books, 1996), 145–9.
10. Naipaul, *The Mimic Men* (1967; repr., London: Picador, 2002), 32.
11. Naipaul, 'Argentina and the Ghost of Eva Perón, 1972–1991.' In *The Writer and the World* (New York: Alfred A. Knopf, 2002), 360.

12. Nana Wilson-Tagoe, *Historical Thought and Literary Representation in West Indian Literature* (Gainesville: University Press of Florida, 1998), 5, 54–6.
13. See Naipaul, *An Area of Darkness* (London: André Deutsch, 1963), 113–7, 133–7.

BIBLIOGRAPHY

Adesanmi, Pius. 'Entanglement and *Durée*: Reflections on the Francophone African Novel.' *Comparative Literature* 56, no. 3 (Summer 2004): 227–42.

Adorno, Theodor W. *Aesthetic Theory*. Edited by Gretel Adorno and Rolf Tiedemann. Translated by C. Lenhardt. 1970. Reprint, London: Routledge and Kegan, 1984.

Antoine-Dunne, Jean. 'Time and Space in their Indissoluble Connection: Towards an Audio-Visual Caribbean Aesthetic.' In *The Montage Principle: Einstein in New Cultural and Critical Contexts.* Edited by Jean Antoine-Dunne with Paula Quigley. Amsterdam: Rodopi, 2004, 125–52.

Antoni, Robert. *Divina Trace*. London: Robin Clark Ltd, 1991.

Baugh, Edward. 'Cuckoo and Culture: *In the Castle of My Skin.' ARIEL* 8, no.3 (1977): 23–33.

———. 'Let Us Praise Naipaul.' *The Jamaica Observer*, April 4, 1993.

Bawer, Bruce. 'Civilization and V.S. Naipaul.' *The Hudson Review* 55, no. 3 (2002): 371–84.

Bayley, John. 'Country Life.' *New York Review of Books*, April 9, 1987.

Beck, Ervin. 'Naipaul's B. Wordsworth.' *The Explicator* 60, no. 3 (Spring 2002): 175–6.

Beja, Morris. 'Epiphany and Epiphanies.' *A Companion to Joyce Studies.* Edited by Zack Bowen and James F. Carens. London: Greenwood, 1984.

Berger, John. 'Afterword.' In *Nineteen Nineteen.* Edited by Hugh Brody, Michael Ignatieff and John Berger. London: Faber & Faber, 1985.

Bhabha, Homi. *The Location of Culture*. London: Routledge, 1994.

———. 'Minority Maneuvers and Unsettled Negotiations.' Editor's Introduction. *Critical Inquiry* 23, no. 3 (1997): 431–59.

———. 'Remembering Fanon: Self, Psyche and the Colonial Condition.' In *Colonial Discourse and Post-colonial Theory: A Reader.* 112–23. Edited by Patrick Williams and Laura Chrisman. New York: Prentice Hall, Harvester Wheatsheaf, 1994.

———. 'The World and the Home.' *Social Text*, No. 31/32, Third World and Post-Colonial Issues (1992): 141–53.

Birbalsingh, Frank. 'Jamaica Kincaid: From Antigua to America.' *Frontiers of Caribbean Literature in English*. 135–51. Edited by Frank Birbalsingh. London: Macmillan, 1996.

Brathwaite, Edward Kamau. *The Arrivants*. London: Oxford University Press, 1973.

———. *Born to Slow Horses*. Middletown, Connecticut: Wesleyan University Press, 2005.

———. *Contradictory Omens: Cultural Diversity and Integration in the Caribbean*. Mona, Jamaica: Savacou Publications, 1974.

Bray, Joe. 'The "Dual" Voice of Free Indirect Discourse: A Reading Experiment.' *Language and Literature* 16 (2007): 37–52.

Breiner, Laurence. 'Laureate of Nowhere.' *The Caribbean Review of Books* 10 (November 2006): 32–35.

Bryce, Jane. 'Review of Oonya Kempadoo, *Buxton Spice* and Shani Mootoo, *Cereus Blooms at Night*.' *Wasafiri* 30 (Autumn 1999): 72–73.

Burnett, D. Graham. "'It's Impossible to Make a Step without the Indians": Nineteenth-Century Geographical Exploration and the Amerindians of British Guiana.' *Ethnohistory* 49, no. 1 (Winter 2002): 3–40.

Caldas-Coulthard, Carmen Rosa. 'Cross-Cultural Representation of "Otherness" in Media Discourse.' In *Critical Discourse Analysis: Theory and Interdisciplinarity*. 272–96. Edited by Gilbert Weiss and Ruth Wodak. New York: Palgrave Macmillan, 2003.

Camus, Albert. *The Myth of Sisyphus*. Translated by Justin O'Brien. London: Hamish Hamilton, 1955.

———. *The Rebel*. Translated by Anthony Bower. London: Penguin Books, 1962.

Cirlot, J.E. *A Dictionary of Symbols*. Mineola, New York: Dover Publications, 2002.

Clifford, James. *Routes: Travel and Translation in the Late Twentieth Century*. Cambridge: Harvard University Press, 1997.

Constable, John. 'The History of Landscape Painting.' Third Lecture at the Royal Institution, 1836.

Courtright, Paul. *Ganesha: Lord of Obstacles, Lord of Beginnings*. New York: Oxford University Press, 1985.

Cudjoe, Selwyn. *V.S. Naipaul: A Materialist Reading*. Amherst: The University of Massachusetts Press, 1988.

Donne, John. 'A Hymne to God the Father.' *The Poems of John Donne*. 337–38. Edited by Sir Herbert Grierson. London: Oxford University Press, 1937.

Donnell, Alison. *Twentieth-Century Caribbean Literature: Critical Moments in Anglophone Literary History*. London: Routledge, 2006.

Dostoevsky, Fydor. *Notes from Underground*. Translated by Richard Pevear and Larissa Volokhonsky. First Vintage Classics Edition. New York: Random House, 1993.

Eliot, Thomas S. 'The Wasteland.' *Collected Poems 1909–1962*. 51–69. San Diego: Harcourt Brace Jovanovich, 1998.

Emmot, Catherine. *Narrative Comprehension: A Discourse Perspective*. Oxford: Clarendon, 1997.

Escoffery, Gloria. 'Reflections on the Rain.' *Daily Gleaner*, August 25, 1981.

Espinet Ramabai. 'Indian Cuisine.' *The Massachusetts Review* 35, nos. 3–4 (Autumn–Winter, 1994): 563–73.

Eytle, Earnest. *Frank Worrell*. London: Hodder & Stoughton, 1963.

Fichtner, Margaria. 'V.S. Naipaul's Way in the World.' *The Miami Herald* (International Edition), May 29, 1994.

Francis, Donette. 'Uncovered Stories: Politicizing Sexual Histories in Third Wave Caribbean Women's Writing.' *Renaissance Noire* 6, no. 1 (Fall 2004): 61–81.

French, Patrick. *The World is What it Is: The Authorised Biography of V.S. Naipaul*. London: Picador, 2008.

Gates, Henry Jr. *The Signifying Monkey: A Theory of African American Literary Criticism*. New York and Oxford: Oxford University Press, 1988.

Gilbert, Harriett. 'V.S. Naipaul talks to BBC World Service about the threat to Britain from "council house culture,"' September 23, 2004. http://www.bbc.co.uk/print/pressoffice/ pressreleases/stories/204/09_september/23/Naipaul.

Glissant, Édouard. *Caribbean Discourse: Selected Essays*. 1989. Reprint, Charlottesvillle: University Press of Virginia, 1999.

———. *Poetics of Relation*. Translated by Betsy Wing. Ann Arbor: University of Michigan Press, 1997.

Gorra, Michael. 'Postcolonial Studies.' *New York Times Book Review*, October 28, 2001.

Graham, Phil. 'Critical Discourse Analysis and Evaluative Meaning: Interdisciplinarity as a Critical Turn.' In *Critical Discourse Analysis: Theory and Interdisciplinarity.* 110–29. Edited by Gilbert Weiss and Ruth Wodak. New York: Palgrave Macmillan, 2003.

Gussow, Mel. 'Naipaul in Search of Himself: A Conversation.' *New York Times,* April 24, 1994. http://www.nytimes.com/books/98/06/07/specials/naipaul-center.html.

———. 'V.S. Naipaul: "It Is Out of This Violence I've Always Written."' *The New York Times on the Web*, September 16, 1984. http://www.nytimes.com/books/98/06/07/specials/naipaul-violence.html.

———. 'Writer without Roots.' *The New York Times Magazine*, (December 26, 1976): 8–9, 18–19.

Hall, Stuart. 'Cultural Identity and Diaspora.' In *Colonial Discourse and Post Colonial Theory: A Reader.* 401–402. Edited by Patrick Williams and Laura Chruman. London: Harvester Wheatsheaf, 1994.

———. '*Myths of Caribbean Identity.*' The Walter Rodney Memorial Lectures. October 1991. Centre for Caribbean Studies, Coventry, UK.

———. 'New ethnicities.' In *Stuart Hall: Critical Dialogues in Cultural Studies.* 392–403. Edited by David Morley and Kuan-Hsing Chen. London: Routledge, 1996.

Hardwick, Elizabeth. 'Meeting V.S. Naipaul.' *The New York Times Book Review*, May 13, 1979.

Harney, Stefano. *Nationalism and Identity: Culture and the Imagination in a Caribbean Diaspora.* London: Zed Books, 1996.

Harris, Wilson. 'Creoleness: The Crossroads of a Civilization?' *Selected Essays: The Unfinished Genesis of the Imagination.* 237–47. Edited by Andrew Bundy. London: Routledge, 1999.

———. *The Four Banks of the River Space.* London: Faber and Faber, 1990.

———. 'The Native Phenomenon.' In *Common Wealth.* Edited by Anna Rutherford. Aarhus: Akademisk Boghandel, 1971.

———. 'The Phenomenal Legacy.' In *Explorations: A Selection of Talks and Articles, 1966–1981.* Edited by Hena Maes-Jelinek. Mundelstrup: Dangaroo, 1981.

———. 'The Quest for Form.' *Kunapipi* (1983): 23.

———. *Tradition, the Writer and Society: Critical Essays.* 28–47. London: New Beacon Publications, 1967.

———. *The Tree of the Sun.* London: Faber and Faber, 1978.

———. 'The Unfinished Genesis of the Imagination.' *Selected Essays: The Unfinished Genius of the Imagination*. 248–60. Edited by Andrew Bundy. London and New York: Routledge, 1999.

Hayward, Helen. *The Enigma of V.S. Naipaul: Sources and Contents.* Oxford: Macmillan, 2002.

Hearne, John. Review of *The Middle Passage. Caribbean Quarterly* 8, no. 4 (December 1962): 65–66.

Henzell, Perry, dir. *The Harder they Come.* Screenplay by Perry Henzell and Trevor Rhone. International Films, Inc., 1972.

Herman, David. 'Towards a Formal Description of Narrative Metalepsis.' *Journal of Literary Semantics* 26, no. 2 (1997): 132–52.

Hoagland, Edward. 'Staking His Life on One Grand Vision.' *New York Times on the Web*, September 16, 1984. http://www.nytimes.com/books/98/06/07/specials/naipaul-center.html.

Hodge, Merle. *Crick Crack Monkey.* 1970. Reprint, London: Heinemann, 1981.

Huntington, Samuel P. *The Clash of Civilizations and the Remaking of World Order.* 1997. Reprint, *London: Simon and Schuster, 2002.*

Jahn, Manfred. *Narratology: A Guide to the Theory of Narrative.* English Department, University of Cologne, 2005.

Jussawalla, Feroza, ed. *Conversations with V.S. Naipaul.* Jackson: University Press of Mississippi, 1997.

Kelso, Paul. 'Naipaul Derides Novels of Forster "A Nasty Homosexual."' *The Guardian* (UK) August 2, 2001.

Kent, George. 'A Conversation with George Lamming.' *Black World* 22, no. 5 (March 1973): 4– 15, 88–97.

Kermode, Frank. 'In the Garden of the Oppressor.' *The New York Times Book Review*. March 22, 1987.

Khan, Aisha. *Callaloo Nation: Metaphors of Race and Religious Identity among South Asians in Trinidad.* Jamaica, Barbados and Trinidad and Tobago: The University Press of the West Indies, 2004.

———. 'What is "a Spanish"?: Ambiguity and "Mixed" Ethnicity in Trinidad.' *Trinidad Ethnicity.* 180–207. Edited by Kelvin Yelvington. London: The Macmillan Press, 1993.

Kincaid, Jamaica. *Annie John.* New York: Farrrar, Straus and Giroux, 1983.

——— . *Lucy.* New York: Farrrar, Straus and Giroux, 1990.

——— . *My Brother.* New York: Noonday Press, 1997.

———. *A Small Place*. London: Farrar, Straus and Giroux, 1988.

King, Jane. 'A Small Place Writes Back.' *Callaloo* 25, no. 3 (2002): 885–90.

Kinsley, David R. *The Sword and the Flute: Kali and Querns Dark Visions of the Terrible and the Sublime in Hindu Mythology*. Berkeley: University Press of California, 1975.

Kurfiss, Joanne. 'Helping Faculty Foster Students' Critical Thinking in the Disciplines.' *New Directions for Teaching and Learning*. no. 37, San Francisco: Jossey-Bass, 1989.

Kurkland, Daniel. *I Know What it Says… What Does it Mean?* Kentucky: Wadsworth Publishing, 1995.

Labov, William. *Language in the Inner City: Studies in the Black English Vernacular Sociolinguistic Patterns*. Philadelphia: University of Pennsylvania Press, 1972.

Lamming, George. *In the Castle of My Skin*. New York: Macmillan, 1970.

———. *The Pleasures of Exile*. London: Michael Joseph, 1960.

———. *Season of Adventure*. London: Michael Joseph, 1960.

Lascelles, Angelo. 'Take the High Road on Morals.' *Daily Nation* (July 12, 2005): 10.

Lipner, Julius. *Hindus: Their Religious Beliefs and Practices*. London: Routledge, 1994.

Lovelace, Earl. *Salt*. New York: Persea Books, 1997.

Lutgendorf, Philip. *Hanuman's Tale: The Messages of a Divine Monkey*. Oxford: Oxford University Press, 2007.

Macedo, Lynne. *Fiction and Film. The Influence of Cinema on Writers from Jamaica and Trinidad*. Chichester: Dido, 2003.

Malina, Debra. *Breaking the Frame: Metalepsis and the Construction of the Subject*. Columbus: Ohio State University Press, 2002.

Mcdougall, Russell. 'Walter Roth, Wilson Harris and a Caribbean/Postcolonial Theory of Modernism.' *University of Toronto Quarterly* 67, no. 2 (Spring 1998). http:/www.utpjournals.com/product/utq/672/672_mcdougall.html (accessed February 8, 2007).

Michener, Charles. 'The Dark Visions of V.S. Naipaul,' *Newsweek*. November 16, 1981.

Mootoo, Shani. *Cereus Blooms at Night*. London: Granta Publishers, 1999.

———. *He Drown She in the Sea*. Berkeley: Grove Press, 2005.

———. *Out on Main Street*. Vancouver: Press Gang Publishers, 1993.

Morris, Mervyn. 'Sir Vidia and the Prize.' *World Literature Today* 76, (Spring 2002): 11–14.

Naipaul, Seepersad. *The Adventures of Gurudeva and Other Stories.* London: André Deutsch, 1976.

Naipaul, V.S. *An Area of Darkness.* London: André Deutsch, 1963; Harmondsworth: Penguin Books, 1964.

———. *A Bend in the River.* London: André Deutsch, 1979; New York: Vintage Books, 1980.

———. *Between Father and Son: Family Letter.* With Introduction by Gillon Aitken. New York: Random House, 1999.

———. *The Enigma of Arrival: A Novel.* London: Penguin Books, 1987; New York: Vintage, 1988.

———. *Finding the Centre.* London: André Deutsch, 1984; Harmondsworth: Penguin, 1985.

———. *A Flag on the Island.* London: André Deutsch, 1967.

———. Foreword to *The Adventures of Gurudeva and Other Stories* by Seepersad Naipaul. London: André Deutsch, 1976.

———. *Half A Life.* New York: Alfred A. Knopf, 2001; London: Picador, 2002.

———. *A House for Mr Biswas.* 1961. Reprint, Harmondsworth: Penguin, 1969; London: Penguin Books, 1982.

———. *In a Free State.* London: André Deutsch, 1971; Harmondsworth: Penguin Books, 1973.

———. *India: A Wounded Civilization.* Harmondsworth: Penguin Books, 1997.

———. Interview by Bhoendradatt Tewarie, April 11, 2007. Video presentation at the University of the West Indies, St Augustine, Trinidad and Tobago, in the Campus celebration of V.S. Naipaul.

———. 'Introduction.' *East Indians in the Caribbean,* Edited by B. Brereton and W. Dookeran. Millwood, NY: Kraus Thomson, 1982.

———. *Letters Between a Father and a Son.* With Introduction and notes by Gillon Aitken. London: Little, Brown and Company, 1999; Letters Between Father and Son: Family Letters with Introduction by Gillon Aitken. New York: Random House, 1999.

———. *Literary Occasions: Essays,* ed. Pankaj Mishra. 2003. Reprint, London: Picador (paperback), 2004.

———. 'London,' *Times Literary Supplement*, August 15, 1958. Reprinted in *The Overcrowded Barracoon.*

———. *The Loss of El Dorado – A History*. London: André Deutsch, 1969; Harmondsworth: Penguin, 1973; New York: Alfred P. Knopf, 1970; London: Picador, 2001.

———. *The Middle Passage*. 1962. Reprint, Harmondsworth: Penguin Books, 1969; *The Middle Passage: The Caribbean Revisited.* 1979. Reprint, London: Penguin Books, 1988; *The Middle Passage: A Caribbean Journey.* London: Picador, 1996; *The Middle Passage: Impressions of Five Societies, British, French and Dutch, in the West Indies and South America.* London: Picador, 2001.

———. *Miguel Street*. 1959. Reprint, Harmondsworth: Penguin, 1971; Reprint, London: Heinemann, 1974; Reprint, New York: Vintage Books, 1984.

———. *The Mimic Men*, London: André Deutsch, 1967; Harmondsworth: Penguin, 1969; London: Picador, 2002.

———. *Mr Stone and the Knights Companion*. London: Four Square, 1966.

———. *The Mystic Masseur*. London: Penguin Books, 1957; London: Penguin, 1964; Harmondsworth: Penguin, 1978.

———. *The Overcrowded Barracoon*. Harmondsworth: Penguin, 1976; *The Overcrowded Barracoon and Other Articles*. London: André Deutsch, 1972.

———. *Reading and Writing: A Personal Account*. New York: New York Review of Books, 2000.

———. *The Return of Eva Perón*. 1974. Reprint, Harmondsworth: Penguin, 1980; *The Return of Eva Perón with the Killings in Trinidad.* New York: Knopf, 1980.

———. 'Sporting Life *Beyond a Boundary*.' *Encounter* 21 (1963): 73–75.

———. *The Suffrage of Elvira*. 1958. Reprint, Harmondsworth: Penguin, 1969.

———. 'Two Worlds.' The Nobel Lecture, Börssalen, Swedish Academy, Stockholm, December 7, 2001. http://nobelprize.org/nobel_prizes/literature/laureates/2001/naipaul-lecture-e.html; *Caribbean Voice* (accessed March 14, 2007). www.caribvoice.org/CaribbeanDocuments/Naipaul.html; the-south-asian.com, January 2002 (accessed December 9, 2007). www.the-south-asian.com/Jan2002/Naipaul-Nobel-Lecture1.htm.

———. *A Way in the World.* New York: Alfred A. Knopf, 1994; New York: Vintage, 1995; London: Minerva, 1995.

———. *The Writer and the World.* Edited by Pankaj Mishra. 1990. Reprint, London: Picador, 2003. Reprint, New York: Alfred A. Knopf, 2002.

———. *A Writer's People: Ways of Looking and Feeling.* London: Picador, 2007.

Nietzsche, Freidrich. *The Gay Science.* Translated by Walter Kaufmann. New York: Vintage Books, 1974.

Nightingale, Margaret. 'V.S. Naipaul as Historian: Combating Chaos.' *Southern Review: Literary and Interdisciplinary Essays* 13, no. 3 (1980): 239–50.

Niven, Alastair. 'V.S. Naipaul.' *Writing Across Worlds: Contemporary Writers Talk.* 102–12. Edited by Susheila Nasta. London: Routledge, 2004.

O'Callaghan, Evelyn. 'V.S. Naipaul's Legacy: Made in the West Indies – for Export.' *Lucayos* 1 (Spring 2008): 106–17.

Pantin, Raoul. 'V.S. Naipaul.' *The Express*, December 14, 1984.

Persaud, Lakshmi. *Butterfly in the Wind.* London: Peepal Tree Press, 1990.

Phillips, Caryl. 'V.S. Naipaul.' *A New World Order: Selected Essays.* 187–219. London: Vintage, 2002.

Piedra, José. 'From Monkey Tales to Cuban Songs: On Signification.' *MLN* 1000, no. 2, Hispanic Issue (March, 1985): 361–90.

Pound, Ezra. 'E. P. Ode Pour L'Election de Son Sepulcre.' *Ezra Pound: Selected Poems.* 61–5. New York: New Directions, 1957.

Rahim, Jennifer. 'No Place to Go: Homosexual Space and the Discourse of Unspeakable Content in Mendes' *Black Fauns* and Kincaid's *My Brother.*' *Journal of West Indian Literature* 3, nos. 1–2 (2005): 119–40.

———. '"A Quartet of Daffodils" Only: Negotiating the Specific and the Relational in the Context of Multiculturalism and Globalisation.' *Caribbean Literature in a Global Context.* Edited by Funso Aiyejina and Paula Morgan. San Juan, Trinidad: Lexicon Trinidad Ltd., 2006.

Rahman, M.F. Letter to the editor. *The Trinidad Guardian*, October 31, 2001.

Ramchand, Kenneth. 'On Minshall and Reading the Mas.' *Caribbean Review of Books* 11 (February 2007): 32–37.

———. 'Partial Truths: A Critical Account of V.S. Naipaul's Later Fiction.' In *Essays on Contemporary Post-Colonial Fiction.* Edited by Hedwig Bock and Albert Wertheim. Munchen: Max Hueber Verlag, 1986; also 'Partial Truths: A Critical Assessment of V.S. Naipaul's Later Fiction.' In *Critical*

Issues in West Indian Literature. 65–87. Edited by Erika Sollish Smilowitz and Roberta Quarles Knowles. St Croix, Virgin Islands: Caribbean Books, 1984.

———. *The West Indian Novel and Its Background.* 2nd edn. London: Heinemann Books, 1983.

Rodríguez, María Cristina. *What Women Lose: Exile and the Construction of Imaginary Homelands in Novels by Caribbean Writers.* New York: Peter Lang, 2005.

Rohlehr, Gordon. 'The Ironic Approach: The Novels of V.S. Naipaul.' *The Islands in Between.* 121–39, 178–93. Edited by Louis James. Oxford: Oxford University Press, 1968; also in Robert Hammer, ed. *Critical Persectives on V.S. Naipaul.* Washington, DC: Three Continents Press, 1977.

———. *Pathfinder: Black Awakening in the Arrivants of Edward Kamau Brathwaite.* Port of Spain: Trinidad, 1981.

Rowe-Evans, Adrian. 'V.S. Naipaul.' *Transition* 40 (December 1971): 56–62.

Rushdie, Salman. *Imaginary Homelands.* New York: Penguin Books, 1991.

Ryan, Marie-Laure. 'Postmodernism and the Doctrine of Panfictionality.' *Narrative* 5, no. 2 (1997): 165–87.

Rhys, Jean. *Wide Sargasso Sea.* 1966. Reprint, London: Penguin, 2000.

Said, Edward 'Interview,' *Newsweek,* August 18, 1980.

Scott, Lawrence. *Witchbroom.* London: Heinemann, 1993.

Sen, Amartya Kumar. *Identity and Violence: The Illusion of Destiny.* New York: W.W. Norton and Co., 2006.

Shenker, Israel. 1977. 'V.S. Naipaul: Man without a Society.' *Critical Perspectives on V.S. Naipaul.* 48–53. Edited by Robert D. Hammer. Washington D.C.: Three Continents Press, 1979.

Sheppard, R. Z. 'Notes from the Fourth World,' *Time,* May 21, 1979.

Singh, Vishnu. 'The Colonial Goes to London.' A paper presented at the symposium, 'V.S. Naipaul: Created in the West Indies,' The University of the West Indies, St Augustine, Trinidad, 2007, 1–6.

Sinha, Jadunath. *Rama Prasada's Devotional Songs: The Cult of Shakti.* Calcutta: Sinha Publishing House Pvt. Ltd., 1966.

Smith, Faith. Preface to 'Genders and Sexualities.' Special Issue of *Small Axe* 7 (March 2000): v–vii.

Smith, Rowland, ed. *Postcolonizing the Commonwealth: Studies in Literature and Culture.* Ontario: Wilfred Laurier University Press, 2000.

Sollors, Werner. 'Ethnicity.' *Critical Terms for Literary Study*. 288–305. Edited by Frank Lentricchia and Thomas McLaughlin. Chicago: University of Chicago Press, 1995.

Stephanides, Stephanos. *Translating Kali's Feast, the Goddess in Indo-Caribbean Ritual and Fiction.* Amsterdam: Rodopi, 2000.

Tewari, Bhoendradatt. 'A Comparative Study of Ethnicity in the Novels of Saul Bellow and V.S. Naipaul.' PhD diss., Pennsylvania State University, 1983.

Theroux, Paul. *Sunrise with Seamonsters: Travels and Discoveries, 1964–84.* Rolling Meadows, MA: Houghton Mifflin Books, 1985.

Thieme, John. *The Web of Tradition: Uses of Allusion in V. S. Naipaul's Fiction.* Hertford: Hansib Publications, 1987.

———.'V.S. Naipaul's Third World.' *Journal of Commonwealth Literature* 10, no. 1 (1975).

Turner, Victor. 'Liminality and Community.' In *Culture and Society Contemporary Debates,* 147–54. Edited by Jeffrey C. Alexander and Steven Seidman. Cambridge: Cambridge University Press, 1990.

van Peer, W., and H. Pander Maat. 'Perspectivization and Sympathy: Effects of Narrative Points of View.' *Empirical Approaches to Literature and Aesthetics.* 143–54. Edited by Roger J. Kreuz and M.S. MacNealy. Norward, NJ: Ablex, 1996.

Walcott, Derek. 'Interview with V.S. Naipaul.' *Conversations with V.S. Naipaul.* 5–9. Edited by Feroza Jussawalla. Jackson: University Press of Mississippi, 1997.

———.'The Garden Path.' In *What the Twilight Says.* London: Faber and Faber, 1998.

———. *Omeros.* London: Faber and Faber, 1990.

———. *Tiepolo's Hound.* New York: Farrar, Straus and Giroux, 2000.

———. *What the Twilight Says.* London: Faber and Faber, 1998.

Warner, Keith. *On Location: Cinema and Film in the Anglophone Caribbean.* London and Oxford: Macmillian, 2000.

Webb, Peter. 'The Master of the Novel.' *Newsweek,* (August 18, 1980): 34–8.

Wheatcroft, Geoffrey. 'A Terrifying Honesty.' *Atlantic Monthly* 289, no. 2 (2002): 88–92.

White, Landeg. *V.S. Naipaul: A Critical Introduction.* London: Macmillan, 1975.

Wilson-Tagoe, Nana. *Historical Thought and Literary Representation in West Indian Literature*. Gainesville: University Press of Florida, 1998.

Wood, James. 'Damage [rev. *Half a Life*].' *The New Republic* (November 5, 2001): 34.

Worcester, Kent. *C.L.R. James: A Political Biography*. Albany: State University of New York Press, 1996.

Wordsworth, William. 'Lines Composed a Few Miles Above Tintern Abbey.' In *The Oxford Anthology of English Literature*. vol. 2. 146–50. Edited by Frank Kermode and John Hollander. New York, London, Toronto: Oxford University Press, 1973.

CONTRIBUTORS

Jean Antoine-Dunne is a Senior Lecturer in Literatures in English at the University of the West Indies, St Augustine. She was the architect and overall coordinator of the new BA in Film at St Augustine, the first of its kind in the Anglophone Caribbean. Dr Antoine-Dunne lectures in modernism and West Indian literature at St Augustine and is also the editor (with Paula Quigley of Trinity College Dublin) of the work, *The Montage Principle: Eisenstein in New Cultural and Critical Contexts*. Many of her essays over the years have sought to demonstrate the impact of film, and in particular montage, on the work of contemporary writers. She is also a cultural commentator and critic and has made extensive contributions to newspapers and journals in Europe and in the Caribbean.

Edward Baugh is Emeritus Professor of English, University of the West Indies, Mona campus. His publications include: *Derek Walcott: Memory as Vision* (Allen & Unwin, 1978), *Derek Walcott* (Cambridge University Press, 2006), *Frank Collymore: A Biography* (Ian Randle Publishers, 2009), and two collections of poetry: *A Tale from the Rainforest* (Sandberry Press, 1988) and *It Was the Singing* (Sandberry Press, 2000). He edited *Critics on Caribbean Literature* (Longman, 1978), Derek Walcott's *Selected Poems* (Farrar, Straus & Giroux, 2007), and Ian McDonald's *Selected Poems* (Macmillan, 2008). Between 1989 and 1992 he was Chairperson of the Association for Commonwealth Literature and Language Studies.

Bridget Brereton is Professor of History at The University of the West Indies, St Augustine, Trinidad and Tobago. She is the author of standard works on the history of Trinidad, and the editor or co-editor of several books, including Volume V of the UNESCO General History of the Caribbean, *The Caribbean in the Twentieth Century.* Her most recent publication is *From Imperial College to University of the West Indies: A History of the St Augustine Campus, Trinidad & Tobago*. She is a former Deputy Principal and Interim Principal of the St Augustine campus, a former President of the Association of Caribbean Historians, and she was the first woman to win the Vice-Chancellor's Award for Excellence.

Rhonda Cobham-Sander graduated from the University of the West Indies in 1974, with first class honours in English. She completed a doctoral dissertation on early Jamaican writing at the University of St Andrews in 1982, under the supervision of Professor Peter Bayley, who was also V.S. Naipaul's undergraduate tutor at Oxford. She has taught at the University of the West Indies, Mona, and at the University of Bayreuth, Germany, and is presently Professor of English and Black Studies at Amherst College in Massachusetts, USA. As editorial consultant to The Women's Press during the 1980s and '90s, she collaborated in the production of several literary firsts, including Sistren's *Lionheart Gal*, Pauline Melville's *Shaper Shifter*, and Tsitsi Dangarembga's *Nervous Conditions*. She is the editor of *Watchers and Seekers: New Writing by Black Women in Britain,* as well as special issues of a variety of journals on such topics as Caribbean Culture, African Women's Writing, and Jamaica Kincaid. Her own articles on Caribbean and African literary subjects have appeared in *Transition, Callaloo, Research in African Literatures*, and *The Women's Review of Books*. Cobham-Sander's writing on V.S.Naipaul is part of a forthcoming book called *I and I: Epitaphs for the Self, in the Work of V.S. Naipaul, Kamau Brathwaite, and Derek Walcott.*

Barbara Lalla is Professor of Language and Literature at The University of the West Indies, St Augustine, publishing mainly in language history, literary linguistics and early British literature. Her publications include several books, of which *Postcolonialisms: Caribbean Re-reading of Medieval English Discourse* is recent, but also *Defining Jamaican Fiction: Marronage and the Discourse of Survival,* as well as the companion volumes, *Language in Exile* and *Voices in Exile*. She produced the university's pioneering text for its thrust in Distance Education (*English for Academic Purposes*). Barbara Lalla's first novel, *Arch of Fire* (1998) has subsequently been translated into German. A past President of The Society for Caribbean Linguistics, a Co-Chair of the Cultural Studies Initiative and a winner of the Vice-Chancellor's Award for Excellence, she also served the campus as Public Orator for many years.

Vijay Maharaj received her PhD in Literatures in English from the University of the West Indies, St Augustine. She has worked as a part-time lecturer in the Department of Liberal Arts, Faculty of Humanities and Education at the university since September 2000. The title of the PhD dissertation, 'A Caribbean *Katha:* Revisioning the "Indo-Caribbean" "Crisis of Being and Belonging" through the Literary Imagination', indicates her research interests which may be briefly spelled out as indigenous methods of literary criticism, interrogation of received epistemologies and of conceptions of ontology, and theorisations of power and strategies used by individuals and groups to gain or maintain economic, social, cultural and political power. She has previously published in the Caribbean Studies journal *Anthurium.*

Paula Morgan is a Senior Lecturer in the Faculty of Humanities and Education and an associate of the Centre for Gender and Development Studies, The University of the West Indies, St Augustine. She currently coordinates the graduate programme in Cultural Studies. Dr Morgan's primary focus of research, teaching and publication has been gender issues in the literatures of the Caribbean and the African Diaspora. Dr Morgan has authored *Language Proficiency for Tertiary Level* (1998) and *Writing About Literature* with Barbara Lalla (2005). She has also produced *Caribbean Literature in a Global Context* – an edited collection with Funso Aiyejina (2006) and *Writing Rage: Violence in Caribbean Discourse* – with Valerie Youssef (2006).

Evelyn O'Callaghan is a Professor of West Indian literature in the Department of Language, Linguistics and Literature at Cave Hill (Barbados). She has published extensively. Her essays and chapters appear in a number of seminal journals and books on Caribbean writing, particularly by women. *Woman Version: Theoretical Approaches to West Indian Fiction by Women* (1993) and *The Earliest Patriots* (fiction) in 1986. Her latest book, *Women Writing in the West Indies 1804–1939: A Hot Place, Belonging to Us* was published by Routledge in 2003. She serves as an editor for the *Journal of West Indian Literature* and is a reader for *Callaloo* and *Ariel.*

Sandra Pouchet Paquet taught Caribbean literature and culture at the University of Miami from 1992 to 2010, where she directed the Caribbean Writers Summer Institute from 1992–1996 before starting the Caribbean Literary Studies Programme in 1999. In 2003, she founded *Anthuium: A Caribbean Studies Journal,* and served as the editor of that journal from 2003 to 2010. Professor Paquet is the author of *The Novels of George Lamming*

(1982), *Caribbean Autobiography* (2002), and co-editor of *Music, Memory, Resistance: Calypso and the Caribbean Literary Imagination* (2007). She has published widely on Caribbean literature in leading journals in the field. She retired from the University of Miami in 2010 with plans to continue her research and scholarship, as well as editing and teaching. Paquet's active research interests include the areas of ethnic Caribbean literary studies, nomadism, diaspora studies, and autobiography.

Jennifer Rahim is a Senior Lecturer in Literature in the Department of Liberal Arts, The University of the West Indies, St Augustine, Trinidad and Tobago. She is a critic, poet and short story writer. Her articles on Caribbean literature have appeared in *MaComere, The Journal of West Indian Literature, Small Axe, Anthurium, The Trinidad and Tobago Review* and *The Woman, the Writer and Caribbean Society* edited by Helen Pyne-Timothy (1998). She edited with Barbara Lalla a collection of Cultural Studies essays entitled, *Beyond Borders: Cross Culturalism and the Caribbean Canon* (2009). Her creative publications include three poetry collections: *Mothers Are Not the Only Linguists* (1992) and *Between the Fence and the Forest* (2002) *and Approaching Sabbaths* (2009). She has one collection of short stories, *Songster and Other Stories* (2007). *Approaching Sabbaths* was awarded the 2010 Casa de las Américas Prize for best book in the category Caribbean Literature in English or Creole.

Gordon Rohlehr, Professor of West Indian Literature at the University of the West Indies, St Augustine, Trinidad, was born in Guyana in 1942. He graduated in 1964 from the University College of the West Indies, Jamaica, with a First Class Honours degree in English Literature, after which he wrote a doctoral dissertation entitled 'Alienation and Commitment in the Works of Joseph Conrad' at Birmingham University, England (1964–1967). He is author of *Pathfinder: Black Awakening in The Arrivants of Edward Kamau Brathwaite* (Gordon Rohlehr 1981); *Calypso and Society in Pre-Independence Trinidad* (Gordon Rohlehr 1990); *My Strangled City and Other Essays* (Longman Trinidad 1992); *The Shape of That Hurt and Other Essays* (Longman Trinidad 1992); and *A Scuffling of Islands: Essays on Calypso* (Lexicon Trinidad Ltd. 2004). He is also co-editor of *Voiceprint: An Anthology of Oral and Related Poetry from the Caribbean* (Longman 1989).

Between 1968 and 2006, he wrote more than 100 essays on West Indian Literature, Oral Poetry, the calypso and popular culture in the Caribbean. He has held over 300 interviews, prepared and participated in nearly 100 radio and television programmes, and lectured extensively throughout the Caribbean, US, Canada, and the UK. He has been visiting Professor to Harvard University (Sept–Dec 1981); the Johns Hopkins University (Sept–Dec 1985); Tulane University (Jan–May 1997); Stephen F. Austin State University (Jan–May 2000); Miami University Writers' Workshop (June–July 1995); York University Toronto (January–Feb 1996) and Dartmouth College, New Hampshire (June–August, 2004).He has been the recipient of the University of the West Indies' Vice-Chancellor's Award for Excellence in the combined fields of Teaching, Research, Administration and Public Service (1995).

Lawrence Scott is from Trinidad and Tobago. His novel, *Aelred's Sin* (1998), was awarded a Commonwealth Writers' Prize, Best Book in Canada and the Caribbean. His first novel *Witchbroom* (1992) was short-listed for a Commonwealth Writers' Prize (1993), Best First Book. This was followed by *Ballad for the New World* (1994), including the Tom-Gallon Award (1986) prize-winning short-story *The House of Funerals*. His most recent novel, *Night Calypso* (2004) was also short-listed for a Commonwealth Writers' Prize, Best Book Award, and long-listed for the International IMPAC Dublin Literary Award (2006), and translated into French as *Calypso de Nuit* (2005). His most recent publication is *Golconda Our Voices Our Lives* an anthology of oral-histories and other stories from the sugar-belt in Trinidad (2009). He divides his time between writing and teaching creative-writing. He lives in London and Port of Spain.

Bhoendradatt Tewarie is Pro Vice Chancellor for Planning and Development at the University of the West Indies. He conceptualised the Nobel Laureates Celebration series, of which V.S. Naipaul was the first, during his tenure as Principal of the St Augustine Campus of UWI. Dr Tewarie has written one book on Naipaul (*VS Naipaul Revisited: Ethnicity ,Marginality and the Triumph of Individual Will*, 2007) and guest edited a *Caribbean Quarterly* volume dedicated to Naipaul to commemorate his winning the Nobel Prize, 2002. Dr Tewarie has crossed multidisciplinary boundaries in his writing having published *Trade, Investment and Development in the*

Contemporary Caribbean (2007 with Roger Hosein) and *Governance in the Twenty-first-Century University: Approaches to Effective Leadership and Strategic Management* (with Dennis Gayle and A. Quinton White). He has recently completed two chapters for a book on Higher education in Small States, soon to be published by UNESCO and is currently leading a UNESCO project on Higher Education funding strategies for Small States which will result in a policy document. Dr Tewarie has served Trinidad and Tobago and the Caribbean in many capacities as Member of Parliament, as Minister of Government, Chairman of Boards and as a Board Member of regional Institutions such as the Caribbean Examinations Council and the Caribbean Court of Justice Trust Fund.

INDEX

LaVergne, TN USA
10 September 2010
196632LV00003B/2/P

9 789766 374129